COLLECTED

POEMS

COLLECTED

POEMS

ROBERT BLY

W. W. NORTON & COMPANY

Independent Publishers Since 1923

New York | London

Silence in the Snowy Fields. © 1962 by Robert Bly. Published by Wesleyan University Press. Used by permission. *Morning Poems*. Copyright © 1997 by Robert Bly. Printed by arrangement with HarperCollins Publishers. All rights reserved. *The Night Abraham Called to the Stars*. Copyright © 2001 by Robert Bly. Printed by arrangement with HarperCollins Publishers. All rights reserved. *My Sentence Was a Thousand Years of Joy*. Copyright © 2005 by Robert Bly. Printed by arrangement with HarperCollins Publishers. All rights reserved. Some versions of these poems that appeared originally in other volumes were revised for *Jumping Out of Bed* (1987) and *Reaching Out to the World: New and Selected Prose Poems* (2009). © 1987 and 2009 by Robert Bly. Published by White Pine Press. Reprinted with permission.

For information about permission to reproduce selections from this book, write to Permissions, W. W. Norton & Company, Inc., 500 Fifth Avenue, New York, NY 10110

For information about special discounts for bulk purchases, please contact W. W. Norton Special Sales at specialsales@wwnorton.com or 800-233-4830

Manufacturing by Worzalla
Book design by JAM Design
Production manager: Anna Oler

Library of Congress Cataloging-in-Publication Data

Names: Bly, Robert, author.
Title: Collected poems / Robert Bly.
Description: First edition. | New York : W. W. Norton & Company, [2018] | Includes index.
Identifiers: LCCN 2018028547 | ISBN 9780393652444 (hardcover)
Classification: LCC PS3552.L9 A6 2018 | DDC 811/.54—dc23
LC record available at https://lccn.loc.gov/2018028547

W. W. Norton & Company, Inc., 500 Fifth Avenue, New York, N.Y. 10110
www.wwnorton.com

W. W. Norton & Company Ltd., 15 Carlisle Street, London W1D 3BS

1 2 3 4 5 6 7 8 9 0

For Ruth

CONTENTS

THE LIGHT AROUND THE BODY (1967)

SLEEPERS JOINING HANDS (1973)

JUMPING OUT OF BED (1973)

THE MORNING GLORY (1975)

THIS BODY IS MADE OF
CAMPHOR AND GOPHERWOOD (1977)

THIS TREE WILL BE HERE
FOR A THOUSAND YEARS (1979)

THE MAN IN THE BLACK COAT TURNS (1981)

LOVING A WOMAN IN TWO WORLDS (1985)

MEDITATIONS ON THE INSATIABLE SOUL (1994)

MORNING POEMS (1997)

THE NIGHT ABRAHAM CALLED TO THE STARS (2001)

MY SENTENCE WAS A THOUSAND YEARS OF JOY (2005)

TALKING INTO THE EAR OF A DONKEY (2011)

ACKNOWLEDGMENTS

I am deeply grateful to Thomas R. Smith, who has over many years given me keen advice on poem after poem. His vast and constant efforts to sort and select versions of some of these poems has helped greatly to fulfill my vision for this book.

I am grateful too to my editor at Norton, Jill Bialosky, for her enthusiasm and support for this mammoth gathering, and to her assistant, Drew Weitman, who shepherded it so carefully through the many intricate stages of production.

The poems in this volume first appeared in the following collections: *Silence in the Snowy Fields*, Wesleyan University Press, 1962; *The Light Around the Body*, Harper and Row, 1967; *The Teeth Mother Naked at Last*, City Lights, 1970; *Sleepers Joining Hands*, Harper and Row, 1973; *Jumping Out of Bed*, Barre Publishers, 1973, revised 1987; *The Point Reyes Poems*, Mudra, 1974; *The Morning Glory*, Harper and Row, 1975; *This Body Is Made of Camphor and Gopherwood*, Harper and Row, 1977; *This Tree Will Be Here for a Thousand Years*, Harper and Row, 1979, revised 1992; *The Man in the Black Coat Turns*, Dial Press, 1981; *Loving a Woman in Two Worlds*, Dial Press, 1985; *Meditations on the Insatiable Soul*, HarperCollins, 1994; *Morning Poems*, HarperCollins, 1997; *The Night Abraham Called to the Stars*, HarperCollins, 2001; *My Sentence Was a Thousand Years of Joy*, HarperCollins, 2005; *Talking into the Ear of a Donkey*, W. W. Norton, 2011. Thanks to the publishers for permission to reprint.

My grateful acknowledgment to Dennis Maloney at White Pine Press for permission to reprint revised versions of poems from *Jumping Out of Bed* (1987) and revised versions of some prose poems from *Reaching Out to the World: New and Selected Prose Poems* (2009).

SILENCE
IN
THE
SNOWY
FIELDS

(1962)

We are all asleep in the outward man.

—Jacob Boehme

ELEVEN POEMS OF SOLITUDE

THREE KINDS OF PLEASURES

I

Sometimes, riding in a car, in Wisconsin
Or Illinois, you notice those dark telephone poles
One by one lift themselves out of the fence line
And slowly leap on the gray sky—
And past them, the snowy fields.

II

The darkness drifts down like snow on the picked cornfields
In Wisconsin: and on these black trees
Scattered, one by one,
Through the winter fields—
We see stiff weeds and brownish stubble,
And white snow left now only in the wheeltracks of the combine.

III

It is a pleasure, also, to be driving
Toward Chicago, near dark,
And see the lights in the barns.
The bare trees more dignified than ever,
Like a fierce man on his deathbed,
And the ditches along the road half full of a private snow.

RETURN TO SOLITUDE

I
It is a moonlit, windy night.
The moon has pushed out the Milky Way.
Clouds are hardly alive, and the grass is leaping.
It is the hour of return.

II
We want to go back, to return to the sea,
The sea of solitary corridors,
And halls of wild nights,
Explosions of grief,
Diving into the sea of death,
Like the stars of the wheeling Bear.

III
What shall we find when we return?
Friends changed, houses moved,
Trees perhaps, with new leaves.

WAKING FROM SLEEP

Inside the veins there are navies setting forth,
Tiny explosions at the waterlines,
And seagulls weaving in the wind of the salty blood.

It is the morning. The country has slept the whole winter.
Window seats are covered with fur skins, the yard is full
Of stiff dogs, and hands that clumsily hold heavy books.

———

Now we wake, and rise from the bed, and eat breakfast!—
Shouts rise from the harbor of the blood,
Mist, and masts rising, the knocks of wooden tackle in the sunlight.

Now we sing, and do tiny dances on the kitchen floor.
Our whole body is like a harbor at dawn;
We know that our master has left us for the day.

HUNTING PHEASANTS IN A CORNFIELD

I
What is so strange about a tree alone in an open field?
It is a willow tree. I walk around and around it.
The body is strangely torn, and cannot leave it.
At last I sit down beneath it.

II
It is a willow tree alone in acres of dry corn.
Its leaves are scattered around its trunk, and around me,
Brown now, and speckled with delicate black,
Only the cornstalks now can make a noise.

III
The sun is cold, burning through the frosty distances of space.
The weeds are frozen to death long ago.
Why then do I love to watch
The sun moving on the chill skin of the branches?

IV
The mind has shed leaves alone for years.
It stands apart with small creatures near its roots.
I am happy in this ancient place,

A spot easily caught sight of above the corn,
If I were a young animal ready to turn home at dusk.

SURPRISED BY EVENING

There is unknown dust that is near us,
Waves breaking on shores just over the hill,
Trees full of birds that we have never seen,
Nets drawn down with dark fish.

The evening arrives; we look up and it is there,
It has come through the nets of the stars,
Through the tissues of the grass,
Walking quietly over the asylums of the waters.

The day shall never end, we think:
We have hair that seems born for the daylight;
But, at last, the quiet waters of the night will rise,
And our skin shall see far off, as it does underwater.

THINKING OF WALLACE STEVENS ON THE FIRST SNOWY DAY IN DECEMBER

This new snow seems to speak of virgins
With frail clothes made of gold,
Just as the old snow shall whisper
Of concierges in France.

The new dawn sings of beaches
Dazzling as sugar and clean as the clouds of Greece,

Just as the exhausted dusk shall sing
Of the waves on the western shore.

This new strength whispers of the darkness of death,
Of the frail skiff lost in the giant cave,
Just as in the boat nearing death you sang
Of feathers and white snow.

SUNSET AT A LAKE

The sun is sinking. Here on the pine-haunted bank, the mos-
quitoes fly around drowsily, and moss stands out as if it wanted to
speak. Calm falls on the lake, which now seems heavier and inhos-
pitable. Far out, rafts of ducks drift like closed eyes, and a thin line
of silver caused by something invisible slowly moves toward shore
in the viscous darkness under the southern bank. Only a few birds,
the troubled ones, speak to the darkening roof of earth; small weeds
stand abandoned, the clay is sending her gifts back to the center of
the earth.

FALL

Because it is the first Sunday of pheasant season, men gather
in the lights of cars to divide pheasants, and the chickens, hud-
dling near their electricity, and in some slight fear of the dark,
walk for the last time about their little hut, whose floor now
seems so bare.

The dusk has come, a glow in the west, as if seen through the
isinglass on old coal stoves, and the cows stand around the barn
door; now the farmer looks up at the paling sky reminding him of

death, and in the fields the bones of the corn rustle faintly in the last wind, and the half-moon stands in the south.

Now the lights from barn windows can be seen through bare trees.

APPROACHING WINTER

I
September. Clouds. The first day for wearing jackets.
The corn is wandering in dark corridors,
Near the well and the whisper of tombs.

II
I sit alone surrounded by dry corn,
Near the second growth of the pigweeds,
And hear the corn leaves scrape their feet on the wind.

III
Fallen ears are lying on the dusty earth.
The useful ears will dry in cribs, but the others, missed
By the picker, will lie here touching the ground the whole winter.

IV
Snow will come, and cover the husks of the fallen ears
With flakes, infinitely delicate, like jewels of a murdered Gothic
 prince
Which were lost centuries ago during a great battle.

DRIVING TOWARD THE LAC QUI PARLE RIVER

I

I am driving; it is dusk; Minnesota.
The stubble field catches the last growth of sun.
The soybeans are breathing on all sides.
Old men are sitting before their houses on carseats
In the small towns. I am happy,
The moon rising above the turkey sheds.

II

The small world of the car
Plunges through the deep fields of the night,
On the road from Willmar to Milan.
This solitude covered with iron
Moves through the fields of night
Penetrated by the noise of crickets.

III

Nearly to Milan, suddenly a small bridge,
And water kneeling in the moonlight.
In small towns the houses are built right on the ground;
The lamplight falls on all fours in the grass.
When I reach the river, the full moon covers it;
A few people are talking low in a boat.

POEM IN THREE PARTS

I

Oh, on an early morning I think I shall live forever!
I am wrapped in my joyful flesh,
As the grass is wrapped in its clouds of green.

II

Rising from a bed, where I dreamt
Of long rides past castles and hot coals,
The sun lies happily on my knees;
I have suffered and survived the night
Bathed in dark water, like any blade of grass.

III

The strong leaves of the box-elder tree,
Plunging in the wind, call us to disappear
Into the wilds of the universe,
Where we shall sit at the foot of a plant,
And live forever, like the dust.

AWAKENING

UNREST

A strange unrest hovers over the nation:
This is the last dance, the wild tossing of Morgan's seas,
The division of spoils.
A lassitude enters into the diamonds
Of the body. In high school the explosion begins,
The child is partly killed. When the fight is over,
And the land and the sea
Ruined, two shapes inside us rise, and move away.

But the baboon whistles on the shores of death—
Climbing and falling, tossing nuts and stones,
He gambols by the tree
Whose branches hold the expanses of cold,
The planets whirling and the black sun,
The cries of insects, and the tiny slaves
In the prisons of bark:
Charlemagne, we are approaching your islands!

We are returning now to the snowy trees,
Charlemagne, through which you rode all night
With stiff hands. Now
The darkness is falling, in which we sleep
And wake, a darkness in which thieves shudder

And the insane have a hunger for snow,
And stiff-faced men like me
Fall on their knees in the dungeons of sleep.

AWAKENING

We are approaching sleep: the chestnut blossoms in the mind
Mingle with thoughts of pain,
And the long roots of barley, bitterness
As of the oak roots staining the water dark
In Louisiana, the wet streets soaked with rain
And sodden blossoms, out of this
We have come, a tunnel softly hurtling into darkness.

The storm is coming. The small farmhouse in Minnesota
Is hardly strong enough for the storm.
Darkness, darkness in the grasses, darkness in trees.
Even the water in wells trembles.
Bodies give off darkness, and chrysanthemums
Are dark, and horses, who are bearing great loads of hay
To the deep barns where the dark air is moving from the corners.

Lincoln's statue, and the traffic. From the long past
Into the long present
A bird forgotten in these pressures, warbling,
As the great wheel turns around, grinding
The living in water.
Washing, continual washing, in water now stained
With blossoms and rotting logs, cries half-
Muffled, from beneath the earth, the living finally as awake as the dead.

POEM AGAINST THE RICH

Each day I live, each day the sea of light
Rises, I seem to see
The tear inside the stone
As if my eyes were gazing beneath the earth.
The rich man in his red hat
Cannot hear
The weeping in the pueblos of the lily,
Or the dark tears in the shacks of the corn.
Each day the sea of light rises
I hear the sad rustle of the darkened armies,
Where each man weeps, and the plaintive
Orisons of the stones.
The stones bow as the saddened armies pass.

POEM AGAINST THE BRITISH

I
The wind through the box-elder trees
Is like rides at dusk on a white horse,
Wars for your country, and fighting the British.

II
I wonder if Washington listened to the trees.
All morning I have been sitting in grass,
Higher than my eyes, beneath trees,
And listening upward, to the wind in leaves.
Suddenly I realize there is one thing more:
There is also the wind through the high grass.

III

There are palaces, boats, silence among white buildings,
Iced drinks on marble tops, among cool rooms;
It is good also to be poor, and listen to the wind.

WHERE WE MUST LOOK FOR HELP

The dove returns; it found no resting place;
It was in flight all night above the shaken seas.
Beneath Ark eaves
The dove shall magnify the tiger's bed;
Give the dove peace.
The split-tail swallows leave the sill at dawn;
At dusk blue swallows shall return.
On the third day the crow shall fly;
The crow, the crow, the spider-colored crow,
The crow shall find new mud to walk upon.

REMEMBERING IN OSLO THE OLD PICTURE
OF THE MAGNA CARTA

The girl in a housedress, pushing open the window,
Is also the fat king sitting under the oak tree,
And the garbagemen, thumping their cans, are
Crows still cawing,
And the nobles are offering the sheet to the king.
One thing is also another thing, and the doomed galleons,
Hung with trinkets, hove by the coast, and in the blossoms
Of trees are still sailing on their long voyage from Spain;
I too am still shocking grain, as I did as a boy, dog tired,
And my great-grandfather steps on his ship.

SUMMER, 1960, MINNESOTA

I
After a drifting day, visiting the bridge near Louisburg,
With its hot muddy water flowing
Under the excited swallows,
Now, at noon,
We plunge through the hot beanfields,
And the sturdy alfalfa fields, the farm groves
Like heavy green smoke close to the ground.

II
Inside me there is a confusion of swallows,
Birds flying through the smoke,
And horses galloping excitedly on fields of short grass.

III
Yet, we are falling,
Falling into the open mouths of darkness,
Into the Congo as if into a river,
Or as wheat into open mills.

WITH PALE WOMEN IN MARYLAND

With pale women in Maryland,
Passing the proud and tragic pastures,
And stupefied with love
And the stupendous burdens of the foreign trees,
As all before us lived, dazed
With overabundant love in the reach of the Chesapeake,
Past the tobacco warehouse, through our dark lives
Like those before, we move to the death we love
With pale women in Maryland.

DRIVING THROUGH OHIO

I

We slept that night in Delaware, Ohio:
A magnificent and sleepy country,
Oak country, sheep country, sod country.
We slept in a huge white tourist home
With *National Geographics* on the table.

II

North of Columbus there is a sort of torpid joy:
The slow and muddy river,
The white barns leaning into the ground,
Cottonwoods with their trunks painted white,
And houses with small observatories on top,
As if Ohio were the widow's coast, looking over
The dangerous Atlantic.

III

Now we drive north past the white cemeteries
So rich in the morning air!
All morning I have felt the sense of death;
I am full of love, and love this torpid land.
Someday I will go back, and inhabit again
The sleepy ground where Harding was born.

AT THE FUNERAL OF GREAT-AUNT MARY

I

Here we are, all dressed up to honor death!
No, it is not that;
It is to honor this old woman
Born in Bellingham.

II

The church windows are open to the green trees.
The minister tells us that, being
The sons and daughters of God,
We rejoice at death, for we go
To the mansions prepared
From the foundations of the world.
Impossible. No one believes it.

III

Out in the bare, pioneer field,
The frail body must wait till dusk
To be lowered
In the hot and sandy earth.

ON THE FERRY ACROSS CHESAPEAKE BAY

On the orchard of the sea, far out are whitecaps,
Water that answers questions no one has asked,
Silent speakers of the grave's rejoinders;
Having accomplished nothing, I am traveling somewhere else;
O deep green sea, it is not for you
This smoking body plows toward death;
It is not for the strange blossoms of the sea
I drag my thin legs across the Chesapeake Bay;
Though perhaps by your motion the body heals;
For though on its road the body cannot march
With golden trumpets—it must march—
And the sea gives up its answers as it falls into itself.

A MAN WRITES TO A PART OF HIMSELF

What cave are you in, hiding, rained on?
Like a wife, starving, without care,
Water dripping from your head, bent
Over ground corn . . .

You raise your face into the rain
That drives across the valley.
Forgive me, your husband,
On the streets of a distant city, laughing,
With many appointments,
Though at night going also
To a bare room, a room of poverty,
To sleep beside a bare pitcher and basin
In a room with no heat—

Which of us two then is the worse off?
And how did this separation come about?

DEPRESSION

I felt my heart beat like an engine high in the air,
Like those scaffolding engines standing only on planks;
My body hung about me like an old grain elevator,
Useless, clogged, full of blackened wheat.
My body was sour, my life dishonest, and I fell asleep.

I dreamt that men came toward me, carrying thin wires;
I felt the wires pass in; they were old Tibetans,
Dressed in padded clothes, to keep out cold;
Then three work gloves, lying fingers to fingers,
In a circle, came toward me, and I awoke.

Now I want to go back among the dark roots;
Now I want to see the day pulling its long wing;
I want to see nothing more than two feet high;
I want to see no one, I want to say nothing,
I want to go down and rest in the black earth of silence.

DRIVING TO TOWN LATE TO MAIL A LETTER

It is a cold and snowy night. The main street is deserted.
The only things moving are swirls of snow.
As I lift the mailbox door, I feel its cold iron.
There is a privacy I love in this snowy night.
Driving around, I will waste more time.

GETTING UP EARLY

I am up early. The box-elder leaves have fallen.
The eastern sky is the color of March.
The sky has spread out over the world like water.
The bootlegger and his wife are still asleep.

I saw the light first from the barn well.
The cold water fell into the night-chilled buckets,
Deepening the somber blue of the southern sky.
Over the new trees, there was a strange light in the east.

The light was dawn. Like a man who has come home
After seeing many dark rivers, and will soon go again,
The dawn stood there with a quiet gaze;
Our eyes met through the top leaves of the young ash.

Dawn has come. The clouds floating in the east have turned white.
The fenceposts have stopped being a part of the darkness.
The depth has disappeared from the puddles on the ground.
I look up angrily at the light.

A LATE SPRING DAY IN MY LIFE

A silence hovers over the earth:
The grass lifts lightly in the heat
Like the ancient wing of a bird.
A horse gazes steadily at me.

LOVE POEM

When we are in love, we love the grass,
And the barns, and the lightpoles,
And the small mainstreets abandoned all night.

"TAKING THE HANDS"

Taking the hands of someone you love,
You see they are delicate cages . . .
Tiny birds are singing
In the secluded prairies
And in the deep valleys of the hands.

AFTERNOON SLEEP

I

I was descending from the mountains of sleep.
Asleep I had gazed east over a sunny field,
And sat on the running board of an old Model A.
I awoke happy, for I had dreamt of my wife,
And the loneliness hiding in grass and weeds
That lies near a man over thirty, and suddenly enters.

II

When Joe Sjolie grew tired, he sold his farm,
Even his bachelor rocker, and did not come back.
He left his dog behind in the cob shed.
The dog refused to take food from strangers.

III

I drove out to that farm when I awoke;
Alone on a hill, sheltered by trees.
The matted grass lay around the house.
When I climbed the porch, the door was open.
Inside were old abandoned books,
And instructions to Norwegian immigrants.

IMAGES SUGGESTED BY MEDIEVAL MUSIC

For Margaret and Joseph Scheinin

"A thousand singing herons I saw passing
Flying overhead, sounding a thousand voices
Exulting: Glory be in the heavens," etc.

I

Once more in Brooklyn Heights
A child is born, and it has no father,
And it is right to rejoice: our past life appears
As a wake behind us, and we plunge on into the sea of pain.

II

I have felt this joy before, it is like the harsh grasses
On lonely beaches, this strange sweetness
Of medieval music, a hoarse joy,
Like birds', or the joy of trackless seas,
Columbus's ships covered with ice,
Palace children dancing among finely worked gold:

III

As I listen, I am a ship, skirting
A thousand harbors, as once, sailing off the coast of Crete,
And turning in, we will find the steep climb from the harbor;
The voyage goes on. The joy of sailing and the open sea!

SOLITUDE LATE AT NIGHT IN THE WOODS

I

The body is like a November birch facing the full moon
And reaching into the cold heavens.

In these trees there is no ambition, no sodden body, no leaves,
Nothing but bare trunks climbing like cold fire!

II
My last walk in the trees has come. At dawn
I must return to the trapped fields,
To the obedient earth.
The trees shall be reaching all the winter.

III
It is a joy to walk in the bare woods.
The moonlight is not broken by the heavy leaves.
The leaves are down, and touching the soaked earth,
Giving off the odor that partridges love.

WATERING THE HORSE

How strange to think of giving up all ambition!
Suddenly I see with such clear eyes
The white flake of snow
That has just fallen in the horse's mane!

IN A TRAIN

There has been light snow.
Dark car tracks move in out of the darkness.
I stare at the train window marked with soft dust.
I have awakened at Missoula, Montana, utterly happy.

SILENCE ON THE ROADS

AFTER WORKING

I
After many strange thoughts,
Thoughts of distant harbors, and new life,
I came in and found the moonlight lying in the room.

II
Outside it covers the trees like pure sound,
The sound of tower bells, or of water moving under the ice,
The sound of the deaf hearing through the bones of their heads.

III
We know the road; as the moonlight
Lifts everything, so in a night like this
The road goes on ahead, it is all clear.

THE CLEAR AIR OF OCTOBER

I can see outside the gold wings without birds
Flying around, and the wells of cold water
Without walls standing eighty feet up in the air,
I can feel the crickets' singing carrying them into the sky.

I know these cold shadows are falling for hundreds of miles,
Crossing lawns in tiny towns, and the doors of Catholic churches;
I know the horse of darkness is riding fast to the east,
Carrying a thin man with no coat.

And I know the sun is sinking down great stairs,
Like an executioner with a great blade walking into a cellar,
And the gold animals, the lions, and the zebras, and the pheasants,
Are waiting at the head of the stairs with robbers' eyes.

LAZINESS AND SILENCE

I
On a Saturday afternoon in the football season,
I lie on a bed near the lake,
And dream of moles with golden wings.

While the depth of the water trembles on the ceiling,
Like the tail of an enraged bird,
I watch the dust floating above the bed, content.

I think of ships leaving lonely harbors,
Dolphins playing far at sea,
Fish with the faces of old men come in from a blizzard.

II
A dream of moles with golden wings
Is not so bad; it is like imagining
Waterfalls of stone deep in mountains,
Or a wing flying alone beneath the earth.

I know that far out in the Minnesota lake
Fish are nosing the mouths of cold springs,
Whose water causes ripples in the sleeping sand,
Like a spirit moving in a body.

It is Saturday afternoon. Crowds are gathered,
Warmed by the sun, and the pure air.
I thought of this strange mole this morning,
After sleeping all night by the lake.

SEPTEMBER NIGHT WITH AN OLD HORSE

I
Tonight I rode through the cornfield in the moonlight!
The dying grass is still, waiting for winter,
And the dark weeds are waiting, as if underwater . . .

II
In Arabia, the horses live in the tents,
Near dark gold, and water, and tombs.

III
How beautiful to walk out at midnight in the moonlight
Dreaming of animals.

NIGHT

I
If I think of a horse wandering about sleeplessly
All night on this short grass covered with moonlight,

I feel a joy, as if I had thought
Of a pirate ship plowing through dark flowers.

II

The box elders around us are full of joy,
Obeying what is beneath them.
The lilacs are sleeping, and the plants are sleeping;
Even the wood made into a casket is asleep.

III

The butterfly is carrying loam on its wings;
The toad is bearing tiny bits of granite in his skin.
The leaves at the crown of the tree are asleep
Like the dark bits of earth at its root.

IV

Alive we are like a sleek black water beetle,
Skating across still water in any direction
We choose, and soon to be swallowed
Suddenly from beneath.

AFTER DRINKING ALL NIGHT WITH A FRIEND, WE GO OUT IN A BOAT AT DAWN TO SEE WHO CAN WRITE THE BEST POEM

These pines, these fall oaks, these rocks,
This water dark and touched by wind—
I am like you, you dark boat,
Drifting over water fed by cool springs.

Beneath the waters, since I was a boy,
I have dreamt of strange and dark treasures,

Not of gold or strange stones, but the true
Gift, beneath the pale lakes of Minnesota.

This morning also, drifting in the dawn wind,
I sense my hands, and my shoes, and this ink—
Drifting, as all of the body drifts,
Above the clouds of the flesh and the stone.

A few friendships, a few dawns, a few glimpses of grass,
A few oars weathered by the snow and the heat,
So we drift toward shore, over cold waters,
No longer caring if we drift or go straight.

OLD BOARDS

I
I love to see boards lying on the ground in early spring:
The ground beneath them is wet, and muddy—
Perhaps covered with chicken tracks—
And they are dry and eternal.

II
This is the wood one sees on the decks of ocean ships,
Wood that carries us far from land,
With a dryness of something used for simple tasks,
Like a horse's tail.

III
This wood is like a man who has a simple life,
Living through the spring and winter on the ship of his own desire.
He sits on dry wood surrounded by half-melted snow
As the rooster walks away springily over the dampened hay.

LATE AT NIGHT DURING A VISIT OF FRIENDS

I
We spent all day fishing and talking.
At last, late at night, I sit at my desk alone,
And rise and walk out in the summery night.
A dark thing hopped near me in the grass.

II
The trees were breathing, the windmill slowly pumped.
Overhead the rain clouds that rained on Ortonville
Covered half the stars.
The air was still cool from their rain.

III
It is very late.
I am the only one awake.
Men and women I love are sleeping nearby.

IV
The human face shines as it speaks of things
Near itself, thoughts full of dreams.
The human face shines like a dark sky
As it speaks of those things that oppress the living.

SILENCE

The fall has come, clear as the eyes of chickens.
Strange muffled sounds come from the sea,
Sounds of muffled oarlocks,
And swampings in lonely bays,
Surf crashing on unchristened shores,
And the wash of tiny snail shells in the wandering gravel.

My body also wanders among these doorposts and cars,
Cradling a pen, or walking down a stair
Holding a cup in my hand,
And not breaking into the pastures that lie in the sunlight.
This is the sloth of the man inside the body,
The sloth of the body lost among the wandering stones of kindness.

Something homeless is looking on the long roads—
A dog lost since midnight, a small duck
Among the odorous reeds,
Or a tiny box-elder bug searching for the windowpane.
Even the young sunlight is lost on the windowpane,
Moving at night like a diver among the bare branches silently
 lying on the floor.

SNOWFALL IN THE AFTERNOON

I
The grass is half-covered with snow.
It was the sort of snowfall that starts in late afternoon,
And now the little houses of the grass are growing dark.

II
If I reached my hands down, near the earth,
I could take handfuls of darkness!
A darkness that was always there, which we never noticed.

III
As the snow grows heavier, the cornstalks fade farther away,
And the barn moves nearer to the house.
The barn moves all alone in the growing storm.

IV

The barn is full of corn, and moving toward us now,
Like a hulk blown toward us in a storm at sea;
All the sailors on deck have been blind for many years.

THE
LIGHT
AROUND
THE
BODY

(1967)

I

THE TWO WORLDS

For according to the outward man, we are in this world, and according
to the inward man, we are in the inward world. . . . Since then we are
generated out of both worlds, we speak in two languages, and we must
be understood also by two languages.

—Jacob Boehme

THE EXECUTIVE'S DEATH

Merchants have multiplied more than the stars of heaven.
Half the population are like the long grasshoppers
That sleep in the bushes in the cool of the day:
The sound of their wings is heard at noon, muffled, near the earth.
The crane handler dies, the taxi driver dies, slumped over
In his taxi. Meanwhile, high in the air, an executive
Walks on the cool floor, and suddenly falls.
He dreams he is lost in a snowstorm in a mountain,
On which he crashed, carried at night by great machines.
As he lies on the wintery slope, cut off and dying,
A pine stump talks to him of Goethe and Jesus.
Commuters arrive in Hartford at dusk like moles
Or hares flying from a fire behind them,
And the dusk in Hartford is full of their sighs;
Their trains come through the air like a dark music,
Like the sound of horns, the sound of thousands of small wings.

THE BUSY MAN SPEAKS

Not to the mother of solitude will I give myself
Away, not to the mother of love, nor to the mother of conversation,
Nor to the mother of art, nor the mother
Of tears, nor the mother of the ocean;
Not to the mother of sorrow, nor the mother
Of the downcast face, nor the mother of the suffering of death;
Not to the mother of the night full of crickets,
Nor the mother of the open fields, nor the mother of Christ.

But I will give myself to the father of righteousness, the father
Of cheerfulness, who is also the father of rocks,
Who is also the father of perfect gestures;
From the Chase National Bank
An arm of flame has come, and I am drawn
To the desert, to the parched places, to the landscape of zeroes;
And I shall give myself away to the father of righteousness,
The stones of cheerfulness, the steel of money, the father of rocks.

JOHNSON'S CABINET WATCHED BY ANTS

1
It is a clearing deep in a forest: overhanging boughs
Make a low place. Here citizens we know during the day,
The ministers, the department heads,
Appear changed: the stockholders of large steel companies
In small wooden shoes: Here are the generals dressed as
 gamboling lambs.

2
Tonight they burn the rice supplies; tomorrow
They lecture on Thoreau; tonight they move around the trees,

Tomorrow they pick the twigs from their clothes;
Tonight they throw the firebombs, tomorrow
They read the Declaration of Independence; tomorrow they are in
 church.

3
Ants are gathered around an old tree.
In a choir they sing, in harsh and gravelly voices,
Old Etruscan songs on tyranny.
Toads nearby clap their small hands, and join
The fiery songs, their five long toes trembling in the soaked earth.

WATCHING TELEVISION

Sounds are heard too high for ears,
From the body cells there is an answering bay;
Soon the inner streets fill with a chorus of barks.

We see the landing craft coming in,
The black car sliding to a stop,
The Puritan killer loosening his guns.

Wild dogs tear off noses and eyes
And run off with them down the street—
The body tears off its own arms and throws them into the air.

The detective draws fifty-five million people into his revolver,
Who sleep restlessly as in an air raid in London;
Their backs become curved in the sloping dark.

The filaments of the soul slowly separate:
The spirit breaks, a puff of dust floats up,
Like a house in Nebraska that suddenly explodes.

SMOTHERED BY THE WORLD

Chrysanthemums crying out on the borders of death,
Lone teeth walking in the icy waters,
Once more the heavy body mourns!
It howls outside the hedges of life,
Pushed out of the enclosure.
Now it must meet the death outside the death.
Living outside the gate is one death,
Cold faces gather along the wall,
A bag of bones warms itself in a tree.
Long and bitter antlers sway in the dark,
The hairy tail howls in the dirt . . .

A DREAM OF SUFFOCATION

Accountants hover over the earth like helicopters,
Dropping bits of paper engraved with Hegel's name.
Badgers carry the papers on their fur
To their den, where the entire family dies in the night.

A chorus girl stands for hours behind her curtains
Looking out at the street.
In a window of a trucking service
There is a branch painted white.
A stuffed baby alligator grips that branch tightly
To keep away from the dry leaves on the floor.

The honeycomb at night has strange dreams:
Small black trains going round and round—
Old warships drowning in the raindrop.

ROMANS ANGRY ABOUT THE INNER WORLD

What shall the world do with its children?
There are lives the executives
Know nothing of,
A leaping of the body,
The body rolling—and I have felt it—
And we float
Joyfully on the dark places;
But the executioners
Move toward Drusia. They tie her legs
On the iron horse. "Here is a woman
Who has seen our mother
In the other world!" Next they warm
The hooks. The two Romans had put their trust
In the outer world. Irons glowed
Like teeth. They wanted her
To assure them. She refused. Finally they took burning
Pine sticks, and pushed them
Into her sides. Her breath rose
And she died. The executioners
Rolled her off onto the ground.
A light snow began to fall
And covered the mangled body,
And the executives, astonished, withdrew.
The other world is like a thorn
In the ear of a tiny beast!
The fingers of the executives are too thick
To pull it out!
It is like a jagged stone
Flying toward them out of the darkness.

II

THE VARIOUS ARTS OF POVERTY AND CRUELTY

When we think of it with this knowledge, we see that we have been locked up, and led blindfold, and it is the wise of this world who have shut and locked us up in their art and their rationality, so that we have had to see with their eyes.

—Boehme

Our fathers ate manna in the wilderness and they died.

—old liturgy

What a distressing contrast there is between the radiant intelligence of the child, and the feeble mentality of the average adult.

—Freud

COME WITH ME

Come with me into those things that have felt this despair for so
 long—
Those removed Chevrolet wheels that howl with a terrible
 loneliness,
Lying on their backs in the cindery dirt, like men drunk and naked,
Staggering off down a hill at night to drown at last in a pond.
Those shredded inner tubes abandoned on the shoulders of
 thruways,

Black and collapsed bodies, that tried and burst, and were left behind.
And those curly steel shavings, scattered about on garage benches,
Sometimes still warm, gritty when we hold them,
Who have given up, and blame everything on the government;
And those roads in South Dakota that feel around in the darkness. . . .

THOSE BEING EATEN BY AMERICA

The cry of those being eaten by America,
Others pale and soft being stored for later eating

And Jefferson
Who saw hope in new oats

The wild houses go on
With long hair growing from between their toes
The feet at night get up
And run down the long white roads by themselves

The dams reverse themselves and want to go stand alone in the desert

Ministers who dive headfirst into the earth
The pale flesh
Spreading guiltily into new literatures

That is why these poems are so sad
The long-dead running over the fields

The mass sinking down
The light in children's faces fading at six or seven

The world will soon break up into small colonies of the saved

WRITTEN IN DEJECTION NEAR ROME

What if these long races go on repeating themselves
Century after century, living in houses painted light colors
On the beach,
Black spiders,
Having turned pale and fat,
Men walking thoughtfully with their families,
Vibrations
Of exhausted violin-bodies,
Horrible eternities of sea pines!
Some men cannot help but feel it,
They will abandon their homes
To live on rafts tied together on the ocean;
Those on shore will go inside tree trunks,
Surrounded by bankers whose fingers have grown long and slender,
Piercing through rotting bark for their food.

LISTENING TO PRESIDENT KENNEDY LIE
ABOUT THE CUBAN INVASION

There is another darkness,
A darkness in the fences of the body,
And in moles running, and telephone wires,
And the frail ankles of horses;
Darkness of dying grass, and yellow willow leaves;
There is the death of broken buttonholes,
Of brutality in high places,
Of lying reporters,
There is a bitter fatigue, adult and sad.

THE GREAT SOCIETY

Dentists continue to water their lawns even in the rain;
Hands developed with terrible labor by apes
Hang from the sleeves of evangelists;
There are murdered kings in the lightbulbs outside movie theaters;
The coffins of the poor are hibernating in piles of new tires.

The janitor sits troubled by the boiler,
And the hotelkeeper shuffles the cards of insanity.
The President dreams of invading Cuba.
Bushes are growing over the outdoor grills,
Vines over the yachts and the leather seats.

The city broods over ash cans and darkening mortar.
On the far shore, at Coney Island, dark children
Play on the chilling beach: a sprig of black seaweed,
Shells, a skyful of birds,
While the mayor sits with his head in his hands.

SUDDENLY TURNING AWAY

Someone comes near, the jaw
Tightens, bullheads bite
The snow, moments of intimacy waved away,
Half-evolved antennas of the sea snail
Sink to the ground.
The sun
Glints on us! But the shadows
Of not-love come.
It cannot be stood against.
And we suffer. The gold discs
Fall from our ears.
The sea grows cloudy.

THREE PRESIDENTS

Andrew Jackson
I want to be a white horse!
I want to be a white horse on the green mountains!
A horse that runs over wooden bridges, and sleeps
In abandoned barns. . . .

Theodore Roosevelt
When I was President, I crushed snails with my bare teeth.
I slept in my underwear in the White House.
I ate the Cubans with a straw, and Lenin dreamt of *me* every night.
I wore down a forest of willow trees. I ground the snow,
And sold it.
The mountains of Texas shall heal our cornfields,
Overrun by the yellow race.
As for me, I want to be a stone! Yes!
I want to be a stone laid down thousands of years ago,
A stone with almost invisible cracks!
I want to be a stone that holds up the edge of the lake house,
A stone that suddenly gets up and runs around at night,
And lets the marriage bed fall; a stone that leaps into the water,
Carrying the robber down with him.

John F. Kennedy
I want to be a stream of water falling—
Water falling from high in the mountains, water
That dissolves everything,
And is never drunk, falling from ledge to ledge, from glass to glass.
I want the air around me to be invisible, resilient,
Able to flow past rocks.
I will carry the boulders with me to the valley.
Then ascending I will fall through space again:
Glittering in the sun, like the crystal in sideboards,

Goblets of the old life, before it was ruined by the Church.
And when I ascend the third time, I will fall forever,
Missing the earth entirely.

HEARING MEN SHOUT AT NIGHT ON MACDOUGAL STREET

How strange to awake in a city,
And hear grown men shouting in the night!
On the farm the darkness wins,
And the small ones nestle in their graves of cold:
Here is a boiling that only exhaustion subdues,
A bitter moiling of muddy waters
At which the voices of white men feed!

The sea is a street, and mud boils up
When the anchor is lifted, for now at midnight there is about to sail
The first New England slave-ship with the Negroes in the hold.

THE CURRENT ADMINISTRATION

1
Here Morgan dies like a dog among whispers of angels;
The saint is born among tin cans in the orchard;
A rose receives the name of "The General Jackson."
Here snow-white blossoms bloom in the bare homes
Of bankmen, and with a lily the Pope meets
A delegation of waves, and blesses the associations
Of the ocean; I walk with a coarse body through winds
That carry the birds on their long roads to the poles,
And see the ghost of Locke above the railroad tracks.

2

Snow fell all night on a farmyard in Montana.
And the Assyrian lion blazed above the soybean fields.
The last haven of Jehovah, down from the old heavens,
Hugged a sooty corner of the murdered pine.
 Arabic numerals
Walked the earth, dressed as bankers and sportsmen,
And at night diamonds in slippers invade our sleep.
Black beetles, bright as Cadillacs, toil down
The long dusty road into the mountains of South Dakota.

3

One night we find ourselves near the giant's house.
At dawn, mist blows over the great meadow.
Outside the steps, we find an aunt and uncle
Dead for twenty years working with hoes.
In their beds are small old men growing from the ground.
A mill grinding. We go in. Chairs
In the great room, hacked from redwood.
Tiny loaves of bread with ears lie on the President's table.
Steps coming! The Father will soon return!

ANDREW JACKSON'S SPEECH

Dido to Aeneas: "I have broke faith with the ashes of Sichaeus!"

I heard Andrew Jackson say, as he closed his Virgil:

"The harsh ravishers in Detroit, inheritors of the soot
Of chimney boys, when they raised the mighty poor,
Broke faith with the cinders of Sichaeus.

"I shot to save the honour of my wife;
And I would shoot again, to save my people.
The Republic lies in the blossoms of Washington.

"The poor have been raised up by the Revolution.
Washington, riding in cold snow at Valley Forge,
Warned the poor never to take another husband."

His voice rose in the noisy streets of Detroit.

SLEET STORM ON THE MERRITT PARKWAY

I look out at the white sleet covering the still streets
As we drive through Scarsdale—
The sleet began falling as we left Connecticut,
And the winter leaves swirled in the wet air after cars
Like hands suddenly turned over in a conversation.
Now the frost has nearly buried the short grass of March.
Seeing the sheets of sleet untouched on the wide streets,
I think of the many comfortable homes stretching for miles,
Two and three stories, solid, with polished floors,
With white curtains in the upstairs bedrooms,
And small perfume flagons of black glass on the windowsills,
And warm bathrooms with guest towels, and electric lights—
What a magnificent place for a child to grow up!
And yet the children end in the river of price-fixing,
Or in the snowy field of the insane asylum.
The sleet falls—so many cars moving toward New York—
Last night we argued about the Marines invading Guatemala in 1947,
The United Fruit Company had one water spigot for two hundred
 families,
And the ideals of America, our freedom to criticize,
The slave systems of Rome and Greece, and no one agreed.

III

THE VIETNAM WAR

AFTER THE INDUSTRIAL REVOLUTION, ALL THINGS HAPPEN AT ONCE

Now we enter a strange world, where the Hessian Christmas
Still goes on, and Washington has not reached the other shore;
The Whiskey Boys
Are gathering again on the meadows of Pennsylvania
And the Republic is still sailing on the open sea.

I saw a black angel in Washington dancing
On a barge, saying, "Let us now divide kennel dogs
And hunting dogs"; Henry Cabot Lodge, in New York,
Talking of sugarcane in Cuba; Ford,
In Detroit, drinking mother's milk;
Henry Cabot Lodge, saying, "Remember the *Maine*!"
Ford, saying, "History is bunk!"
And Wilson saying, "What is good for General Motors . . ."

Who is it, singing? Don't you hear singing?
It is the dead of Cripple Creek;
Coxey's army
Like turkeys are singing from the tops of trees!
And the Whiskey Boys are drunk outside Philadelphia.

ASIAN PEACE OFFERS REJECTED WITHOUT PUBLICATION

These suggestions by Asians are not taken seriously.
We know Rusk smiles as he passes them to someone.
Men like Rusk are not men only—
They are bombs waiting to be loaded in a darkened hangar.
Rusk's assistants eat hurriedly,
Talking of Teilhard de Chardin,
Longing to get back to their offices
So they can cling to the underside of the steel wings shuddering
 faintly in the high altitudes.
They land first, and hand the coffee cup to the drawn pilot.
They start the projector, and show the movie about the mad professor.

Lost angels huddled on a night branch!
The waves crossing
And recrossing beneath—
The sound of the rampaging Missouri—
Bending the reeds again and again—something inside us
Like a ghost train in the Rockies
About to be buried in snow!
Its long hoot
Making the owl in the Douglas fir turn his head . . .

WAR AND SILENCE

The bombers spread out, temperature steady
A Negro's ear sleeping in an automobile tire
Pieces of timber float by saying nothing

Bishops rush about crying, There is no war,
And bombs fall,
Leaving a dust on the beech trees

.

One leg walks down the road and leaves
The other behind, the eyes part
And fly off in opposite directions

.

Filaments of death grow out.
The sheriff cuts off his black legs
And nails them to a tree

COUNTING SMALL-BONED BODIES

Let's count the bodies over again.

If we could only make the bodies smaller,
The size of skulls,
We could make a whole plain white with skulls in the moonlight!

If we could only make the bodies smaller,
Maybe we could get
A year's kill in front of us on a desk!

If we could only make the bodies smaller,
We could fit
A body into a finger-ring, for a keepsake forever.

AS THE ASIAN WAR BEGINS

There are longings to kill that cannot be seen,
Or are seen only by a minister who no longer believes in God,
Living in his parish like a crow in its nest.

And there are flowers with murky centers,
Impenetrable, ebony, basalt . . .

Conestogas go past, over the Platte, their contents
Hidden from us, murderers riding under the canvas . . .

Give us a glimpse of what we cannot see,
Our enemies, the soldiers and the poor.

AT A MARCH AGAINST THE VIETNAM WAR

WASHINGTON, NOVEMBER 27, 1965

Newspapers rise high in the air over Maryland

We walk about, bundled in coats
 and sweaters in the late November sun

Looking down, I see feet moving
Calmly, gaily,
Almost as if separated from their bodies

But there is something moving in the dark somewhere
Just beyond
The edge of our eyes: a boat
Covered with machine guns
Moving along under trees

It is black,
The hand reaches out
And cannot touch it—
It is that darkness among pine boughs
That the Puritans brushed
As they went out to kill turkeys

At the edge of the jungle clearing
It explodes
On the ground

We long to abase ourselves

We have carried around this cup of darkness
We have longed to pour it over our heads

We make war
Like a man anointing himself

HATRED OF MEN WITH BLACK HAIR

I hear voices praising Tshombe, and the Portuguese
In Angola, these are the men who skinned Little Crow!
We are all their sons, skulking
In back rooms, selling nails with trembling hands!

We distrust every person on earth with black hair;
We send teams to overthrow Chief Joseph's government;
We train natives to kill Presidents with blowdarts;
We have men loosening the nails on Noah's Ark.

The State Department floats in the heavy jellies near the bottom
Like exhausted crustaceans, like squids who are confused,
Sending out beams of black light to the open sea,
Fighting their fraternal feeling for the great landlords.

We have violet rays that light up the jungles at night, showing
The friendly populations; we are teaching the children of ritual
To overcome their longing for life, and we send
Sparks of black light that fit the holes in the generals' eyes.

Underneath all the cement of the Pentagon
There is a drop of Indian blood preserved in snow:
Preserved from the trail of blood that once led away
From the stockade, over the snow, the trail now lost.

DRIVING THROUGH MINNESOTA DURING THE HANOI BOMBINGS

We drive between lakes just turning green;
Late June. The white turkeys have been moved
To new grass.
How long the seconds are in great pain!
Terror just before death,
Shoulders torn, shot
From helicopters, the boy
Tortured with the telephone generator,
"I felt sorry for him,
And blew his head off with a shotgun."
These instants become crystals,
Particles
The grass cannot dissolve. Our own gaiety
Will end up

In Asia, and in your cup you will look down
And see
Black Starfighters.
We were the ones we intended to bomb!
Therefore we will have
To go far away
To atone
For the sufferings of the stringy-chested
And the small rice-fed ones, quivering
In the helicopter like wild animals,
Shot in the chest, taken back to be questioned.

IV

IN PRAISE OF GRIEF

O dear children, look in what a dungeon we are lying, in what lodging we are, for we have been captured by the spirit of the outward world; it is our life, for it nourishes and brings us up, it rules in our marrow and bones, in our flesh and blood, it has made our flesh earthly, and now death has us.

—Jacob Boehme

MELANCHOLIA

1
A light seen suddenly in the storm, snow
Coming from all sides, like flakes
Of sleep, and myself
On the road to the dark barn,
Halfway there, a black dog near me.

2
Light on the wooden rail.
Someone I knew and loved.
As we hear the dates of his marriage
And the years he moved,
A wreath of dark fir and shiny laurel
Slips off the coffin.

3

A cathedral: I see
Starving men, weakened, leaning
On their knees. But the bells ring anyway,
Sending out over the planted fields
A vegetation, sound waves with long leaves.

4

There is a wound on the trunk,
Where the branch was torn off.
A wind comes out of it,
Rising, swelling,
Swirling over everything alive.

TURNING AWAY FROM LIES

1

If we are truly free, and live in a free country,
When shall I be without this heaviness of mind?
When shall I have peace? Peace this way and peace that way?
I have already looked beneath the street
And there I saw the bitter waters going down,
The ancient worms eating up the sky.

2

Christ did not come to redeem our sins
The Christ Child was not obedient to his parents
The Kingdom of Heaven does not mean the next life
No one in business can be a Christian
The two worlds are both in this world

3

The saints rejoice out loud upon their beds!
Their song moves through the troubled sea
The way the holy tortoise moves
From dark blue into troubled green,
Or ghost crabs move above the dolomite.
The thieves are crying in the wild asparagus.

A HOME IN DARK GRASS

In the deep fall the body awakes
And we find lions on the seashore—
Nothing to fear.
The wind rises; the water is born,
Spreading white tomb-clothes on a rocky shore,
Drawing us up
From the bed of the land.

We did not come to remain whole.
We came to lose our leaves like the trees,
The trees that are broken
And start again, drawing up from the great roots;
So men captured by the Moors
Wake rowing in the cold ocean
Air, living a second life.

That we should learn of poverty and rags,
That we should taste the weed of Dillinger,
And swim in the sea,
Not always walking on dry land,
And, dancing, find in the trees a savior,
A home in dark grass,
And nourishment in death.

LOOKING AT NEW-FALLEN SNOW FROM A TRAIN

Snow has covered the next line of tracks,
And filled the empty cupboards in the milkweed pods;
It has stretched out on the branches of weeds,
And softened the frost-hills, and the barbed-wire rolls
Left leaning against a fencepost—
It has drifted onto the window ledges high in the peaks of barns.

 A man throws back his head, gasps
 And dies. His ankles twitch, his hands open and close,
 And the fragment of time that he has eaten is exhaled from
 his pale mouth to nourish the snow.
 A salesman falls, striking his head on the edge of the counter.

Snow has filled out the peaks on the tops of rotted fenceposts.
It has walked down to meet the slough water,
And fills all the steps of the ladder leaning against the eaves.
It rests on the doorsills of collapsing children's houses,
And on transformer boxes held from the ground forever in the
 center of cornfields.

A man lies down to sleep.
Hawks and crows gather around his bed.
Grass shoots up between the hawks' toes.
Each blade of grass is a voice.
The sword by his side breaks into flame.

IN DANGER FROM THE OUTER WORLD

This burning in the eyes as we open doors,
This is only the body burdened down with leaves,
The opaque flesh, heavy as November grass,
Growing stubbornly, triumphant even at midnight.

And another day disappears into the cliff,
And the Eskimos come to greet it with sharp cries—
The black water swells up over the new hole,
The grave moves forward from its ambush,

Moving over the hills on black feet,
Living off the country,
Leaving dogs and sheep murdered where it slept;
Some shining thing, inside, that has served us well

Shakes its bamboo bars—
It may be gone before we wake . . .

THE FIRE OF DESPAIR HAS BEEN OUR SAVIOUR

Today, autumn.
Heaven's roots are still.
O holy trees, rejoicing ruin of leaves,
How easily we see spring coming in your black branches!
Not like the Middle Ages! Then iron ringing iron
At dawn, chill wringing
The grass, clatter of saddles,
The long flight on borrowed stone
Into the still air sobered by the hidden joy of crows.

Or the Ice Age!
Another child dead,
Turning bone stacks for bones, sleeves of snow blowing
Down from above, no tracks in the snow, in agony
Man cried out—like the mad hog, pierced, again,
Again, by teeth-spears, who
Grew his horny scales
From sheer despair—instants
Finally leading out of the snowbound valley!

This autumn, I
Cannot find the road
That way: the things that we must grasp,
The signs, are gone, hidden by spring and fall, leaving
A still sky here, a dusk there,
A dry cornleaf in a field; where has the road gone? All
Trace lost, like a ship sinking,
Where what is left and what goes down both bring despair.
Not finding the road, we are slowly pulled down.

LOOKING AT SOME FLOWERS

Light is around the petals, and behind them:
Some petals are living on the other side of the light.
Like sunlight drifting onto the carpet
Where the casket stands, not knowing which world it is in.
And fuzzy leaves, hair growing from some animal
Buried in the green trenches of the plant.
Or the ground this house is on,
Only free of the sea for five or six thousand years.

V

A BODY NOT YET BORN

But when this had given me many a hard blow, doubtless from the Spirit that had a desire for me, I finally fell into great sadness and melancholy, when I viewed the great depth of this world, the sun and the stars and the clouds, rain and snow, and contemplated in my mind the whole creation of this world.

So then I found in all things good and evil, love and wrath, in creatures of reason as well as in wood, in stone, in earth, in the elements, in men and animals. Withal, I considered the little spark "man" and what it might be esteemed to be by God in comparison with this great work of heaven and earth.

In consequence I grew very melancholy, and what is written, though I knew it well, could not console me.

—Jacob Boehme

LOOKING INTO A FACE

Conversation brings us so close! Opening
The surfs of the body,
Bringing fish up near the sun,
And stiffening the backbones of the sea!

I have wandered in a face, for hours,
Passing through dark fires.

I have risen to a body
Not yet born,
Existing like a light around the body,
Through which the body moves like a sliding moon.

HURRYING AWAY FROM THE EARTH

The poor and the dazed and the idiots
Are with us, they live in the casket of the sun
And the moon's coffin, as I walk out tonight
Seeing the night wheel its dark wheelbarrow
All about the plains of heaven,
And the stars inexorably rising.
Dark moon! Sinister tears!
Shadows of slums and of the conquering dead!

One man pierced his chest with a long needle
To stop his heart from beating anymore.
Another put blocks of ice in his bed
So he would die; a woman
Washed her hair, and hanged herself
In the long braids. Climbing a high
Elm above her lawn, another
Opened a box, and swallowed poisonous spiders.

The time for exhortation is past. I have heard
The iron chairs scraping in asylums,
As the cold bird hunches into the winter
In the windy night of November.
The coal miners rise from their pits
Like a flash flood,
Like a rice field disintegrating.
Men cry when they hear stories of someone rising from the dead.

THE HERMIT

Darkness is falling through darkness,
Falling from ledge
To ledge.
There is a man whose body is perfectly whole.
He stands, the storm behind him,
And the grassblades are leaping in the wind.
Darkness is gathered in folds
About his feet.
He is no one. When we see
Him, we grow calm,
And sail on into the tunnels of joyful death.

MAX ERNST AND THE TORTOISE'S BEAK

1

Floating in turtle blood, going backward and forward,
We wake up like a mad sea-urchin
On the bloody fields near the secret pass—
There the dead sleep in jars. . . .

2

Or we go at night slowly into the tunnels of the tortoise's claws,
Carrying chunks of the moon
To light the tunnels,
Listening for the sound of rocks falling into the sea. . . .

3

Waking, we find ourselves in the tortoise's beak,
As he carries us high
Over New Jersey—going swiftly
Through the darkness between the constellations. . . .

4
At dawn we are still transparent, pulling
In the starlight; high up near the stars,
We are still falling like a room
Full of moonlight through the air. . . .

MOVING INWARD AT LAST

The dying bull is bleeding on the mountain!
But inside the mountain, untouched
By the blood,
There are antlers, bits of oak bark,
Fire, herbs are thrown down.

When the smoke touches the roof of the cave,
The green leaves burst into flame,
The air of night changes to dark water,
The mountains alter and become the sea.

RIDERLESS HORSES

An owl on the dark waters
And so many torches smoking
By mossy stone
And horses that are seen riderless on moonlit nights
A candle flutters as a black hand
Reaches out
All of these mean
A man with coins on his eyes

The vast waters
The cry of seagulls

EVOLUTION FROM THE FISH

This grandson of fishes holds inside him
A hundred thousand small black stones.
This nephew of snails, six feet long, lies naked on a bed
With a smiling woman. His head throws off light
Under marble; he is moving toward his own life
Like fur, walking. And when the frost comes, he is
Fur, mammoth fur, growing longer
And silkier, passing the woman's dormitory,
Kissing a stomach, leaning against a pillar,
He moves toward the animal, the animal with furry head!

What a joy to smell the flesh of a new child!
Like new grass! And this long man with the student girl,
Coffee cups, her pale waist, the spirit moving around them,
Moves, dragging a great tail into the darkness.
In the night we blaze up, drawing pictures
Of spiny fish; we throw off the white stones!
Serpents rise from the ocean floor with spiral motions;
A man goes inside a jewel, and sleeps. Do
Not hold my hands down! Let me raise them!
A fire is passing up through the soles of my feet!

WANTING TO EXPERIENCE ALL THINGS

A blind horse stands among cherry trees.
And legbones poking from cool earth.
The heart leaps
Almost up to the sky! But laments
And filaments pull us back into the dark.
Night takes hold of us.
But a paw

Comes out of the dark
To light the road. I'll be all right.
I follow my own fiery traces through the night.

OPENING AN OYSTER
For Max Ernst

We think of Charlemagne
As we open oysters.
Looking down, we see
Crowds waving from islands inside the oyster shell.
The neck swings to bite the dog.
When the fishermen take in their floats
They lift nets some giant fish
Broke through at night.
At dusk we start north with twenty dogs.
Blowing snow
Makes us lower our heads
And miles of snow crust
Go past between the runners!

Westward the ice peaks
Like vast maternity hospitals turned white by oyster shells!
Going around the war hospital,
We see a pebble
That has drawn in the malignancy of the shark,
Like a mammoth hair
That melts an entire Russian county, drowning
Chickens and cows—then we know that in attics there are
Cloths folded that murdered the great princes!

WHEN THE DUMB SPEAK

There's a joyful night in which we lose
Everything, and drift
Like a radish
Rising and falling, and the ocean
At last throws us into the ocean;
And on the water we are sinking
As if floating on darkness.
The body raging,
And driving itself, disappearing in smoke:
Walks in large cities late at night,
Reading the Bible in Christian Science windows,
Or reading a history of Bougainville:
Then the images appear—
Images of grief,
Images of the body shaken in the grave,
And the graves filled with seawater;
Fires in the sea,
Bodies smoldering like ships,
Images of wasted life,
Life lost, imagination ruined,
The house fallen,
The gold sticks broken!
Then shall the talkative be silent
And the dumb will speak.

SLEEPERS
JOINING
HANDS

(1973)

SIX WINTER PRIVACY POEMS

I

About four, a few flakes.
I empty the teapot out in the snow,
Feeling shoots of joy in the new cold.
By nightfall, wind;
The curtains on the south sway softly.

II

My shack has two rooms; I use one.
The lamplight falls on my chair and table,
And I fly into one of my own poems—
I can't tell you where—
As if I appeared where I am now,
In a wet field, snow falling.

III

More of the fathers are dying each day.
It is time for the sons.
Bits of darkness are gathering around them.
The darkness appears as flakes of light.

IV

Listening to Bach's Cello Concerto
Inside this music there is someone
Who is not well-described
By the names of Jesus, or Jehovah, or the Lord of Hosts.

V

There is a solitude like black mud!
Sitting in the darkness singing,
I can't tell if this joy
Is from the body, or the soul, or a third place!

VI

When I wake, new snow has fallen,
I am alone, yet someone else is with me,
Drinking coffee, looking out at the snow.

THE TURTLE

How shiny the turtle is, coming out
of the water, climbing the rock, as if
the body inside shone through!
As if swift turtle wings swept out of darkness,
crossed some barriers,
and found new eyes.
An old man falters with his stick.
Later, walkers find holes in black earth.
The snail climbs up the wet trunk glistening
like an angel-flight trailing long black banners.
No one finds the huge turtle eggs
lying inland on the floor of the old sea.

CHINESE TOMB GUARDIANS

Oh yes, I love you, book of my confessions,
Where what was swallowed, pushed away, sunken,
Driven down, begins to rise from the earth

Once more, and the madness and rage from the wells.
The buried is still buried, like cows who eat
In a collapsed strawpile all winter to get out.

Something inside me is still imprisoned in winter straw,
Or far back in the mountain where Charlemagne sleeps,
Or under the water, hard to get to, guarded by women.
Enough rises from that place to darken my poems;
Perhaps too much; and what remains down there
Makes a faint glow in the dead leaves.

I am less than half risen. I see how carefully
I have covered my tracks as I wrote,
How well I have brushed over the past with my tail.
Faces look at me from the shallow waters,
Where I have pushed them down—
Father and mother pushed into the dark.

What am I in my ambition and loneliness?
I am the dust that fills the cracks on the ocean floor.
Floating like the stingray, used to the weight
Of the ocean floor, retreating to a cave,
I live as a lizard or a winged shark,
Darting out at times to wound others, or get food.

How do we know that the hidden will ever rise?
How do we know that the buried will be revealed?
Some beings get used to life underneath.
Some dreams do not want to move into the light.
Some want to, but they can't; they can't make their way out,
Because someone is guarding the posts of the door.

Have you seen those Chinese tomb guardians
Left at the closed door? They stand with one knee raised;
They half-stand, half-dance, half-rage, half-shout—

Hot-tempered muscle-bulgers, big-kneed brow-bulgers.
They scowl for eternity at the half-risen.
What do you have that can get past them?

SHACK POEM

1
I don't even know these roads I walk on,
I see the backs of white birds.
Whales rush by, their teeth ivory.

2
Far out at the edge of the heron's wing,
where the air is disturbed by the last feather,
there is the Kingdom. . . .

3
Hurrying to brush between the Two Fish,
the wild woman flies on . . .
blue glass stones a path on earth mark her going.

4
I sit down and fold my legs. . . .
The half-dark in the room is delicious.
How marvelous to be a thought entirely surrounded by brains!

IN A MOUNTAIN CABIN IN NORWAY

I look down the mountainside. Just below my window
several grasses growing raggedly together.

The noise of the snow-fed river
winds into the ear, far back into the head.
At three a.m. the big peaks are still lit.

I look over to the other mountainside.
So many pines the eyes can't count them!
Sparks of darkness float around me.
No one comes to visit us for a week.

A CONVERSATION

Judgment
The doctor arrives to inject the movie star against delirium tremens.
Hands that lie so often calm on the horse's mane are shaking.
His hair hangs down like a skier's hair after a fall.
From a whirlpool drops of black water fly up,
And thousands and thousands of years go by—
Like an infinite procession of walnut shells.

That hair that fell to the floor of the barbershop over thirty years
Lives on in some other place outlasting death.
And those shoelaces, shiny and twisted, that we tossed to the side,
Live on in their place, and the Hippopotamus horde arrives;
The newly dead kneel, and a tip of the lace sends them on into fire!

Affinity
I say the clumps of hair weep.
Because hair does not long for immense states;
Hair does not hate the poor.
Hair is merciful,
Like the arch of night under which the juvenile singer lolls back drunk.

Hair is excitable as a child of four or five;
It is a hammock on which the sleeper lies,
Dizzy with heat and the earth's motion.

There are golden pins lying in bureau drawers,
Whose faces shine with power. They shine
Like the cheekbones of saints radiant in their beds,
Or their great toes that light up the whole room!

Judgment
Prince Philip becomes irritable, the royal sports car
Shoots down the narrow roads;
Judy Garland is led hysterical to the Melbourne plane.
The general joins the Jehovah's Witnesses.

There are men who look, and cannot find the road,
And die coughing particles of black flesh onto neighboring roofs.

Nailheads that have been brooding on Burton's *Melancholy* under
 Baltimore rowhouses
Roll out into the street under tires,
And catch the Secretary of State
As he goes off to threaten the premiers of underdeveloped nations.

So many things are borne down by the world,
By bad luck, corpses pulled down by years of death,
Veins clogged with flakes of sludge,
Mouths from which bats escape at death,
Businessmen reborn as black whales sailing under the Arctic ice.

Affinity
I say it is all right. The earth has hair cathedrals.
The priest comes down the aisle wearing caterpillar fur.
In his sermons the toad defeats the knight.

The dying man waves his son away.
He wants his daughter-in-law to come near
So that her hair will fall over his face.

The senator's plane falls in an orchard in Massachusetts.
And there are bitter places, knots
That leave dark pits in the sawdust. . . .
The nick on the hornblade through which the mammoth escapes.

TAO TE CHING RUNNING

If we could only not be eaten by the steep teeth,
if we could only leap like the rough marble into the next world,
if the anteater that loves to rasp its tongue over the rough eggs of
 the lizard
could walk into a room the carpenters have just left,
or if the disturbed county commissioners could throw themselves
 like a waved hand up into the darkness,
if the fragments in the unconscious would grow big as the beams
 in hunting lodges,
then the tiny black eggs the salmon lays in the luminous ears of
 nuns would be visible,
then we would find holy books in our beds,
then the *Tao Te Ching* would coming running across the field!

CONDITION OF THE WORKING CLASSES: 1970

You United States, frightened by dreams of Guatemala,
building houses with eight-mile-long wings to imprison the Cubans,

eating a bread made of the sound of sunken buffalo bones,
drinking water turned dark by the shadow of Negroes.
You remember things seen when you were still unable to speak—
white wings lying in a field.
And when you try to pass a bill,
long boards fly up, suddenly,
in Nevada,
in ghost towns.

You wave your insubstantial food timidly in the damp air.
You long to return to the shell.
Even at the start Chicago was a place where the cobblestones
got up and flew around at night,
and anarchists fainted as they read *The Decline and Fall*.
The ground is soaked with water used to boil dogs.

Your sons dream they have been lost in kinky hair,
no one can find them,
neighbors walk shoulder to shoulder for three days,
but your sons are lost in the immense forest.

And the harsh deer drop,
the businessmen climb into their F-4s,
the chocks are knocked out,
the F-4 shoots off the deck,
 trailing smoke,
dipping slightly,
 as if haunted by the center of the ocean,
then pulling up again as Locke said it would.

Our spirit is inside the baseball rising into the light.

So the crippled ships go out into the deep,
sexual orchids fly out to meet the rain,
 the singer sings from deep in his chest,

memory stops,
> black threads string out in the wind,
the eyes of the nation go blind.

The building across the street suddenly explodes,
wild horses run through the long hair on the ground floor.
Cripple Creek's survivors peer out from an upper-story window,
> blood pours from their ears,
the Sioux dead sleep all night in the rain troughs on the Treasury
> Building.

The moonlight crouches over the teenager's body thrown from a car

The weeping child like a fish thrown from the herring block
the black-nosed Avenger leaping off the deck

Women who hear the cry of small animals in their furs
and drive their cars at a hundred miles an hour into trees

CALLING TO THE BADGER

Come, let us write of Niagara and the Huron squaws,
The Puritans with their black robes, Dillinger
Like a dark wind. Bring in the advertising men,
So that the strong-haunched woman
By the blazing stove of the sun, the moon,
May come home to us, sitting on the naked wood
In another world, and all the Shell stations folded in a faint light.

Come, let us write of the sadness of the Indian fighters,
The sadness that rises from the death of the Diggers,
From the death of Logan alone in his house,
And the Cherokees forced to eat the tail of the Great Bear.

The old are being driven to Florida
Like Geronimo, and young men are still calling to the badger
And the otter, alone on the mountains of South Dakota.

PILGRIM FISH HEADS

It is a Pilgrim village; heavy rain is falling.
Fish heads lie smiling at the corners of houses.
Inside, words like "Samson" hang from the rafters.
Outdoors the chickens squawk in woody hovels,
yet the chickens are walking on Calvinist ground.
The women move through the dark kitchen, their heavy
skirts bear them down like drowning men.
Upstairs beds are like thunderstorms on the bare floor,
leaving the covers always moist by the rough wood.
And the eggs! Strange, white, perfect eggs!
Eggs that even the rain could not move,
white, painless, with tails even in nightmares.
And the Indian, damp, musky, asking for a bed.
The Mattapoisett is in league with rotting wood,
he has made a conspiracy with the salamander,
he has made treaties with the cold heads of fishes.
In the grave he does not rot, but vanishes into water.
The Indian goes on living in the rain-soaked stumps.
This is our enemy, this is the outcast,
the one from whom we must protect our nation,
the one whose dark hair hides us from the sun.

THE TEETH MOTHER NAKED AT LAST

1

Massive engines lift beautifully from the deck.
Wings appear over the trees, wings with eight hundred rivets.

Engines burning a thousand gallons of gasoline a minute sweep
 over the huts with dirt floors.

The chickens feel the new fear deep in the pits of their beaks.
Buddha with Padmasambhava.

Meanwhile, out on the China Sea,
Immense gray bodies are floating,
Born in Roanoke,
The ocean on both sides expanding, "buoyed on the dense marine."

Helicopters flutter overhead. The death-
Bee is coming. Super Sabres
Like knots of neurotic energy sweep
Around and return.
This is Hamilton's triumph.
This is the advantage of a centralized bank.
B-52s come from Guam. All the teachers
Die in flames. The hopes of Tolstoy fall asleep in the ant heap.
Do not ask for mercy.

Now the time comes to look into the past-tunnels,
The hours given and taken in school,
The scuffles in coatrooms,
Foam leaps from his nostrils,
Now we come to the scum you take from the mouths of the dead,
Now we sit beside the dying, and hold their hands, there is hardly
 time for goodbye.

The staff sergeant from North Carolina is dying—you hold his hand,
He knows the mansions of the dead are empty, he has an empty place
Inside him, created one night when his parents came home drunk.
He uses half his skin to cover it,
As you try to protect a balloon from sharp objects. . . .

Artillery shells explode. Napalm canisters roll end over end.
Eight hundred steel pellets fly through the vegetable walls.
The six-hour infant puts his fists instinctively to his eyes to keep out
 the light.
But the room explodes;
The children explode;
Blood leaps on the vegetable walls.

Yes, I know, blood leaps on the walls—
Don't cry at that—
Do you cry at the wind pouring out of Canada?
Do you cry at the reeds shaken at the edge of the sloughs?
The Marine battalion enters.
This happens when the seasons change,
This happens when the leaves begin to drop from the trees too early
"Kill them: I don't want to see anything moving."
This happens when the ice begins to show its teeth in the ponds.
This happens when the heavy layers of lake water press down on the
 fish's head, and send him deeper, where his tail swirls slowly, and
 his brain passes him pictures of heavy reeds, of vegetation fall on
 vegetation. . . .

2
Excellent Roman knives slip along the ribs.

A stronger man starts to jerk up the strips of flesh.

"Let's hear it again, you believe in the Father, the Son, and the Holy Ghost?"

A long scream unrolls.

More.

*"From the political point of view, democratic institutions are being built in
Vietnam, wouldn't you agree?"*

A green parrot shudders under the fingernails.
Blood jumps in the pocket.
The scream lashes like a tail.

"Let us not be deterred from our task by the voices of dissent. . . ."

The whines of the jets
Pierce like a long needle.

3
The ministers lie, the professors lie, the television reporters lie, the
 priests lie.
What are these lies? They mean that the country wants to die.
Lie after lie starts out into the prairie grass,
Like mile-long caravans of Conestoga wagons crossing the Platte.

And a long desire for death goes with them, guiding it all from beneath:
"A death longing if all longing else be in vain,"
Stringing together the vague and foolish words.

It is a desire to eat death,
To gobble it down,
To rush on it like a cobra with mouth open.
It is a desire to take death inside,
To feel it burning inside, pushing out velvety hairs,
Like a clothes brush in the intestines—

That is the thrill that leads the President on to lie.

Now the Chief Executive enters, and the press conference begins.
First the President lies about the date the Appalachian Mountains rose.
Then he lies about the population of Chicago,
Then the weight of the adult eagle, and the acreage of the Everglades.
Next he lies about the number of fish taken every year in the Arctic.

He has private information about which city *is* the capital of Wyoming.
He lies next about the birthplace of Attila the Hun,
Then about the composition of the amniotic fluid.

He insists that Luther was never a German,
And only the Protestants sold indulgences.
He declares that Pope Leo X *wanted* to reform the Church, but the
 liberal elements prevented him.
He declares the Peasants' War was fomented by Italians from the
 North.
And the Attorney General lies about the time the sun sets.

4
These lies mean we have a longing to die.
What is there now to hold us on earth?
It is the longing for someone to come and take us by the hand to
 where they are all sleeping:
Where the Egyptian pharaohs are asleep, and our own mothers,
And all those disappeared children, who went around with us on the
 rings at grade school.

Do not be angry at the President—
He is longing to take in his hands the locks of death-hair:
To meet his own children, dead, or never born. . . .

He is drifting sideways toward the dusty places.

5

This is what it's like to watch the altimeter needle going mad

Baron 25, this is 81. Are there any friendlies in the area? 81 from 25, negative on the friendlies. I'd like you to take out as many structures as possible located in those trees within 200 meters east and west of my smoke mark.

diving, the green earth swinging, cheeks hanging back, red pins
 blossoming ahead of us, 20-millimeter cannon fire, leveling
 off, rice fields shooting by like telephone poles, smoke rising,
 hut roofs loom up huge as landing fields, slugs going in, half
 the huts on fire, small figures running, palm trees burning,
 shooting past, up again; . . . blue sky . . . cloud mountains . . .

This is what it's like to have a gross national product.

It is because we have so few women sobbing in back rooms,
Because we have so few children's heads torn apart by high-
 velocity bullets,
Because we have so few tears falling on our own hands
That the Super Sabre turns and screams down toward the earth.

6

A car is rolling toward a rock wall.
The treads in the face begin to crack.
We feel like tires being run down roads under heavy cars.

The teenager imagines herself floating through the Seven Spheres.
Oven doors are found
Open.
Soot collects over the doorframe, has children, takes courses, goes
 mad, and dies.

There is a black silo inside our bodies.
Bits of black paint are flaking off,
Where the motorcycles roar, around and around,
Rising higher on the silo walls,
The bodies bent toward the horizon,
Driven by angry women dressed in black.

7
I know that books are tired of us.
I know they are chaining the Bible to chairs.
Books don't want to remain in the same room with us anymore.
New Testaments are escaping . . . dressed as women . . . they slip
 out after dark.
And Plato! Plato . . . Plato
Wants to hurry back up the river of time,
So he can end as a blob of seaflesh rotting on an Australian beach.

8
Why are they dying? I have written this so many times.
They are dying because the President has opened a Bible again.
They are dying because gold deposits have been found among the
 Shoshoni Indians.
They are dying because money follows intellect,
And intellect is like a fan opening in the wind.

The Marines think that unless they die the rivers will not move.
They are dying so that the mountain shadows will continue to fall
 east in the afternoon,
So that the beetle can move along the ground near the fallen twigs.

9
But if one of those children came near that we have set on fire,
Came toward you like a gray barn, walking,
You would howl like a wind tunnel in a hurricane,

You would tear at your shirt with blue hands,
You would drive over your own child's wagon trying to back up,
The pupils of your eyes would go wild—

If a child came by burning, you would dance on a lawn,
Trying to leap into the air, digging into your cheeks,
You would ram your head against the wall of your bedroom
Like a bull penned too long in his moody pen—

If one of those children came toward me with both hands
In the air, fire rising along both elbows,
I would suddenly go back to my animal brain,
I would drop on all fours, screaming,
My vocal cords would turn blue; so would yours;
It would be two days before I could play with my own children again.

10
I want to sleep awhile in the rays of the sun slanting over the snow.
Don't wake me.
Don't tell me how much grief there is in the leaf with its natural oils.
Don't tell me how many children have been born with stumpy hands
All those years we lived in St. Augustine's shadow.

Tell me about the dust that falls from the yellow daffodil shaken in
 the restless winds.
Tell me about the particles of Babylonian thought that still pass
 through the earthworm every day.
Don't tell me about "the frightening laborers who do not read books."

Now the whole nation starts to whirl,
The end of the Republic breaks off,
Europe comes to take revenge,
The mad beast covered with European hair rushes toward the mesa
 bushes in Mendocino County.

Pigs rush toward the cliff.
The waters underneath part: in one ocean luminous globes float
 up (in them hairy and ecstatic men);
In the other ocean—the Teeth Mother, naked at last.

Let us drive cars
Up
The light beams
To the stars . . .

Then return to earth crouched inside the drop of sweat
That falls
From the chin of the Protestant tied in the fire.

II

SLEEPERS JOINING HANDS

A Long Poem

THE SHADOW GOES AWAY

The woman chained to the shore stands bewildered as night comes
I don't want to wake up in the weeds, and find the light
gone out in the body, and the cells dark. . . .
I see the cold ocean rise to take us
as I stand without feathers on the shore
and watch the blood-colored moon gobbling up the sand. . . .

The owl senses someone in the hole of his tree,
and lands with wings closing, claws out. . . .

I fall asleep, and dream I am working in the fields. . . .
Now I show the father the coat stained with goat's blood. . . .
The shadow goes away,
we are left alone in the father's house.
I knew that. . . . I sent my brother away.
I saw him turn and leave. It was a schoolyard.
I gave him to the dark people passing.
He learned to sleep alone on the high buttes.
I heard he was near the Missouri, taken in by traveling Sioux.
They taught him to wear his hair long,

to glide about naked, drinking water from his hands,
to tether horses, follow the faint trail through bent grasses. . . .

Men bound my shadow. That was in high school.
They tied it to a tree, I saw it being led away.
I dreamt that I sat in a big chair,
and every other second I disappeared.
This was during Stanley's visit to Africa.

In high school I was alone, asleep in the Law.
I slipped off one night into the water,
 swam to shore with no one watching,
left my brother alone on the ship!
On 66th Street I noticed he was gone.
I sat down and wept.
Hairs of depression come up through the palm laid on the
 ground,
little impulses shoot up in the dark,
in the dark the sleeping marmoset opens his eyes.
There are nights in which everything is torn
away, all piers gone. . . .
I walk through the trees, and come into the Indian encampment.
The Sioux are struggling up the mountain in disordered lines,
the field littered with robes, dogbones, thongs,
the great cooking iron in which my shadow was boiling!

Walking through the camp, I notice an old chest of drawers.
I open a drawer and see small white horses gallop away toward
 the back.
I see the birds inside me,
with massive shadows like humpbacked Puritan ministers,
a headstrong beak ahead,
and wings supple as the stingray's,
ending in claws, lifting over the shadowy peaks.

Looking down, I see dark marks on my shirt.
My mother gave me that shirt, and hoped that her son would be
 the one man in the world
who would have a happy marriage,
but look at me now—
I have been divorced five hundred times,
six hundred times yesterday alone.

I hear the sound of hoofs . . . coming. . . . Now the men
move in, smashing and burning. The huts
of the Shadowy People are turned over, the wood
utensils broken, straw mats set on fire,
digging sticks jumped on, clay bowls
smashed with dropped stones. . . .

Thousands of men come,
like dwarf antelopes in long streaming herds,
or hair flying behind the skidding racer. . . .

No ministers or teachers come out,
I am flying over my bed alone. . . .
I am flying over the Josephine forests, where only the rat builds
 his nest of leaves,
and keeps his mistress in the white dusk. . . .

The moon swims through the clogging veins,
the sun leaps from its dying bed,
divorced men and women drown in the paling, reddening sea.

The Marines turn to me. They offer me money.
I turn and leave. The sun sinks toward the darkening hills.
My mother's bed looms up in the dark.
The noose tightens,

servants of the armor brain, terrified hired men whom the sharks feed,
scales everywhere, "glittering on their bodies as they fall."

The Sea of Tranquility scattered with dead rocks,
and black dust resembling diesel oil.
The suppressed race returns: snakes and transistors filling the beaches,
pilots in armored cockpits finding their way home through moonlit
 clouds.

MEETING THE MAN WHO WARNS ME

I wake and find myself in the woods, far from the castle.
The train hurtles through lonely Louisiana at night.
The sleeper turns to the wall, delicate
aircraft dive toward earth.

A woman whispers to me, urges me to speak truths.
"I am afraid that you won't be honest with me."
Half or more of the moon rolls on in shadow.
Owls talk at night, loons wheel cries through lower waters,
fragments of the mother lie open in all low places.

I have been alone two days, and still everything is cloudy.
The body surrounds me on all sides.
I walk out and return.
Rain dripping from pine boughs, boards soaked on porches,
gray water awakens, fish slide away underneath.
I fall asleep. I meet a man from a milder planet.
I say to him: "I know Christ is from your planet!"
He lifts his eyes to me with a fierce light.
He reaches out and touches me on the tip of my cock,
and I fall asleep.

I dream that the fathers are dying.
Jehovah is dying, Jesus's father is dying,
the hired man is asleep inside the oat straw.
Samson is lying on the ground with his hollow hair.

Who is this that visits us from beneath the earth?
I see the dead like great conductors
carrying electricity under the ground,
the Eskimos suddenly looking into the womb of the seal. . . .
Water shoots into the air from manhole covers,
the walker sees it astonished and falls;
before his body hits the street
he is already far down the damp steps of the Tigris,
seeing the light given off under the door by shining hair.

Something white calls to us:
it is the darkness we saw outside the cradle.
My shadow is underneath me,
floating in the dark, in his small boat bobbing among reeds.
A fireball floats in the corner of the Eskimo's house—
It is a light that comes nearer when called!
A light the spirits turn their heads for,
suddenly shining over land and sea!
I taste the heaviness of the dream,
the northern lights curve up toward the roof of my mouth.
The energy is inside us. . . .
I start toward it, and I meet an old man.
He looms up in the road, his white hair standing up:
"Who is this who is ascending the red river?
Who is this who is leaving the dark plants?"
I don't want to leave, and walk back and forth,
looking toward the old landing.

I dream that I cannot see half of my life.
I look back, it is like the blind spot in a car.
So much just beyond the reach of our eyes,
what tramples the grasses while the horses are asleep,
the hoof marks all around the cave mouth . . .
what slips in under the door at night, and lies exhausted on the
 floor in the morning.

What cannot be remembered and cannot be forgotten,
the chaff blowing about my father's feet.
And the old man cries out: "I am here.
Either talk to me about your life, or turn back."
I look from bridges at cattle grazing,
the lizard moving stiffly over the November road,
the night frogs who give out the croak of the planet turning,
the great knees of horses loyal to the earth risen in their will.
"I am the dark spirit that lives in the dark.
Each of my children is under a leaf he chose from all the leaves in
 the universe.
When I was alone, for three years, alone,
I passed under the earth through the night-water,
I was for three days inside a warm-blooded fish.
'Purity of heart is to will one thing.'
I saw the road. . . ." "Go on! Go on!"
"A whale bore me back home, we flew through the air. . . .
Then I was a boy who had never seen the sea!
It was like a King coming to his own shores.
I feel the naked touch of the knife,
I feel the wound,
this joy I love is like wounds at sea. . . ."

THE NIGHT JOURNEY IN THE COOKING POT

I was born during the night sea-journey.
I love the whale with his warm organ pipes
 in the mouse-killing waters,
I love the men who drift, asleep, for three nights in octopus waters,
the furry men gathering wood, piling the chunks by walls,
I love the snow, I need privacy as I move,
I am all alone, floating in the cooking pot
on the sea, through the night I am alone.

 The crow nests high in the fir.
 Birds leap through the snowy branches,
 uttering small cries,
The mice run dragging their tails in the new-fallen snow.

 The old trees move in the wind.
 Sitting I leap from branch to branch,
 the old man calls out,
long prayers at dawn, the deer antlers abandoned in the snow.

I float on solitude as on water . . . there is a road. . . .
I felt the road first in New York, in that great room
reading Rilke in the womanless loneliness.
How marvelous the great wings, sweeping along the floor,
inwardness, inwardness, inwardness,
the inward path I still walk on,
I felt the wings brushing the floors of the dark,
trailing longer wings,
the wing marks left in the delicate sand of the corridors,
the face shining far inside the mountain.

There is a certainty that makes the fingers love each other,
and makes the body give up sleep.
The animals open their mouths, and come, glad,
in a ring.
The snow begins falling.
A winter of privacy is before us,
winter privacy,
the vast halls inside the heads of animals
lie before us, the slow
breaking of day, warm blood moving, moving,
and immense pine trees.

For the first time in months I love the dark.
A joy pierces into me, it arrives like a runner,
a radio signal from inside a tree trunk,
a smile spreads over the face, the eyes fall.

Someone is asleep in the back of my house.
I feel the blood galloping in the body,
the baby whirling in the womb.
Dark bodies pass by far out at the horizon,
trailing lights like flying saucers,
the shadows go by long after the bodies have passed.
Nuns with faces smoothed by prayer
peer out from holes in the earth.

The mouse goes down the tunnel where the mice-infants light the
 whole room!
I start down, after him,
I see owls with blue flames coming from the tops of their heads,
watching from firs on each side of the road,
and snow just beginning to fall.

They broke from the house, walked in the trees, and were lost,
slept in the earth, brooded like wells in the deep ground,
sleeping in anguish like grain, whole, blind in the old grave.

Who is it that visits us from beneath the snow?
Something shining far down in the ice.
Deep in the mountain the sleeper is glad.
Men with large shoulders covered with furs,
eyes closed, inexplicable.
Holy ones with eyes closed,
the cracking sound in the ice under our feet,
the frozen lake marked with caribou feet . . .

Leaves slip down, falling through their own branches.
The tree becomes naked and joyful.
Leaves fall in the tomby woods.
Some men need so little, and even that I need very little.
Suddenly I love the dancers, leaping
in the dark, jumping
into the air, and the singers and dancers and leapers!
I start to sing, and rove around the floor,
singing like "a young Lioun."

I want to rise far into the piney tops.

I am not going farther from you,
I am coming nearer,
green rain carries me nearer you,
I weave drunkenly about the page,
I love you,
I never knew that I loved you
until I was swallowed by the invisible,
my black shoes evaporating, rising about my head. . . .

For we are like the branch bent in the water . . .
Taken out, it is whole, it was always whole. . . .

I see the road ahead,
and my body cries out, and leaps into the air,
and throws itself on the floor, knocking over the chairs.
I think I am the body,
the body rushes in and ties me up,
and then goes through the house. . . .

I am on the road, and the next instant in the ditch,
 face down on the earth,
wasting energy talking to idiots.
Clumsy wings flop around the room,
I know what I must do,
I am ashamed looking at the fish in the water.

The barn doors are open. His first breath touches the manger hay
and the King a hundred miles away
stands up. He calls his ministers.
"Find him.
There cannot be two rulers in one body."
He sends his wise men out along the arteries,
along the winding tunnels, into the mountains,
to kill the child in the old moonlit villages of the brain.

The mind waters run out on the rug.
Pull the mind in,
pull the arm in,
it will be taken off by a telephone post.

Suddenly I am those who run large railroads at dusk,
who stand around the fallen beast howling,

who cannot get free,
the man the lion bounding catches in the African grass.
I stop, a hand turns over in my stomach,
this is not the perfect freedom of the saints.

I decide that death is friendly,
Finally death seeps up through the tiniest capillaries of my toes.
I fall into my own hands,
 fences break down under horses,
cities starve, whole towns of singing women carrying to the burial
 fields the look I saw on my father's face,
I sit down again, I hit my own body,
I shout at myself, I see what I have betrayed.
What I have written is not good enough.
Who does it help?
I am ashamed sitting on the edge of my bed.

WATER DRAWN UP INTO THE HEAD

Now do you understand the men who laugh all night in their sleep?
Here is some prose:

> *Once there was a man who went to a far country*
> *to get his inheritance and then returned.*

There are places for our feet to go.

When we come face to face with you,
the holder laughs and is glad!
He laughs like the mad condor in his sticky nest!

The feminine creature at the edge of town,
men with rifles all around.

I am passive, listening to the lapping waves,
I am divine, drinking the air,
consciousness fading or sweeping out over the husky soybean
 fields like a revolving beacon all night,
horses at the end of their tethering ropes,
the wing of affection passes over,
flying bulls glimpsed passing the moon disc.

We know the world with all its visible stars,
earth, water, air, and fire,
but when alone we see that great tomb is not God.
There are spirits,
 who wheel with sparks at night in a room,
but everyone knows they are not God.
We know of Christ, who raised the dead and started time.
He is not God, and is not called God.

When the waterholes go, the fish
 flop about
in the caked mud, they can moisten each other faintly.
 That is good, but best
is to let them lose themselves in a river.
So rather than saying that Christ is God or he is not,
it is better to forget all that
and lose yourself in the curved energy.
I entered that energy one day,
that is why I have lived alone in old places,
that is why I have knelt in churches, weeping,
that is why I have become a stranger to my father.
We have no name for you, so we say:
he makes grass grow upon the mountains,
and gives food to the dark cattle of the sea,
he feeds the young ravens that call on him.

I have sat here alone for two hours. . . .
I have sat here alone for two years!
There is another being living inside me.
He is looking out of my eyes.
I hear him
in the wind through the bare trees.

I met the King coming through the traffic.
He said, I shall give to you more pain than wounds at sea.

That is why I am so glad in fall.
I walk out, throw my arms up, and am glad.
The thick leaves fall,
falling past their own trunk,
and the tree goes naked,
leaving only the other one.

*An Extra Joyful Chorus for Those
Who Have Read This Far*

I sit alone late at night.
I sit with eyes closed, thoughts shoot through me.
I am not floating, but fighting.
In the marshes the mysterious mother calls to her moor-bound
 chicks.
I love the Mother.
I am an enemy of the Mother, give me my sword.
I leap into her mouth full of seaweed.

I am the single splinter that shoots through the stratosphere leaving
 fire trails!
I walk upright, robes flapping at my heels,
I am fleeing along the ground like a frightened beast.
I am the ball of fire the woodman cuts out of the wolf's stomach,
I am the sun that floats over the Witch's house,
I am the horse sitting in the chestnut tree singing,
I am the man locked inside the oakwomb,
waiting for lightning, only let out on stormy nights.
I am the steelhead trout that hurries to his mountain mother,
to live again in the stream where he was born,
gobbling up the new water.

Sometimes when I read my own poems late at night,
I sense myself on a long road,
I feel the naked thing alone in the universe,
the hairy body padding in the fields at dusk. . . .

I have floated in the eternity of the cod heaven,
I have felt the silver of infinite numbers brush my side—
I am the crocodile unrolling and slashing through the mudded water,
I am the baboon crying out as her baby falls from the tree,
I am the light that makes the flax blossom at midnight!
I am an angel breaking into three parts over the Ural Mountains!
I am no one at all.

•

I am a thorn enduring in the dark sky,
I am the one whom I have never met,
I am a swift fish shooting through the troubled waters,
I am the last inheritor crying out in deserted houses
I am the salmon hidden in the pool on the temple floor
I am what remains of the beloved
I am an insect with black enamel knees hugging the curve of insanity

I am the evening light rising from the ocean plains
I am an eternal happiness fighting in the long reeds.

Our faces shine with the darkness reflected from the Tigris,
cells made by the honeybees that go on growing after death,
a room darkened with curtains made of human hair.

The panther rejoices in the gathering dark.
Hands rush toward each other through miles of space.
All the sleepers in the world join hands.

JUMPING

OUT

OF

BED

(1973)

All around me men are working;
but I am stubborn, and take no part.
The difference is this:
I prize the breasts of the Mother.

—Tao Te Ching

I came out of the Mother naked,
and I will be naked when I return.
The Mother gave, and the Mother takes away,
I love the Mother.

—Old Testament, restored

TURTLE CLIMBING FROM A ROCK

For Wang Hui-Ming

How shiny the turtle is, coming out
of the water, climbing the rock, as if
Buddha's body were to shine!
As if swift turtle wings swept out of darkness,
crossed some barriers,
and found new eyes.
An old man falters with his stick,
later, walkers find holes in black earth.
The snail climbs up the wet trunk glistening
like an angel-flight trailing long black banners.
No one finds the huge turtle eggs
lying inland on the floor of the old sea.

THINKING OF "THE AUTUMN FIELDS"

1

Already autumn begins here in the mossy rocks.
The sheep bells moving from the wind are sad.
I have left my wife foolishly in a flat country,
I have set up my table looking over a valley.
There are fish in the lake but I will not fish;
I will sit silently at my table by the window.
From whatever appears on my plate,
I will give a little away to the birds and the grass.

2

How easy to see the road the liferiver takes!
Hard to move one living thing from its own path.
The fish adores being in the deep water;
The bird easily finds a tree to live in.

In the second half of life a man accepts poverty and illness;
praise and blame belong to the glory of the first half.
Although cold wind blows against my walking stick,
I will never get tired of the ferns on this mountain.

3
Music and chanting help me overcome my faults;
the mountains and woods keep my body fiery.
I have two or three books only in my room.
The sun shining off the empty bookcase warms my back.
Going out I pick up the pinecones the wind has thrown away.
When night comes, I will open a honeycomb.
On the floor-throw covered with tiny red and blue flowers,
I bring my stocking feet closer to the faint incense.

LIKE THE NEW MOON I WILL LIVE MY LIFE

When your privacy is beginning over,
how beautiful the things are that you did not notice before!
A few sweetclover plants
along the road to Bellingham,
culvert ends poking out of driveways,
wooden corncribs, slowly falling,
what no one loves, no one rushes toward or shouts about,
what lives like the new moon,
and the wind
blowing against the rumps of grazing cows.

Telephone wires stretched across water,
a drowning sailor standing at the foot of his mother's bed,
grandfathers and grandsons sitting together.

SOME NOVEMBER PRIVACY POEMS

I am comforted
by a crack in dry ground
nearly smoothed over with winter dust.

.

How marvelous to look out and see
the boulders
that have been gloomy since the earth began
now with a faint dusting of snow.

.

Mist: no one on the other shore.
It may be the trees I see have consciousness
and this desire to weep comes from them.

.

Most birds have gone south.
Grass heels over in the wind.
The feminine hooves of the horse
stand side by side as he eats.

ON A MOONLIT ROAD IN THE NORTH WOODS

I sit on the forest road,
cross-legged.
I am an oyster
breathing on his own shore.

.

Cars seldom use this road.
I looked up and down,
 no car coming, none would,
perhaps for hours. . . .

 •

All day my thoughts ran on in small rivulets
near some bigger flood.
Several times water
 carried me away:
then I was a cedar twig,
 a fish scale. . . .

 •

And what does the oyster think
on this forest road?
He thinks of his earlier life,
of meeting her again.

THE WALNUT TREE ORCHARDS

*(An answering poem in which Wang Wei writes the first poem, then his friend
P'ei Ti writes a poem answering it.)*

WANG WEI: In the old days the serious man was not an "important
 person."
 He thought making decisions was too complicated for
 him.
 He took whatever small job came along.
 Essentially he did nothing, like these walnut trees.

P'EI TI: I soon found doing nothing was a great joy to me.
 Look, you see, here I am! Keeping my ancient promise.
 Let's spend today just strolling around these walnut trees.
 The two of us will nourish the ecstasies Chuang Tzu loved.

THE HILL OF HUA-TZU

WANG WEI: The birds fly away into the air that never ends;
 the magnificence of fall comes back to the mountain.
 Whenever I walk up or down Hua-Tzu hill,
 my whole body feels confusion and inner suffering.

P'EI TI: The sun goes down; there is wind sound in the pines.
 Walking home I notice dew on the grass.
 The white clouds look up at me from the tracks of my
 shoes.
 The blue from the mountain touches my clothes.

CHRYSANTHEMUMS
(planted for Tao Yuan Ming, who likes them)

1
Tonight I rode again in the moonlight!
I saddled late at night.
The horse picked his way down a dead-furrow,
guided by the deep shadows.

2
A mile from the yard the horse rears,
glad. How magnificent to be doing nothing,
moving aimlessly through a nighttime field,
and the body alive, like a plant!

3
Coming back up the pale driveway,
how calm the wash looked on the line!
And when I entered my study, beside the door,
white chrysanthemums in the moonlight!

AFTER LONG BUSYNESS

I start out for a walk at last after weeks at the desk.
Moon gone, plowing underfoot, no stars; not a trace of light!
Suppose a horse were galloping toward me in the open field?
Every day I did not spend in solitude was wasted.

SOME IMAGES FOR DEATH

Death throws a shadow on us, as if it were a tree.
It is a swinging lamp, swaying from the motion of the planet.
It rushes up through tunnels where only chill air rushes.
The mammoths feel the wind in their hollow legs.
 The leaves above us rustle.

A NIGHT IN DECEMBER

On this windy December night two children lost their way.
"Birds ate the womb-shaped seeds we dropped in the moonlight."
("You know we left so early the moon was still out.")
"Come in, do not be frightened, children."

How odd that I feel a connection between the feminine
And this windy December night! Or is it the feminine?
When Paris took Helen away, he kept the moon in a pouch.
Inside the salmon's stomach, the cook finds the wedding ring.

"Come in, do not be frightened, children!"
Why do men need this fear? Some are torn in pieces,
Other men lengthen out years on islands. . . .
This night calls: men will die for this night.

SLEEPING FACES

Tonight the first fall rain washes away my sly distance.
I have decided to blame no one for my life.
This water falls like a great privacy.
Letters sink into the desk,
The desk sinks away, leaving an intelligence
Slowly learning to talk of its own suffering.
The muttering of thunder is a gift
That reverberates in the roof of the mouth.
Another gift is a child's face in a dark room
I see as I check the house during the storm.
My life is a blessing, a triumph, a car racing through the rain.

THE CREEK BY THE LUAN HOUSE

WANG WEI: Autumn rain and sudden winds.
 The water plunges, bouncing off the rocks.
 Waves leap aimlessly over each other.
 The white heron is alarmed and lands.

P'EI TI: A man could hear the water-sound far off.
 I walk down looking for the ford.
 Ducks and egrets swim away, and then
 veer back, longing to be near people.

THE MAGNOLIA GROVE

For Michael Bullock

WANG WEI: The mountain receives the last sunshine of fall.
 Flocks fly off following the first that leaves.
 Occasionally something emerald flashes in the trees.
 The evening dark has nowhere to settle down.

P'EI TI: Settling down at dusk from the dome of light
 bird voices get mingled with the river sounds.
 The path beside the river winds off into the distance.
 Joy of solitude, will you ever come to an end?

ANOTHER DOING NOTHING POEM

There is a bird that flies through the water.
It is like a whale ten miles high!
Before it went into the ocean,
it was just a bit of dust from under my bed!

WALKING IN THE DITCH GRASS

The spring wind blows dissatisfactions
and mad architects, two-mile-long tails,

and my shoes like whales
eat the grass, they sweep through
the grass, eating
up the darkness.

The night is windy. Sleek cows fly
across the sky. Samson
is angry.
So much of women
in this uneven grass.

TONGUES WHIRLING

You open your mouth, I put my tongue in,
and this wild universe-thing begins!

Our tongues together are two seagulls
 whirling high above the Great Lakes,
two jellyfish floating under a Norwegian moon!

Suddenly we are with the fallen leaves,
 blowing along the soaked roads.
My hand closes so firmly around you
and I feel the sea rising
 and falling
as we go ashore . . .

We are two turtles with wings!

We are rolling together, head down,
through oceans of mother air!

We are two tumbleweeds hurrying through the universe.

A DOING NOTHING POEM

After walking about all afternoon
Barefoot, in my shack,
I have grown long and transparent . . .
Like the sea slug
Who has lived alone doing nothing
For eighteen thousand years.

JUMPING OUT OF BED

Coming nearer and nearer the resonating chamber,
the poem begins to throw itself around
wildly,
silent stretches of snow,
grass waving for hundreds of miles.

We leap up from our Sadducean pillow,
every spot is forgotten,
our hair is crinkly and gold.

The moon hovers over the drunk's hut.
The teaspoon gleams in the trunk of the car.

THE POEM

Coming nearer and nearer the resonating chamber,
the poem begins to throw itself around
fiercely,
silent stretches of snow,
grass waving for hundreds of miles.

Intent pierces into hard wood, which grows dense
from inside, something mad penetrates
the wood,
something alive, something
human, like a violin that reverberates with thought.

A fierce intent that nature does not know of
drives inside the poem,
changes it,
thickens it with sober weight;
it is something dense, a human madness.

LOOKING AT CLOUD BANKS BELOW THE PLANE WINDOW

Hills of cloud, mountains of mist below.
What are they? Troll-heads,
Tufts of forgetfulness,
Childhood stories, dreams of someone's death.

Perhaps a burbling up of blind affection . . .
The clouds are affectionate creatures
With their backs turned to us,
Crouched over a smiling landscape beneath.

How different these tuffy bodies are from ours!
They are secretive, but do not cling,
Are not afraid of a storm,
Willing to dissipate in the wind . . .

THE
MORNING
GLORY

(1975)

There is an old occult saying: whoever wants to see the invisible has to penetrate more deeply into the visible. All through Taoist and "curving lines" thought, there is the idea that our disasters come from letting nothing live for itself, from the longing we have to pull everything, even our friends, in to ourselves, and let nothing alone. If we examine a pine carefully, we see how independent it is of us. When we first sense that a pine tree doesn't really need us, that it has a physical life and a moral life and a spiritual life that is complete without us, we feel alienated and depressed. The second time we feel it, we feel joyful. As Bashō says in his wonderful poem:

The morning glory—
another thing
that will never be my friend.

I

A BIRD'S NEST MADE OF WHITE REED FIBER

The nest is white as the foam thrown up when the sea hits rocks! It is translucent as those cloudy transoms above Victorian doors, and swirled like the hair of those intense nurses, gray and tangled after long nights in Crimean wards. It is something made and then forgotten, like our own lives, that we will entirely forget in the grave, when we are floating, nearing the shore where we will be reborn, ecstatic and black.

LEONARDO'S SECRET
(THE VIRGIN AND ST. ANNE)

The Virgin is thinking of a child—who will drive the rioters out of the Temple—and her face is smiling. Her smile is full, it reminds you of a cow's side, or a stubble field with water standing in it.

Behind her head, jagged blue rocks. The pointed rocks slope up quietly, and fall back, washed by a blue light, like the light in an octopus's eye. The rocks, though no one is there, are not empty of people.

The rocks have not been forgotten by the sea either. They are the old brains of the sea. They glow for several seconds every morning, as the old man who lives in a hut on the shore drinks down his glass of saltwater.

LOOKING AT A DEAD WREN IN MY HAND

Forgive the hours spent listening to radios, and the words of gratitude I did not say to teachers. I love your tiny ricelike legs, that are bars of music played in an empty church, and the feminine tail, where no worms of Empire have ever slept, and the intense yellow chest that makes tears come. Your tail feathers open like a picket fence, and your bill is brown, with the sorrow of a rabbi whose daughter has married an athlete. The black spot on your head is your own mourning cap.

SITTING ON SOME ROCKS IN SHAW COVE

I sit in a cliff hollow, surrounded by fossils and furry shells. The sea breathes and breathes under the new moon. Suddenly it rises, hurrying into the long crevices in the rock shelves, it rises like a woman's belly as if nine months have passed in a second; rising like the milk to the tiny veins, it overflows like a snake going over a low wall.

I have the sensation that half an inch under my skin there are nomad bands, stringy-legged men with firesticks and wide-eyed babies. The rocks with their backs turned to me have something spiritual in them. On these rocks I am not afraid of death; death is like the sound of the motor in an airplane as we fly. And I still haven't found the woman I loved in some former life—how could I, when I have loved only twice on this rock, though twice in the moon, and three times in the rising water. My two daughters run toward me, laughing, arms in the air. A bird with long wings comes flying toward me in the dusk, pumping just over the darkening waves. He has flown around the whole planet; it has taken him centuries. He returns to me the lean-legged runner laughing as he runs through the stringy grasses, and gives back to me my buttons, and the soft sleeves of my sweater.

AT A FISH HATCHERY IN STORY, WYOMING

A ranger is lifting fingerling trout from a pickup with his scoop. They are weighing the fingerlings for stocking. The man in black boots pours them out of his scoop into a tub set on a scale. The fish slip off the scoop shovel, five or six inches long, shiny, gleaming, full of life! How they twist and turn in the Wyoming sun, about to fall! They are immense reserves of pure energy, like snowbanks, like mountains, like millions of hands . . . and when they do fall, they leave behind pure strokes in the air, vanishing into the wash-tub of fish, that contains so much, like the white stones dropped by glaciers, and washed by chilly streams . . . or the furs wrapped around old shoulders in the back of caves, where the skins have been chewed by women with luminous faces, who glow because their child has come into the universe . . . and now lies on their naked breast, which gleams in the risen light like a fish.

AN OCTOPUS

I hear a ticking on the Pacific stones. A white shape is moving in the furry air of the seacoast. The moon narrow, the sea quiet. He comes close; a long time the stick ticks on over the rock faces. Is it a postal employee saddened by the sleet? It comes nearer. I talk. The shape talks, it is a Japanese man carrying a spear and a heavy-bellied little bag. The spear has a hook on the end. What are you looking for, clams? No! Octopus!

Did you get any? I found three. He sits down. I get up and walk over. May I see them? He opens the plastic bag. I turn on the flashlight. Something wet, fantastic, womblike, horse intestine-like. May I take hold of one? His voice smiles. Why not? I reach in. Dry things stick to my hands, like burrs from burdocks, compelling, pleading, dry, poor, in debt. You boil them, then sauté them. I look and cannot find the eyes. He is a cook. He ate them in Japan.

So the octopus is gone now from the mussel-ridden shelf with the low roof, the pool where he waited under the thin moon, but the sea never came back, no one came home, the door never opened. Now he is taken away in the plastic bag, not understood, illiterate.

A HOLLOW TREE

I bend over an old hollow cottonwood stump, still standing, waist high, and look inside. Early spring. Its Siamese temple walls are all brown and ancient. The halls have been worked on by the intricate ones. Inside the hollow walls there is privacy and secrecy, dim light. And yet some creature has died here.

On the temple floor feathers, gray feathers, many of them with a fluted white tip. Many feathers. In the silence many feathers.

LOOKING INTO A TIDE POOL

It is a tide pool, shallow, water coming in, clear, tiny white shell-people on the bottom, asking nothing, not even directions! On the surface, the noduled seaweed, lying like hands, slowly drawing back and returning, hands laid on fevered bodies, moving back and forth, as the healer sings wildly, shouting to Jesus and his dead mother.

SEEING CREELEY FOR THE FIRST TIME

Creeley sits on a chair, pulling up his knees to laugh, like a boy, looking very insecure, unsure, like a boy at school with pants too short. He looks astoundingly like a crow—it is unbelievable—even

his hair is somehow "crow hair." Shining black, falling over his head that is full of determination to pester owls if he sees any. The beak is a crow beak, and the sideways look he gives, the head shoved slightly to the side by the bad eye, finishes it. And I suppose his language is crow language—no long open vowels, like the owl, no howls like the wolf, but instead short, faintly hollow, harsh sounds, that all together make something absolutely genuine, crow speech coming up from every feather, every source of that crow body and crow life.

The crows take very good care of their children, and are the most intelligent of birds, wary of human company, though when two or three fly over the countryside together, they look almost happy.

THE HOCKEY POEM
For Bill Duffy

1. *The Goalie*

The Boston College team has gold helmets, under which the long black hair of the Roman centurion curls out.... And they begin. How weird the goalies look with their African masks! The goalie is so lonely anyway, guarding a basket with nothing in it, his wide lower legs wide as ducks'.... No matter what gift he is given, he always rejects it.... He has a number like 1, a name like Mrazek, sometimes wobbling on his legs waiting for the puck, or curling up like a baby in the womb to hold it, staying a second too long on the ice.

The goalie has gone out to mid-ice, and now he sails sadly back to his own box, slowly; he looks prehistoric with his rhinoceros legs; he looks as if he's going to become extinct, and he's just taking his time....

When the players are at the other end, he begins sadly sweeping the ice in front of his house; he is the old witch in the woods, waiting for the children to come home.

2. *The Attack*

They all come hurrying back toward us, suddenly, knees dipping like oil wells; they rush toward us wildly, fins waving, they are pike swimming toward us, their gill fins expanding like the breasts of opera singers; no, they are twelve hands practicing penmanship on the same piece of paper. . . . They flee down the court toward us like birds, swirling two and two, hawks hurrying for the mouse, hurrying down wind valleys, swirling back and forth like amoebae on the pale slide, as they sail in the absolute freedom of water and the body, untroubled by the troubled mind, only the body, with wings as if there were no grave, no gravity, only the birds sailing over the cottage far in the deep woods. . . .

Now the goalie is desperate . . . he looks wildly over his left shoulder, rushing toward the other side of his cave, like a mother hawk whose chicks are being taken by two snakes. . . . Suddenly he flops on the ice like a man trying to cover a whole double bed. He has the puck. He stands up, turns to his right, and drops it on the ice at the right moment; he saves it for one of his children, a mother hen picking up a seed and then dropping it. . . .

But the men are all too clumsy, they can't keep track of the puck . . . no, it is the *puck*, the puck is too fast, too fast for human beings, it humiliates them constantly. The players are like country boys at the fair watching the con man—The puck always turns up under the wrong walnut shell. . . .

They come down the ice again, one man guiding the puck this time . . . and Ledingham comes down beautifully, like the canoe through white water or the lover going upstream, every stroke right, like the stallion galloping up the valley surrounded by his mares and colts, how beautiful, like the body and soul crossing in a poem. . . .

3. *The Fight*

The player in position pauses, aims, pauses, cracks his stick on the ice, and a cry as the puck goes in! The goalie stands up disgusted, and throws the puck out. . . .

The player with a broken stick hovers near the cage. When the play shifts, he skates over to his locked-in teammates, who look like a nest of bristling owls, owl babies, and they hold out a stick to him. . . .

Then the players crash together, their hockey sticks raised like lobster claws. They fight with slow motions, as if undersea . . . they are fighting over some woman back in the motel, but like lobsters they forget what they're battling for; the clack of the armor plate distracts them, and they feel a pure rage.

Or a fighter sails over to the penalty box, where ten-year-old boys wait to sit with the criminal, who is their hero. . . . They know society is wrong, the wardens are wrong, the judges hate individuality. . . .

4. The Goalie

And this man with his peaked mask, with slits, how fantastic he is, like a white insect who has given up on evolution in this life; his family hopes to evolve after death, in the grave. He is ominous as a Dark Ages knight . . . the Black Prince. His enemies defeated him in the day, but every one of them died in their beds that night. . . . At his father's funeral, he carried his own head under his arm.

He is the old woman in the shoe, whose house is never clean, no matter what she does. Perhaps this goalie is not a man at all, but a woman, all women; in her cage everything disappears in the end; we all long for it. All these movements on the ice will end, the seats will come down, the stadium walls bare. . . . This goalie with his mask is a woman weeping over the children of men, that are cut down like grass, gulls that stand with cold feet on the ice. . . . And at the end, she is still waiting, brushing away the leaves, waiting for the new children developed by speed, by war. . . .

WALKING ON THE SUSSEX COAST

A stone barn. The ground around is green, springy, rolling over into the ocean. The hoof marks in the muck outside the door mean only that the hoofs are glad to be going out, it is not an ominous sign. I stand a long time looking at the barn floor. The ground is fresh and yellow from tumbled bales. A portable wooden gate leans against the stone wall; it is calm, like an altar, some slivers missing. Maybe at night we split up into different beings, and one of them comes back here, to stand inside this barn, with only one eye, loved by the other cows, or at least recognized by the brown patches on my sides. How good to flop down here, our sides touching other cows, protected from seawind by stone walls that will later become the color of night. We know that at dawn we can look out the door and see the green hills again!

A TURTLE

The orange stripes on his head shoot forward into the future. The turtle's slim head stretches out, and it pushes with all its might, caught now on the edge of my palm. The claws—five on the front, four in back—are curiously long and elegant, curved, pale, like a lieutenant's sword. The yellow stripes on the neck and head remind you of racing cars.

The bottom plate is a washed-out rose color from being dragged over the world. The imagination is simplified there, without too much passion, business-like—like the underside of a space ship.

FROST ON THE WINDOWPANE

Frost is glittery, excited, like so many things laid down silently in the night, with no one watching. Through the two lower panes the watcher can dimly see the three trunks of the maple, sober as Europe. The frost wavers, it hurries over the world, it is like the body that lies in the coffin, and the next moment has disappeared! The mind through its skin picks up the radio signals of death, reminders of the molecules flying all about the universe . . . the icy disembarking, chill fingertips, tulips at head and foot.

I look at the upper panes and see more complicated roads . . . ribbons thrown down on the road . . .

MY THREE-YEAR-OLD DAUGHTER BRINGS ME A GIFT

For Mary

She comes and lays him carefully in my hand—a caterpillar! A yellow stripe along his back, and how hairy! Hairs wave like triumphal plumes as he walks.

Just behind his head, a black something slants back, like a crime, a black memory leaning toward the past.

He is not as beautiful as she thinks: the hair falling over his mouth cannot completely hide his face—two sloping foreheads with an eye between, and an obstinate jaw, made for eating through sleeping things without pain of conscience . . .

Now he rears, looking for another world.

LOOKING AT A DRY TUMBLEWEED BROUGHT IN FROM THE SNOW

What is this wonderful thing? Brown and everywhere! It has leaped up on my desk like surf, or like a bull onto a cow! It rushes everywhere in front of me. . . . And my sleeping senses are shouted at, called in from the back of my head, to look at it! Well, it is only a broken-off bush, a tumbleweed, every branch different, and the whole bush the same, so that way it is like the sea. Taken in from the deserted shore, it talks of queens sent away to live in cramped farmhouses, living in the dirt, and it talks of coffins and amazing arrows, no it is a love, some love we forget every day, it is my mother.

WATCHING ANDREI VOZNESENSKY READ IN VANCOUVER

Andrei Voznesensky has a curious look like a wood animal, one that often lives not far from marshes, near places where the deer sink in up to their knees. Waiting to read while the translation is being spoken, he sits with an utterly expressionless face—he is a pool unstirred by wind . . . hair falling over the pale forehead is a little like birch branches swaying over the water . . .

His shoes are elegant Italian cowboy shoes, patent leather. Black trousers and a blue shirt, with a folded silk tie always to protect the throat.

He strolls slowly toward the microphone, his hands put in slit front pockets, the thumbs pointing toward each other. As he begins to read, his knees bend, the right hand swings back and forth like the Neanderthal man complimenting himself after having thrown the first stone.

He looks straight forward, bending over slightly—a fantastic and resonant voice booms out, like enormous dynamos, like immense waterfalls falling, tremendous winds in the west sweep-

ing up, swirling winds carrying bits of chairs, barn doors, dust from chickenhouse floors, fragments of wooden grave markers set up by old Carnation-condensed-milk-drinking trappers; the whirlwind veers off the gravel road onto stubble fields. . . .

Sometimes the deep voice starts with a jolt, brought up from underneath by the right arm swinging forward . . .

then it drops suddenly into the most matter-of-fact tone, emotionless, muttering. . . .

The face has much mother-quality, his poems are mother-quality on fire, tenderness in flames, his voice is rushing water on fire, he is saying, it's OK to be on fire, OK for water, it's OK even for socialist concrete—

The voice is coming from deep in his chest that is bent forward like a javelin about to be thrown. It is the voice of some deep-throated woman shouting at last, her voice rattling the dishes, men covering their ears in the basement, or turning near the kitchen door and going back to the barn. . . . How good it feels to be able to shout about the pet chicken killed by men when you were a girl . . . to shout about the doll bureau painted with roses given to that *other* girl . . . how good it feels to shout at last!

STANDING UNDER A CHERRY TREE AT NIGHT
For the Rapps

The cherry branches sway . . . they are arms that prophesy music, hands that follow the note just about to come. The clumps of blossoms look heavily down, and are women's faces, not angry with us, who forgive and return petals to the earth. And I too sway like these boughs, as if in heavy canyons, hardly making ground, moving upstream against tiny cedar twigs being turned over and over in the cloudy spring river coming down.

All day I walked by the sea! I climbed down the cliffs at times to sit with the black mussels. Finally, I am back here, in the garden,

where the night air is affectionate, the stars are a transparent mountain range . . . and I am a human being standing in the dark, looking at the cherry branches above him swaying against the night sky not far from the sea!

TWO PROSE POEMS ON LOCKED-IN ANIMALS

1. *Lobsters Waiting to Be Eaten in a Restaurant Window*

A Saturday night. The area is cold, deserted. In a water tank set in the window there are many many small lobsters with crossed eyes, that are black and unsure—they make a fantastic forest of waving claws and movable armors. Sometimes they turn up to the sky, as if praying after some catastrophe, or climb over each other like clumsy men in splints; or stare steadily, the white hairs under their chins beating.

2. *Bored Elephants in the Circus Stable*

The elephants rock back and forth, their vast gray heads with indented temples swaying in the light coming down above them. Their bodies gray and wrinkled sway like the sea at dawn. It is a sea with no islands, no vegetation floating on it, no dry sticks even, only fish-shaped animals with no mouths swerving angrily in the gray water.

WATERFALL COMING OVER A CLIFF

HARDANGER, NORWAY

Eight hundred feet up, there is water pouring out of the sky! It drops a few feet, and then the long plunge, after the slanting blow off the cliff. . . . It is a deep plunge, loveless, floating; it falls by the cliff like tufts of sleep . . . the long sleep the truckdriver sinks into

after he has driven three days from the coast, or the clouds that pass across the sky of a dog's eyes, when he dies in a room with human beings . . . or the glimpse the meditator has of something floating under the water, neither moving nor not moving, seeming to slow as it nears the bottom.

IN THE COURTYARD OF THE ISLETA MISSION

Behind the Church in the Isleta Pueblo, here is a courtyard. The sun comes down from the purest ant heavens. On the old flagstones the ants trail after each other, between a fireweed and a rock chip, as they did when the European friars awoke and walked here in the morning. The New Mexico trees are spare and detached; wind moves through branches that do not want the wealth of the world.

Inside the Church, the coffins of the old priests rose every spring. The people stood near the altar and watched. One day a German priest arrived. He said it was only the rising water table, he got ready to bury them again, outside. The Indians collected him one night, covered him with chains, threw him out of the car, padlocked the Church, and closed the rectory.

Now the courtyard is left to the ants and the wind, and the priests rise and fall as they wish, an Indian man carries a six-pack of Pepsi across the desert plaza, and the clear shadows falling on the adobe walls resemble the airiest impulses we have, that want to live, and will, if we agree to put ourselves in the hands of the ants.

A POEM ABOUT TENNESSEE

REELFOOT LAKE, WEST TENNESSEE

For Stephen Mooney

We are in Reelfoot Lake, Green Island Cutoff. It is a wide ditch, cut into the Tennessee earth. Some lily pads rise above the water, like hands held up to receive; others lie flat on the surface, like opened books. A rotted carcass lies on the shore as we pass, sending out reminders, maybe a buffalo fish, or a pig, or an immense beaver; now it is a rotted glove, with the hand still inside. A muskrat swims past like a commuter. Two cardinals in the bushes like red nuns. How heavy the water is, the small swirl near the boat, it is a sculpture disappearing again into the stone.

This is Tennessee, the sun hollering through the lonesome marsh trees. Three pines lean sideways over the exiled Mississippi water, some dead fish float by like neglected wives. There are Indian villages nearby, tears fill the sockets of the Indian grandmothers as they see their grandsons; dreams of luminous bird-points, delicate as wren eyes . . . the setting sun rolls like a puppy over the water, "water that is ours" the Indians said; the low hills of Tennessee, with their frail mimosa-hair half leafed out, hard nights in cabins with tired women, the flint-gun hung like Calvin over the fireplace, lying on upturned deer-feet, long nights when the porcupines ate and Andrew Jackson slept a good sleep, his dreams of the Presidency bordered by coffins and women proud of him . . . the rope ahead of me on the prow is lonely here, so near the immense Mississippi that carries our lonelinesses, and gathers them all together, the Mississippi on which so many black bodies have floated home, near which so many husbands with English names have looked somberly down at the legs of tables in the kitchen, and then longed to disappear into the burning sun, and live there high in eagles' nests, with bare sticks around them. . . . I can hear the water obeying on each side of the boat, this is Tennessee, Tennessee waters, with cypress knees breathing, and men who do care,

and look sideways before they talk, we are all here in the heavy waters, where the cypresses live, "I shall give thanks in Tennessee!" Sputt and Ed throw the rope up on the dock, we come in, the shadows in Rembrandt, the black and white tiles on the floor, the map above on the wall.

THE BLACK CRAB DEMON

The ocean swirls up over the searock. It falls back, returns, and rushes over a whirlhole the shape of a galaxy. A black crab climbs up the searock sideways, like a demon listening in Aramaic.

All at once, I am not married; I have no parents; I wave my black claws and hurry over the rock. I hold fast to the bottom; no night-mother can pry me loose; I am alone inside myself; I love whatever is like me. I am glad no seabeast comes to eat me; I withdraw into the rock caverns and return; I hurry through the womb-systems at night.

Last night in my dream a man I did not know whispered in my ear that he was disappointed in me, and that I had lost his friendship. . . . How often have I awakened with a heavy chest, and yet my life does not change.

A ROCK ISLET ON THE PACIFIC

The sea boils in over underwater rocks, then swiftly pulls back, among currents with different thoughts, everything sweeping and howling. . . . Now the sea is suddenly motionless, making the holes on the rock floor clear.

But thoughts hurry in again, trying to leap up the sides; the whole inlet is like an eyeball, mad sights climbing the walls.

My own nostrils feel the bite of the salt. The sloshing water is

too wild for seaweed, but limpets understand—this sloshing goes on for centuries, but no one gets tired of it . . . there is no one to get tired! The man sitting by the sea sits silent for hours, then suddenly breaks out singing. As the heart pumps it senses the seawaters entering and leaving, jumping up and nearly touching the tern's foot. The jellyfish opens and closes, our mouth longs for the saltwater.

II

THE POINT REYES POEMS

NOVEMBER DAY AT McCLURE'S BEACH

Alone on the jagged rock at the south end of McClure's Beach. The sky low. The sea grows more and more private, as afternoon goes on; the sky comes down closer; the unobserved water rushes out to the horizon—horses galloping in a mountain valley at night. The waves smash up the rock; I find flags of seaweed high on the worn top, forty feet up, thrown up overnight; separated water still pooled there, like the black ducks that fly desolate, forlorn, and joyful over the seething swells, who never "feel pity for themselves," and "do not lie awake weeping for their sins." In their blood cells the vultures coast with furry necks extended, watching over the desert for signs of life to end. It is not our life we need to weep for. Inside us there is some secret. We are following a narrow ledge around a mountain, we are sailing on skeletal eerie craft over the buoyant ocean.

WELCOMING A CHILD IN THE LIMANTOUR DUNES

For Micah

Thinking of a child soon to be born, I hunch down among friendly sand grains. . . . The sand grains love us, for they love whatever lives without force, a young girl who looks out over her life, alone, with no map, no horse, a white dress on. The sand grains love whatever is not rushing blindly forward—I mean the mole who is blinking at the door of his crumbly mole Vatican, and the salmon who one morning senses in her gills the fragrant Oregon waters crashing down. Something seems to love this planet abandoned here at the edge of the Milky Way, and this child floating inside the Pacific of the womb, near the walls, hearing the breakers roaring.

TRESPASSING ON THE PIERCE RANCH

I walk toward Tomales Point over soaked and lonely hills—a wild cat runs away from his inspection of a wet gopher hole as I come near. Wind off the sea. A few sheep, some cows with large udders high above the ocean.

These cliffs are the first land the amazed traveler saw when looking over the rail he suddenly came on a continent . . . in the middle of the endless ocean.

Glancing east, I see the three-quarters moon moving in broad daylight, pale and urgent, through the sky, freeing itself from itself in the clouds. It is a sturdy eye-traveler, sailing eerily forward, orphaned, bold and alone. Formed long ago, it has parted from the Earth as my moon from myself.

Part of me sails steadily through clouds, and the rest of me is down here, among these soaked and lonely hills. These lowlands that are backed by the Coastal Range and again by the Rockies

thicken eastward into Nebraska and the plateau that holds up the heavy pueblos, Taos, San Isidro, Isleta.

There the old men hit the boys lightly with twigs as the boys run past, their heels hitting the earth, racing each other to the plaza, where a Douglas fir has been set up with a dead sheep tied to the very top. One of the winter boys arrives first. Then the clowns prepare to unhook the sheep from the sky.

CLIMBING UP MOUNT VISION WITH MY LITTLE BOY

We started up. All the way he held my hand. Sometimes he falls back to bend over a banana slug, then senses how lonely the slug is, and comes running back. He never complained, and we went straight up. How much I love being with him! How much I love to feel his small leafy hand curl around my finger. He holds on, and we are flying through a cloud. On top we hunker down beneath some bushes to get out of the wind, while the girls go off to play, and he tells me the story of the little boy who wouldn't cut off his hair and give it to a witch, and so she changed him into a hollow log! A boy and girl came along, and stepped on the log—and the log said, "Oww!" They put their feet on it again, and the log said, "Oww!" Then they looked inside and saw a boy's jacket sticking out. A little boy was in there! "I can't come out, I've been changed into a hollow log." That's the end, he said.

Then I remembered a bit more—the boy and the girl went to a wise man . . . he corrected me, "It was a wise woman, Daddy" . . . and said, "How can we get him changed back into a little boy?" She said, "Here is a pearl. If a crow asks you for it, give it to him." So they went along. Pretty soon a crow came and said, "Can I have the buttons on your shirt?" The boy said, "Yes." Then the crow said, "Can I have that pearl in your shirt pocket?" "Yes." Then the crow

said, "Now we'll go to the witch's house." The crow flew up and dropped some moss down the witch's chimney. The chimney got full, the witch started to cough. The crow dropped in some more moss. Then she had to open the door, and run outside! Then the crow took an oyster, a big one, from the Johnson Oyster Company, and flew high into the air, and dropped it right on the witch's head. And that was the end of her. And then the log was changed back again into a little boy.

The land on top is bare, sweeping, forbidding—so unlike a little boy's mind. I asked him what he liked best about the whole walk. He said it was Bethany (an eight-year-old friend of Mary's) going peepee in her pants while hiding.

AN EXCURSION ON TOMALES BAY
For Michael and Barbara Whitt

The blue sky suddenly gone—fog. We cut the engine and drift. We glimpse a derrick on shore—it is a bird—a Great Blue Heron! He turns his head and walks away . . . like some old Hittite empire, all the brutality forgotten, only the rare vases left, and the elegant necks of the women. . . .

Heavy bodies float nearby; we drift among them. Whiskered heads peer over at us attentively, like angels called to look at a baby. They have risen from their sea-mangers to peer at us. Their Magi come to them every day . . . and they gaze at the godless in their wooden boat. . . .

Boulders lie piled on the shore . . . no . . . sea lions, hundreds of them! . . . Some on their backs playing. . . . Now the whole shore starts to roll seaward, barking and flapping. . . .

Meanwhile, the whiskered heads have vanished; they are some-where in the water underneath us. At last one head pops up five feet from the boat, looking neither arrogant nor surprised, but like a billfold found in the water, or a mountain that has been rained on

for three weeks . . . and the Great Blue Heron, each wing as long as Holland, flies off, thin as a grassblade in the fog . . .

CALM MORNING AT DRAKE'S BAY

A sort of roll develops out of the bay, and lays itself all down this long beach. . . the hiss of the water wall, two inches high, coming in, steady as lions, or African grass fires. Two gulls with feet the color of a pumpkin walk together on the sand. A snipe settles down . . . three squawks . . . the gulls agree to chase it away. Then the wave goes out, the waters mingle so beautifully, it is the min-gling after death, the silence, the sweep—so swift!—over darken-ing sand . . . the airplane sweeping low over the African field at night, lost, no tin cans burning, the old woman stomps around her house on a cane, no lamp lit yet. . . .

FINDING A SALAMANDER ON INVERNESS RIDGE

Walking. Afternoon. The war still going on, I stoop down to pick up a salamander. He is halfway across the mossy forest path. He is dark brown, fantastically cold in my hand. This one is new to me—the upper part of his eyeball light green . . . strange bullfrog eyes. The belly is a brilliant orange, color of airplane gasoline on fire; the back is a heavy-duty rubber black, with goose pimples from permanent cold. I make a kind of pulpit of my left hand, and turn him gently upright; his head and front legs look out at me, as his hands rest on my crossing thumb joint. Warmed, he grows lively, pulls himself out, and falls to earth where he raises his chin defiantly. I pick him up again. But he is patient, this war. I hold him again between thumb and forefinger for many minutes, and

his front paws hold onto my thumb resignedly—perhaps I could hold him so for hours. Perhaps he could be held gently this way for days until he died, the green eyes still opening and closing. When I turn my wrist over, I see the long orange-black tail hanging down into the cathedral of the open palm, circling back and forth, rolling and unrolling like a snake. It hangs down like a rudder on some immensely long boat, a rudder that the men and women on board looking over the handrail do not see.

SEAWATER POURING BACK OVER STONES

Waves rush up, pause, and drag pebbles back around stones . . . the sound of pebbles going out. . . . It is a complicated sound, as of small sticks breaking, or kitchen sounds heard from another house, the rustling when bodies turn over at night. . . . Now the retreating wave gets to the boulders, drops down over the stones always wet . . . the gentleness of William Carlos Williams after his stroke . . . Then we hear the sound of harsh death waves that race up the roof of leopard-colored stones, leaving a tiny rattling in the throat as they go out. . . . They leave the ecstatic brown sand stretched out between stones. We know that the anger of some young women is right.

And always another sound: a heavy underground roaring in my ears from the surf farther out, as if the earth were reverberating under the feet of one dancer. That sound is a comforting sound, like the note of Paradise carried to the Egyptian sands; and I hear the driftwood far out singing; the great logs, fifty miles out, still floating in. The water under the waters is singing, what has not yet come to the surface to float, years that are still down somewhere below the chest. Long trunks are out there, too, that have floated all the way from the Pacific islands. . . . And the donkey the disciples will find standing beside the white wall . . .

THE DEAD SEAL NEAR McCLURE'S BEACH

1

Walking north toward the point, I come on a dead seal. From a few feet away, he looks like a brown log. The body is on its back, dead only a few hours. I stand and look at him. There's a quiver in the dead flesh: My God, he's still alive. And a shock goes through me, as if a wall of my room had fallen away.

His head is arched back, the small eyes closed; the whiskers sometimes rise and fall. He is dying. This is the oil. Here on its back is the oil that heats our houses so efficiently. Wind blows fine sand back toward the ocean. The flipper near me lies folded over the stomach, looking like an unfinished arm, lightly glazed with sand at the edges. The other flipper lies half underneath. And the seal's skin looks like an old overcoat, scratched here and there—by sharp mussel shells maybe.

I reach out and touch him. Suddenly he rears up, turns over. He gives three cries: Awaark! Awaark! Awaark!—like the cries from Christmas toys. He lunges toward me; I am terrified and leap back, though I know there can be no teeth in that jaw. He starts flopping toward the sea. But he falls over, on his face. He does not want to go back to the sea. He looks up at the sky, and he looks like an old lady who has lost her hair. He puts his chin back down on the sand, rearranges his flippers, and waits for me to go. I go.

2

The next day I go back to say goodbye. He's dead now. But he's not. He's a quarter mile farther up the shore. Today he is thinner, squatting on his stomach, head out. The ribs show more: each vertebra on the back under the coat is visible, shiny. He breathes in and out.

A wave comes in, touches his nose. He turns and looks at me—the eyes slanted; the crown of his head looks like a boy's leather jacket bending over some bicycle bars. He is taking a long time to

die. The whiskers white as porcupine quills, the forehead slopes. . . . Goodbye, brother, die in the sound of the waves. Forgive us if we have killed you. Long live your race, your inner-tube race, so uncomfortable on land, so comfortable in the ocean. Be comfortable in death then, when the sand will be out of your nostrils, and you can swim in long loops through the pure death, ducking under as assassinations break above you. You don't want to be touched by me. I climb the cliff and go home the other way.

THE LARGE STARFISH

It is low tide. Fog. I have climbed down the cliffs from Pierce Ranch to the tide pools. Now the ecstasy of the low tide, kneeling down, alone. In six inches of clear water I notice a purple starfish— with nineteen arms! It is a delicate purple, the color of old carbon paper, or an attic dress . . . at the webs between the arms sometimes a more intense sunset red glows through. The fingers are relaxed . . . some curled up at the tips . . . with delicate rods . . . apparently globes on top of each, as at World's Fairs, waving about. The starfish slowly moves up the groin of the rock . . . then back down . . . many of its arms rolled up now, lazily, like a puppy on its back. One arm is especially active and curved up over its own body as if a dinosaur were looking behind him.

How slowly and evenly it moves! The starfish is a glacier, going sixty miles a year! It moves over the pink rock, by means I cannot see . . . and into marvelously floating delicate brown weeds. It is about the size of the bottom of a pail. When I reach into it, it tightens and then slowly relaxes. . . . I take an arm and quickly lift. The underside is a pale tan. . . . Gradually, as I watch, thousands of tiny tubes begin rising from all over the underside . . . hundreds in the mouth, hundreds along the nineteen underarms . . . all looking . . . feeling . . . like a man looking for a woman . . . tiny heads blindly feeling for a rock and finding only

air. A purple rim runs along the underside of every arm, with paler tubes. Probably its moving-feet.

I put him back in. He unfolds—I had forgotten how purple he was—and slides down into his rock groin, the snail-like feelers waving as if nothing had happened, and nothing has.

III

GOING IN A HELICOPTER FROM RIVERSIDE TO THE L.A. AIRPORT

We are up. The wheel below my window hangs useless, like a crippled leg, shaking slightly.

Los Angeles in the valley—we can see some white substance, held as if in a breakfast bowl, by the rim of hills. Smog. The particles of combustion slip out along the muffler tunnels, and are alone a few minutes on the freeway, before rising to meet this cloud. The cloud is white, like the watery milk with flies in it that the gold miners drink.

And the freeways hurry through the streets, they are a hand sweeping pencils, photographs, fruit, everything, off the desk.

We start to go down into the smog. It is all around us, ectoplasm coming from the medium now in anguish, beads of sweat stand out on his forehead, demons approach in the fog, the dead move around behind, surround him . . . he can't get back. . . .

THE PORCUPINE IN THE WIND

For Galway Kinnell

In half-light, I make out a shape near a tree trunk—a half-grown porcupine! He hurries clumsily—like a steam shovel—up the tree. Six feet up, he decides he has gone far enough and he waits, occasionally looking at me over a half-turned shoulder. Step-

ping up, I look into his eye, which is black, with little spontaneity, above an expressionless nose. He knows little about climbing, and his claws keep slipping on the gray poplar bark. His body apparently feels no excitement anyway to be climbing higher, toward the immaterial sky: he can't remember any stories he has heard.

Sun already down. The white needle-fur stands out, something pre-Roman, next to the elegant bark. As I listen I become aware of a third thing, still older. It is the wind through miles of leafless forest.

VISITING THOMAS HART BENTON AND HIS WIFE IN KANSAS CITY

The stone driveway is littered with chill leaves, damp in the November mist. We climbed the back porch of stone, the door opens. A man, who looks like a short tractor, comes out saying, "Come on in here!"; brushing us in with his hands. There was labor on the face; this was not the happy poet typing his poems twenty minutes a day, but the cattle driver walking through snow, the wrestler wrestling with the angel, lifting him up and driving him down to earth over and over, the joy of hard work, the thresher defeated at dusk by the weight of the bundles.

We see on the wall a painting of his—a girl with a red hood. She looks at the wolf on the path; she is hesitant; she has seen no evil, having only seen her parents, and those not well; the light brown wolf is curious to talk to her; he has met her before, in another life: she cannot remember, though he can. She does not remember, and is about to lose the battle again (although we know the wolf will twist away toward the river wounded once more).

Here are two boys in a canoe: water curves like lace around the island in the river that resembles an arm sleeping on a kitchen table; and the two farm boys in the canoe head toward the unknown falls of brightness—something they never experienced at home where

their lantern at night fell on the sides of the patient Guernseys standing with their heads in prison.

Thomas Hart Benton's wife comes in, strong, radiant, triumphant, as if she had survived the flesh, like some rocket that has returned from the moon and splashed down in a Russian meadow. Tom, as she called him, sits crouched on the sofa now, muttering strong phrases: "I used to go on tour . . . I've been all over this goddamned country . . . I got as far west as Lubbock in 1934 . . . you from Minnesota? Where's the damn university? Minneapolis? Hell, I've been there." His eighty-two-year-old head is full of Grant Wood memories and Vachel Lindsay. "I lived on the same floor as him in 1912, maybe . . . I didn't know him well . . . in those days we were a poor lot" . . . a gurgling laugh . . .

There's a deep indentation in his forehead, starting near his right eye and going upward . . . above the forehead it forks, then the two forks join again deepening, and the line seems to sink into the upper sensual part of the brain.

On the wall we see girls in short skirts out in the yard during the auction sale, as the mortgage storm comes on. The hungers of some traveling preacher has flowed into the girls who have known only linoleum floors and rickety kitchen tables. The traveling preacher has confused Jesus with the storms of deep sleep . . .

In another painting, as the woman groans in labor, wolves fade back into the woods and the dancing girls drive their sexual energy into the ground (just as men drive nails). The energy flows down into the dead, who carry it to the throats of trees and up into the big branches, under which the half-asleep mule brushes at flies. His cock hangs down like a wagon tongue, and his long ears remind you of the long river down which we all float, sleeping and waking fitfully.

WALKING IN THE HARDANGERVIDDA

The mountain bushes move toughly in the wind. There has been a rain. And I love these stretches of new water, one or two inches deep, fifteen or twenty feet long, with green grass growing straight up out of them! The sun slanting in at late dawn makes little moats of light around the grass stems.

Each grassblade has its own molecules of light around it, as they say a mountain where men are meditating always has white clouds above, as—they say—the roof of the dying saint gathers white storks.

When I bend closer, the little motes of light disappear, and I can see the ecstatic earthbed, the brown blades of grass left from last year, like ruins of things we never did. And a few green blades entirely underwater, joy of the man who has lived.

RENDEZVOUS AT AN ABANDONED FARM

As we walk out at dawn we can still see the remains of the path the cows have beaten into the weedy earth, and the 75-by-40-foot barn that the farmer inherited and, as Thoreau said, "pushed before him all his life." The barn is used now only for storing hay, the buildings rented out. The barn resembles some African trading post, abandoned when the secrets the Europeans hid caught up with them, and no one could give a "simple and sincere account of his own life."

The Germans and Norwegians who opened this land broke into the earth, ignoring the mother-love of the Sioux. The immigrants have sunk back now into their family Bibles; the great hinges have closed on them, and they sleep a coarse sleep—not forgiven. They know they have done wrong, and they go over and over the harness-hours, trying to see how they threw on the harness, how they happened to buckle things in the wrong order. And the souls of the

immigrant women float crippled through the hayloft; the bodies are lacking an arm or foot; the missing parts have been sent to someone as a message, like those hands sent back by kidnappers in the Middle Ages.

It is early dawn. Sunlight bounces from the roofs of the two cars that have brought us. Something is over, has finished here, and there is no comfort, there is no good thing to say.

A CATERPILLAR

Lifting my coffee cup, I notice a caterpillar crawling over my sheet of ten-cent airmail stamps. The head is black as a Chinese box. Nine soft accordions follow it around, with a waving motion, like a flabby mountain. Skinny brushes used to clean pop bottles rise from some of its shoulders. As I pick up the sheet of stamps, the caterpillar advances around and around the edge, and I see his feet: three pairs under the head, four sponge-like pairs under the middle body, and two final pairs at the tip, pink as a puppy's hind legs. As he walks, he rears, six pairs of legs off the stamp, waving around in the air! One of the sponge pairs, and the last two tail pairs, the reserve feet, hold on anxiously. It is the first of September. The leaf shadows are less ferocious on the notebook cover. A man accepts his failures more easily—or perhaps summer's insanity is gone? A man notices ordinary earth, scorned in July, with affection, as he settles down to his daily work, to use stamps.

MORNING BY THE LAKE
For Jim and Sue

Wind blows, and lake water breaks over the bare lake-rocks no one loves. I walk about on bare feet an inch off the ground, and feel

the longing to kneel down, to put my knees against the earth. Something in me flies out over the water like fragments of lightning, or a beam broken up into sparks.

All at once I understand the Virgin and her candles, and I love the great gray body of the whale rolling in the sea, with his sides glistening, and I understand why my hair is up toward the clouds.

That understander in me longs for a room with stone walls, deep bays, and morning sunlight, where a woman with shining arms is sitting.

AUGUST RAIN

After a month and a half without rain, at last, in late August, darkness comes at three in the afternoon, a cheerful thunder begins, and then the rain. I set a glass out on a table to measure the rain, and, suddenly buoyant and affectionate, go indoors to find my children. They are upstairs, playing quietly alone in their doll-filled rooms, hanging pictures, thoughtfully moving "the small things that make them happy" from one side of the room to another. I feel triumphant, without need of money, far from the grave. I walk over the grass, watching the soaked chairs, and the cooled towels, and sit down on my stoop, dragging a chair out with me. The rain deepens. It rolls off the porch roof, making a great puddle near me. The bubbles slide toward the puddle edge, become crowded, and disappear. The black earth turns blacker, it absorbs the rain needles without a sound. The sky is low, everything silent, as when parents are angry. . . . What has failed and been forgiven—the leaves from last year unable to go on, lying near the foundation, dry under the porch, retreat farther into the shadow, they give off a faint hum, as of birds' eggs, or the tail of a dog.

The older we get the more we fail, but the more we fail the more we feel a part of the dead straw of the universe, the corners of barns with cow dung twenty years old, the belts left hanging over the

chairback after the bachelor has died in the ambulance on the way to the city. These objects ride us as the child who holds onto the dog's fur; they appear in our dreams; they are more and more near us, coming in slowly from the wainscoting; they make our trunks heavy, accumulating between trips; they lie against the ship's side, and will nudge the hole open that lets the water in at last.

GRASS FROM TWO YEARS

When I write poems, I need to be near grass that no one else sees, as here, where I sit for an hour under the cottonwood. The long grass has fallen over until it flows. Whatever I am . . . if the great hawks come to look for me, I will be here in this grass. Knobby twigs have dropped on it. The summer's grass still green crosses some dry grass beneath, like the hair of the very old, that we stroke in the morning.

And how beautiful this ring of dry grass is, pale and tan, that curves over the half-buried branch—the grass flows over it, and is pale, gone, ascended, no longer selfish, no longer centered on its mouth; it is centered now on the God "of distance and of absence." Its pale blades lie near each other around the dry wood . . . this stick that the rain has not cared for, and has ignored, as it fell in the night, on men holding horses in the courtyard, and the sunlight was glad that the branch could be ignored, and did not ask to be loved—so I have loved you—and the branch and the grass lie here deserted, a part of the wild things of the world, noticed only for a moment by a heavy, nervous man who sits near them, and feels he has at this moment more joy than anyone alive.

CHRISTMAS EVE SERVICE AT MIDNIGHT
AT ST. MICHAEL'S
For Father Richter

A cold night; the sidewalk we walk on icy; the dark surrounds the frail wood houses that were so recently trees. We left my father's house an hour before midnight, carrying boxes of gifts out to the car. My brother, who had been killed six months before, was absent. We had wept sitting near the decorated tree. Now I see the angel on the right of St. Michael's altar kneeling on one knee, a hand pressed to his chin. The long-needled Christmas pine, who is the being inside us who is green both summer and winter, is hung with red ribbons of triumph. And it is hung with thirty golden balls, each ball representing a separate planet on which that eternal one has found a home. Outdoors the snow labors its old Manichean labors to keep the father and his animals in melancholy. We sing. At midnight the priest walks down one or two steps, finds the infant Christ, and puts him into the cradle beneath the altar, where the horses and the sheep have been waiting.

Just after midnight he turns to face the congregation, lifts up the dry wafer, and breaks it—a clear and terrifying sound. He holds up the two halves . . . frightening . . . like so many acts, it is permanent. With his arms spread, the cross clear on his white chasuble, he tells us that Christ intended to leave his body behind. . . . It is confusing . . . we want to take our bodies with us when we die. I see waters dark and lifting near flights of stairs, waters lifting and torn over which the invisible birds drift like husks over November roads. . . . The cups are put down. The ocean has been stirred and calmed. A large man is flying over the water with wings spread, a wound on his chest.

OPENING THE DOOR OF A BARN I THOUGHT WAS EMPTY ON NEW YEAR'S EVE

I walk over the fields made white with new snow and then open the double-barn doors: Sounds of breathing! Thirty steers are wandering about, the old barn partitions gone. Creatures heavy, shaggy, slowly moving in the dying light. Bodies with no St. Teresa look straight at me. The floor is cheerful with clean straw. Snow gleams in the feeding lot outside. The bony legs of the steers look frail in the pale light from the snow like uncles visiting from the city.

Dust and cobwebs thicken the windowpanes. The dog who came with me stands up on his hind legs to look over the wooden gate. Large shoulders watch him, and he suddenly puts his legs down, frightened. After a while, he puts them up again. A steer's head swings to look at the dog; it stares for three or four minutes unable to get a clear picture from the instinct reservoir—then bolts.

But the steers' enemies are asleep; the whole barn is asleep. The steers do not demand eternal life; they ask only to eat the crushed corn and the hay tasty with dust, and sometimes to feel an affection run down along the heavy nerves. Each steer has a lamp lit inside fluttering on a windy night.

THIS BODY
IS MADE
OF CAMPHOR
AND
GOPHERWOOD

(1977)

Gendron would like to dedicate this book to:
"All the waters of this world."

WALKING SWIFTLY

When I wake, I hear sheep eating apple peels just outside the screen. The trees are heavy, soaked, cold and hushed, the sun just rising. All seems calm, and yet somewhere inside I am not calm. We live in wooden buildings made of two-by-fours, making the landscape nervous for a hundred miles. And the Emperor when he was sixty called for rhinoceros horn, for sky-blue phoenix eggs shaped from veined rock, dipped in rooster blood. Around him the wasps kept guard, the hens continued their patrol, the oysters open and close all questions. The heat inside the human body grows, it does not know where to throw itself—for a while it knots into will, heavy, burning, sweet, then into generosity, that longs to take on the burdens of others, and then into mad love that lasts forever. The artist walks swiftly to his studio, and carves oceanic waves into the dragon's mane.

A DAY ALONE

My friend, this body is made of camphor and gopherwood. Where it goes, we follow, even into the Ark. As the light comes in sideways from the west over damp spring buds and winter trash, the body comes out hesitatingly, and we are shaken, we weep, how is it that we feel no one has ever loved us? This protective lamplit left hand hovering over its own shadow on the page seems more loved than we are. . . . And when we step into a room where we expect to find someone, we walk all the way over the floor and feel the bed. . . .

THE SLEEPER

He came in and sat by my side, and I did not wake up. I went on dreaming of vast houses with rooms I had not seen, of men suddenly appearing whom I did not know, but who knew me, of thistles whose points shone as if a light were inside.

A man came to me and began to play music. One arm lay outside the covers. He put the dulcimer in my hand but I did not play it. I went on, hearing.

Why didn't I wake up? And why didn't I play? Because I am asleep, and the sleeping man is all withdrawn into himself. He thinks the sound of a shutting door is a tooth falling from his head, or his head rolling on the ground.

FINDING THE FATHER

This body offers to carry us for nothing—as the ocean carries logs—so on some days the body wails with its great energy, it smashes up the boulders, lifting small crabs, that flow around the sides. Someone knocks on the door, we do not have time to dress. He wants us to come with him through the blowing and rainy streets, to the dark house. We will go there, the body says, and there find the father whom we have never met, who wandered in a snowstorm the night we were born, who then lost his memory, and has lived since longing for his child, whom he saw only once . . . while he worked as a shoemaker, as a cattle herder in Australia, as a restaurant cook who painted at night. When you light the lamp you will see him. He sits there behind the door . . . the eyebrows so heavy, the forehead so light . . . lonely in his whole body, waiting for you.

THE OWLETS AT NIGHTFALL

The sun is sinking. Each minute the air darker. The night thickens near the ground, pulls my body down to it. And if my body is earth, then what? Then I am down here, thickening as night comes on. The moon will float up there. Some part of me is up there too. How far it is up to that part!

There are earth things, earthly, joined, they are snuggled down in one manger, one sweep of arms holds them, one clump of pine, the owlets sit together in one hollow tree. . . .

When night comes what has been sun in me all day will drop underneath the earth, and travel sizzling along the underearth-ocean-darkness path. . . . There a hundred developed saints lie stretched out, throwing bits of darkness onto the road.

At midnight what has been moon in me will also vanish. I will go down toward utter darkness and find myself in Joseph's prison cell telling dreams to the baker.

GOING OUT TO CHECK THE EWES

My friend, this body is food for the thousand dragons of the air, each dragon light as a needle. This body loves us, and carries us home from our hoeing.

It is ancient, and full of the bales of sleep. In its vibrations the sun rolls along under the earth; the spouts over the ocean curl into our stomach. Water revolves, making spouts seen by skull eyes at mid-ocean. This body of herbs and gopherwood, this blessing, this is a lone ridge patrolled by water. . . . I get up, morning is here. The stars are still out; the black winter sky looms over the unborn lambs. The barn is cold before dawn, the gates slow.

This body longs for itself far out at sea, it floats in the black heavens, it is a brilliant being, locked in the prison of human dullness. . . .

GALLOPING HORSES

The horses gallop east, over the steppes, each with its rider, hard. Each rider carries a strip of red cloth raised above his head. The horses leap over a line of fire. Then a stream, they leap higher, hooves push into the mud. Then a crevice—space stretched out sideways—a few horses fall in. Now they meet their fourth obstacle—flesh. . . . It is a Garden, elephant trunks reach lazily up into tree branches, and the gazelles hurry over the plain like blood corpuscles in a storm, flock on flock, even the monkeys have hair. And the horses slow, they become confused among so many gentle animals, the riders look to the side and behind them, turning in their saddles to see the large animals peacefully grazing behind.

A DREAM OF WHAT IS MISSING

I dreamt all night such glad painful exultant dreams. Each scene was a tile of glazed and luminous clay. What does not have the senses longs for the senses. All longing is terrible and terrifying—a herd of gazelles running over the savannah—and intense and divine, and I saw it lying over the floor in layers there.

All night I longed for my missing limbs. Lines of force at the bottom of Joseph's well sent up lumps of dirt that heal the humpbacked; something rolled upward from the water, became a lion, that prowls around the rocky edges of the desert, keeping the hermit inside his own chest.

THE OLD MAN WITH MISSING FINGERS

This body holds its protective wall around us, it watches us whenever we walk out. Each step we take in conversations with our

friends, moving slowly or flying, the body watches us, calling us into what is possible, into what is not said, into the shuck heap of ruined arrowheads or the old man with missing fingers.

We take our first step in words each day, and instantly fall into a hole in the sounds we make. Overly sane afternoons in a room during our twenties come back to us in the form of a friend who is mad; every longing another person had that we failed to see returns to us as a squinting of the eyes when we talk, and no sentimentality, only the ruthless body performing its magic, transforming each of our confrontations into energy, changing our scholarly labors over white-haired books into certainty and healing power, and our cruelties into an old man with missing fingers.

We talk one morning about the messy lives others lead, and in broad daylight the car slides off the road. Yesterday I offered advice as if I were adult; in my dream I saw a policeman holding a gun to the head of a frightened girl, who was blindfolded. We talk wisely of eternity; looking down, we see an old man with missing fingers.

WALKING TO THE NEXT FARM

It has been snowing all day. Three of us start out across the fields. The boots sink in to the ankles, but go on; our feet move through the most powerful snow energy. There is falling snow above us, and below us, and on all sides. My eyes feel wild, as if a new body were rising, with tremendous swirls in its flow; its whirlpools move with their face upward, as those whirls in the Missouri that draw in green cottonwoods from collapsed earth banks, pull them down with all their branches. And our feet carry the male energy that disappears, as my brother's energy did, in its powerful force field his whole life disappeared, and all the trees on his farm went with it. . . .

There is some sort of energy that comes off the fierce man's

hair. It is not a halo, but a background of flames. The energy increases, while "more and more docile men are being born each day." As the Tibetan exhales, fifty pale men melt back into the ground. Huns fade back into the forest around Vienna, the doctor leaps up from his desk, he curses the stupidity of his life, grinds his teeth. Lenin refuses to eat with others. The carriage goes on through the night.

Then what is asked of us? To stop sacrificing one energy for another. They are not different energies anyway, not "male" or "female," but whirls of different speeds as they revolve. We must learn to worship both, and give up the idea of one god. . . . I taste the snow, lying on a branch. It tastes slow. It is as slow as the whirl in the boulder lying beneath the riverbed. . . . Its swirls take nine thousand years to complete, but they too pull down the buffalo-skin boats into their abysses, many souls with hair go down.

> *The light settles down in front of each snowflake,*
> *And the dark rises up behind it,*
> *And inside its own center it lives!*

THE LOVER'S BODY AS A COMMUNITY OF PROTOZOA

This body is made of bone and excited protozoa . . . and it is with my body that I love the fields. How do I know what I feel but what the body tells me? Erasmus thinking in the snow, translators of Virgil who burn up the whole room, the man in furs reading the Arabic astrologer falls off his three-legged stool in astonishment— this is the body, so beautifully carved inside, with the curves of the inner ear, and the husk so rough, knuckle-brown.

As we walk we enter the magnetic fields of other bodies, and every smell we take in the communities of protozoa see; and a being inside leaps up toward it, as a horse rears at the starting gate. When

you and I come near each other, we are drawn down into the sweet-
est pools of slowly circling energies, slowly circling smells.

> *The sunlight lays itself down before the protozoa,*
> *And night opens itself out behind it,*
> *And inside its own energy it lives!*

So the space between two people diminishes; it grows less and
less; no one to weep; they merge at last. The sound that pours from
the fingertips awakens clouds of cells far inside the other's body,
and beings unknown to us start out in a pilgrimage to their Sav-
iour, to their holy place. Their holy place is a small black stone, that
they remember from Protozoic times, when it was rolled away from
a door . . . and it was after that they found their friends who helped
them to digest the hard grains of this world. . . .

The clouds of cells awaken, intensify, swarm; and they dance
inside a ray of sunlight so thin we cannot even see it. But to them,
each ray is a vast palace with thousands of rooms. From the cells,
praise sentences begin to the rise to the man and woman singing in
the room. He lets his arms climb above his head, and says, "Now
do you still say you cannot choose the Road?"

For Lewis Thomas
and his The Lives of a Cell

COMING IN FOR SUPPER

It is lovely to follow paths in the snow made by human feet. The
paths wind gaily around the ends of drifts, they rise and fall. How
amazed I am, after working hard in the afternoon, that when I sit
down at the table, with my elbows touching the elbows of my chil-
dren, so much love flows out and around in circles. . . . The chil-
dren have been working on a play.

Each child flares up as a small fire in the woods. . . . Biddy

chortles over her new hair, curled for the first time last night, over her new joke song.

> Yankee Doodle went to town,
> Riding on a turtle,
> Turned the corner just in time
> To see a lady's girdle. . . .

Mary knows the inscription she wants on her coffin if she dies young, and says it:

> Where the bee sucks there suck I
> In a cowslip's bell I lie. . . .

She is obstinate and light at the same time, a heron who flies pulling long legs behind, or balances unsteadily on a stump, aware of all the small birds at the edge of the forest, where it is shadowy . . . longing to capture the horse with only one hair from its mane. . . .

Biddy can pick herself up and run over the muddy river bottom without sinking in; she already knows all about holding, and kisses each grownup carefully before going to bed; at the table she faces you laughing, bending over slightly toward you, like a tree bent in wind, protective of this old shed she is leaning over. . . .

And all the books around on the walls are feathers in a great feather bed, they weigh hardly anything! Only the encyclopedias, left lying on the floor near the chair, contain the heaviness of the three-million-year-old life of the oyster-shell breakers, those long dusks—they were a thousand years long then—that fell over the valley from the cave mouth (where we sit). . . . The inventions found, then lost again . . . the last man killed by flu who knew how to weave a pot of river clay the way the wasps do. . . . Now he is dead and only the wasps know in the long river-mud grief. The marmoset curls its toes once more around the slippery branch, remembering the furry chest of its mother, long since sunk into a hole that appeared in the afternoon. . . .

Dinner is finished, and the children pass out invitations composed with felt pens.

You are invited to "The Thwarting of Captain Alphonse"

PRINCESS GARDINER:	*Mary Bly*
CAPTAIN ALPHONSE:	*Wesley Ray*
AUNT AUGUST:	*Biddy Bly*
RAILWAY TRACK:	*Noah Bly*
TRAIN:	*Sam Ray*

Costumes and Sets by Mary Bly and Wesley Ray
Free Will Offering Accepted

HOW THE ANT TAKES PART

Smoke rises from mountain depths, a girl walks by the water. This is the body of water near where we sleep. And the mountain climber picks his way up the rocky scarp. How far up on the mountainside he is! As he disappears over the pass, an ant in the village below hurries up his mound of dirt, a woman turns her face back to the stove. Her man at that instant feels some mistake in his heart. The girl moves her hands, all the images rearrange themselves, the bacteria go in swarms through the ocean-salted blood.

WHEN THE WHEEL DOES NOT MOVE

There is a dense energy that pools in the abdomen and wants to move and does not! It lies there fierce and nomadic, blocking the road, preventing anyone else from going by.

When the sperm wants to move and does not, then it is as if the

earth were not made for me at all, and I cannot walk with the cricket voyaging over his Gobi of wood chips; he is too free for me. I hear a howling in the air.

And what the soul offers, we never see clearly, though the spears fly through the air, crossing above our heads . . . and the naked old man walks by the ecstatically grieving sea, by the tumbling waters . . . And how can the soul walk without its body? When its own seed stops the wheel, then the body lets nothing through its pores, it longs to groan and stretch out, to walk in procession shaking the sistrum, to disappear into the fog. . . .

And it is knotted. The sun hunches over and walks with its eyes on the ground, the moon hardens, it will not pass away, it refuses to become the sickle but holds up its face at the window. . . . The water goes back disappointed to the root, the house of sticks falls, we stand alone on the plain. . . .

TWO DAYS ON THE FARM

Friend, this body is made of camphor and gopherwood. So for two days I gathered ecstasies from my own body, I rose up and down, surrounded only by bare wood and bare air and some gray cloud, and what was inside me came so close to me, and I lived and died!

The grandfather comes back inquiringly to the farm, his son stares down at the pickup tire, the family lawyer loses his sense of incompetence for a moment.

The faint rain of March hits the bark of the half-grown trees. The honeysuckle will drip water, the moon will grow wet sailing, the granary door turns dark on the outside, the oats inside still dry.

THE ORCHARD KEEPER

Snow has fallen on snow for two days behind the Keilen farmhouse . . . no one has walked through it, or looked at it. . . . It makes the sound the porgies hear near the ocean floor, the sound the racer hears before his death, the sound that lifts the buoyant swimmer in the channel.

Wind blows four pigeon-grass heads, scarce and fine, above the snow. They are heron legs in white morning fog, a musical thought that rises as the pianist sits down at her table, the body laboring before dawn to understand its dream. . . .

Everyone else in the house is still asleep. . . . In its dream thin feet come down the mountainside, hooves clatter over the wooden bridges, walk along the stone walls, and then pause, and look in at an orchard, where a fount of water is rising in the air. . . . Men are lying asleep around its base, each with his sword lying under him. And the orchard-keeper, where is he?

WE LOVE THIS BODY

My friend, this body is made of energy compacted and whirling. It is the wind that carries the henhouse down the road dancing, and an instant later lifts all four walls apart. It is the horny thumbnail of the retired railway baron, over which his children skate on Sunday, it is the forehead bone that does not rot, the woman priest's hair still fresh among Shang ritual things. . . .

We love this body as we love the day we first met the person who led us away from this world, as we love the gift we gave one morning on impulse, in a fraction of a second, that we still see every day, as we love the human face, fresh after lovemaking, more full of joy than a wagonload of hay.

WINGS FOLDING UP

The cucumbers are thirsty, their big leaves turn away from the wind. I water them after supper; the hose lies curled near the rhubarb. The wind sound blows through the head; a smile appears on the sitter's face as he sits down under a tree. What can be comforted in us words help, the sunken islands speak to us. . . .

Is this world animal or vegetable? Others love us, the cabbages love the earth, the earth is fond of the heavens—a new age comes close through the dark, an elephant's trunk waves in the darkness, so much is passing away, so many disciplines already gone, but the energy in the double flower does not falter, the wings fold up around the sitting man's face. And these cucumber leaves are my body, and my thighs, and toes stretched out in the wind. . . . Well, waterer, how will you get through this night without water?

SNOWED IN AGAIN

Snow has been falling for three days. The horses stay in the barn. At four I leave the house, sinking to my waist in snow, and push open the door of my writing shack. Snow falls in. At the desk there is a plant in blossom.

The plant faces the window where snow sweeps past at forty miles an hour. So the snow and the flowers are a little like each other. In both there is the same receiving, the longing to circle slowly upward or sink down toward roots. Perhaps the snow and the orangey blossoms are both the same flow, that starts out close to the soil, close to the floor, and needs no commandments, no civilizations, no drawing room lifted on the labor of the claw hammer, but is at home where one or two are present.

The two people sit quietly near each other. In the storm, millions of years come close behind us. Nothing is lost, nothing is

rejected. The body is ready to sing all night, and be entered by whatever wishes to enter the human body singing.

THE CRY GOING OUT OVER PASTURES

I love you so much with this curiously alive and lonely body. My body is a young hawk sitting on a tree by the Mississippi, in early spring, before any green has appeared on the earth beneath. Some days walnut hollows in my chest fill with crackling light and shadows. There birds drink from water drops. . . . My body loves you with what it extracts from the prudent man, hunched over his colony of lizards; and with that it loves you madly, beyond all rules and conventions. Even the six holes in the flute move about under the dark man's fingers, and the piercing cry goes out over the grown-up pastures no one sees or visits at dusk except the deer, out of all enclosures, who has never seen any bed but his own of wild grass.

I first met you when I had been alone for nine days, and now my lonely hawk body longs to be with you, whom it remembers . . . it knew how close we are, we would always be. There is death but also this closeness, this joy when the bee rises into the air above his hive to find the sun, to become the son, and the traveler moves through exile and loss, through murkiness and failure, to touch the earth again of his own kingdom and kiss the ground. . . .

What shall I say of this? I say, praise to the first man who wrote down this joy clearly, for we cannot remain in love with what we cannot name. . . .

THIS
TREE WILL
BE HERE
FOR A
THOUSAND
YEARS

(1979)

After a storm the leafy tree is no longer solid,
but the pine still throws a full shadow.
It has found a place to be.
For a thousand years it will not give up this place.

—Tao Yuan-Ming

I

OCTOBER FROST

Last night the first heavy frost.
Now the brave alfalfa has sobered.
It has folded, as if from great heat,
and turned away from the north.
The horse's winter coat has come
through the bark of the trees.
Our ears hear tinier sounds,
reaching far away east in the early darkness.

WRITING AGAIN

Oval
faces crowding to the window!
I turn away,
disturbed—

When I write of moral things,
the clouds boil
blackly!
By day's end
a room of restless people,
lifting and putting down small things.

Well that is how I have spent this day.
And what good will it do me in the grave?

THE YEARLY FAILURE

There are eyes in the dry wisps of grass,
And invisible claws in the rooster's eyes,
The patient feet of old men in the boards left out all summer.

Something is about to happen!
Christ will return!
But each fall it goes by without happening.

The end of the pickup disappears
Down the road; behind the barn we see
Pigweed bent over like abandoned machines.

SITTING IN FALL GRASS

All day wind had called me,
oceans, a yellow line streaking
across the sky,
bones thrown out.

I walked to my sitting place,
I sat down.

As we close our eyes, what
piles of bones we see!

Ruined castles,
trampled cinnamon,
crinoline crushed in long grass.

And voices that say,
I am not like you . . .
I must live so . . . condemned
by an old yellow lion . . .

NIGHT FARMYARD

The horse lay on his knees sleeping.
A rat hopping across scattered hay
Disappeared under the henhouse,
Where the chickens sat in their stiff darkness.

Asleep they are bark fallen from an old cottonwood.
Yet we know their souls are gone, risen
Far into the upper air about the moon.

DAWN IN THRESHING TIME

The three-bottom plow is standing in the corner of a stubble field. The flax straw lies exhausted on the ground.

The dawning sun slants over the wet pigeon grass, so that the slope of highway ditches is like a face awakening from sleep.

The oat stubble is shiny. The farmer puts on his jacket and goes out. Swaths still to be combined are wet. Every morning as he gets

up after thirty he puts on besides his jacket the knowledge that he is not strong enough to die, which he first felt deep in his wooden cradle at threshing time.

READING IN FALL RAIN

The fields are black once more.
The old restlessness is going.
I reach out with open arms
to pull in the black fields.

All morning rain has fallen
steadily on the roof.
I feel like a butterfly
joyful in its powerful cocoon.

I break off reading:
one of my bodies is gone!
It's outdoors, walking
swiftly away in the rain!

I get up and look out.
Sure enough, I see
the rooster lifting his legs
high in the wet grass.

OCEAN INSECTS

Those insects, golden
and Arabic, sailing in the husks of galleons,
their octagonal heads also
hold sand paintings of the next life.

TO LIVE OR NOT

"To live" means to pick up particles of death
As a child picks up crumbs from beneath the table.
"To exist" means to drop the bread behind you on the path
Hoping the birds will find the crumbs and eat them.
"To live" is to rush forward eating up your own death,
Like a locomotive with its catcher on, hurrying into the night.

CORNPICKER POEM

1
Sheds left out in the darkness,
abandoned granaries, cats merging into the night.

There are hubcaps cooling in a dark yard.

The stiff-haired son has slouched in
and gone to bed.
A low wind sweeps over the moony land.

2
Overshoes stiffen in the entry.
The calendar grows rigid on the wall.

He dreams, and his body grows limber.
He is fighting a many-armed woman,
he is a struggler, he will not yield.
He fights her in the crotch of a willow tree.

He wakes up with jaws set,
and a victory.

3
It is dawn. Cornpicking today.
He leans over, hurtling
his old Pontiac down the road.

Somewhere the sullen chilled machine
is waiting, its empty gas cans around it.

PROPHETS

Inside the body there is a field of white roses
With prophets asleep in it—
I see their long black feet.

LISTENING TO A CRICKET IN THE WAINSCOTING

Its sound is like a boat with black sails
Or a widow under a redwood tree, warning
Passersby that the tree is about to fall
Or a bell made of black tin in a Mexican village
Or the hair in the ear of a hundred-year-old man.

THINKING OF TU FU'S POEM

I get up late and ask what has to be done today.
Nothing has to be done, so the farm looks doubly good.
The blowing maple leaves fit so well with the moving grass,
The shadow of my writing shack looks small beside the growing trees.

Never be with your children, let them get stringy like radishes!
Let your wife worry about the lack of money!
Your whole life is like some drunkard's dream!
You haven't combed your hair for a whole month!

DIGGING WORMS

Here I am, digging worms behind the chickenhouse,
the clods fall open when I hit
them with a tine, worms fall out . . .

Dreams press us on all sides, we stagger
along a wire, our children balance us
on their shoulders, we balance their graves
on ours.

Their graves are light. And we unwind
from some kind of cocoon made by lovers . . .
the old tires we used to swing on,
going faster, around and around, until

with one lurch we grow still and look down at our shoes.
Last night I dreamt my carelessness started stones dislodging near a
 castle. The stones
did not hurt my shoulders when they hit and went through,
but the wall of the castle fell.

WALKING AND SITTING

That's odd—I am trying to sit still,
trying to hold the mind to one thing.
Meanwhile angleworms stretch out thin in the gravel,
while it is thundering.

A LONG WALK BEFORE THE SNOWS BEGAN

1
Nearly winter. All day the sky gray. Earth heavy.
The cornfields dead. I walk over the soaked
cornstalks knocked flat in rows,
a few grains of white sleet on the leaves.

2
White sleet also in the black plowing.
I turn and go west—tracks, pushed deep!
I am walking with an immense deer.
He passed three days ago.

3
It must be that I will die one day!
I see my body lying stretched out.
A woman whose face I cannot see stands near my body.
A column of smoke rises from Vonderharr's field.

4
I reach the creek at last, nearly dusk.
New snow on the river ice, under willow branches,
open places like the plains of North China,
where the mice have been, just a half hour ago.

A DREAM ON THE NIGHT OF FIRST SNOW

I woke from a first-day-of-snow dream.
I met a girl in an attic,
 who talked of operas, intensely.
Snow has bent the poplar over nearly to the ground,
new snowfall widens the plowing.
Outside, maple leaves float on rainwater,
 yellow, matted, luminous.
I saw a salamander . . . I took him up . . .
he was cold. When I put him down again,
 he strode over a log
with such confidence, like a chessmaster,
 the front leg first, then the hind
 leg he rose up like a tractor climbing
 over a hump in the field
and disappeared toward winter, a caravan going deeper into
 mountains,
dogs pulling travois,
feathers fluttering on the lances of the arrogant men.

A WALK

It is a pale tree,
all alone in January snow.
Beneath it a shoot
eaten pale by a rabbit . . .

Looking up I see the farmyards with their grooves—
the pines somber,
made for winter, they knew it would come . . .

———

And the cows inside the barn, caring nothing for all this,
their noses in the incense hay,
half-drunk, dusk comes as it was promised
to them by *their* savior.

FOR MY BROTHER, A YEAR AFTER HIS DEATH

Last night, full moon.
The snowy fields, the roads silent and alone.
Clods rose above the snow in the plowing west,
like mountaintops, or the chests of graves.

PASSING A SPANISH ORCHARD BY TRAIN

Grass high under apple trees:
The bark of the trees rough and sexual,
The grass growing heavy and uneven.
We cannot bear distance,

As the rocks do, swaying nakedly
In open fields. You know an apple
Does not survive a blow.
One slight bruise and we die!

How many men my age died in the war!
I know no one on this train.
A man comes walking down the aisle.
I want to tell him
That I forgive him, that I want him
To forgive me.

I I

WOMEN WE NEVER SEE AGAIN

There are women we love whom we never see again.
They are chestnuts shining in the rain.
Moths hatched in winter disappear behind books.
Sometimes when you put your hand into a hollow tree
you touch the dark places between the stars.
Human war has parted messengers from another planet,
who cross back to each other at night,
going through slippery valleys, farmyards where rain has washed
 out all tracks,
and when we walk there, with no guide, saddened, in the dark
we see above us glowing the fortress made of ecstatic blue stone.

FEAR FOR THE BRIDAL PAIR

A private, misty day,
With the lake as utterly cast down
As a child. Anxious
Wheels I cannot hear turn
Over and over in sand.
Willow leaves I cannot see shed light
"Around the pale bride and groom."

ANT HEAPS BY THE PATH

I love to stare at old wooden doors after working,
the cough the ant family makes in ground,
the blackish stain around screwheads.

How much labor is needed to live our four lives!
Something turns its shoulders. When we do work
holes appear in the mountainside, no labor at all.

THE ARTIST

In his cabin with darkened windows the solitary man
Sang long and joyfully with Johann Sebastian Bach.
When he opened the door he noticed with shock
That the horse had turned his rump to the north;
Snow had settled along the red slope of his back.
The white roof stood calmly among black trees.

Could a stone heron cry out after years of silence
Though we, singing, never hear his cry gathering?
Ah, the story says: Snow fell over the whole farmyard
While the singer remained private, alone in his house.

PULLING A ROWBOAT UP AMONG LAKE REEDS

In the Ashby reeds it is already night,
though it is still day out on the lake.
Darkness has soaked into the shaded sand.
And how many other darknesses it reminds me of!

The darkness a father feels the moment a child is born,
blood pouring from the animal's neck,
the slender metal climbing toward the moon.

MOVING BOOKS TO A NEW STUDY

First snow yesterday, and now more falling.
Each grassblade has its own snow balanced on it.
One mousetrack in the snow ahead,
the tailmark wavering in
between the footprints. Dusk in half an hour.

Looking up I see my parents' grove.
Somehow neither the Norwegian culture
nor the American could keep them warm.
I walk around the barn the long way
carrying the heavy green book I love through the snow.

DRIVING MY PARENTS HOME AT CHRISTMAS

As I drive my parents home through the snow,
their frailty hesitates on the edge of a mountainside.
I call over the cliff,
only snow answers.
They talk quietly
of hauling water, of eating an orange,
of a grandchild's photograph left behind last night.
When they open the door of their house, they disappear.
And the oak when it falls in the forest who hears it through miles
 and miles of silence?
They sit so close to each other . . . as if pressed together by the snow.

AFTER A DAY OF WORK

How lightly the legs walk over the snow-whitened fields!
I wander far off, like a daddy longlegs blown over the water.
All day I worked alone, hour after hour.
It is January, easy walking, the big snows still to come.

WALKING WHERE THE PLOWS HAVE BEEN TURNING

> The most beautiful music of all is the music of what happens.
>
> —old Irish tale

For Gioia Timpanelli

Some intensity of the body came to me at five in the morning. I woke up, I saw the east pale with its excited brood. I slipped from bed, and out the back door, onto the sleek and resigned cottonwood leaves. The horses are out, eating in the ditch . . . I walk down the road toward the west.

I notice a pebble on the road, then a corn-ear lying in the ditch-grass, then an earthbridge into the cornfield. I cross the ditch to the backland where the plows turn, the tractor tires have married it, they love it more than the rest, cozy with bare dirt, the down-turned face of the plow that looked at it each round . . .

In the risen sun the earth provides a cornhusk in one place, a cottonwood in another, for no apparent reason. A branch has dropped onto the fence wire, there are eternities near, the body free of its exasperations, ready to see what will happen. There is a humming in my body, it is jealous of no one. The cricket lays its wings one over the other, a faint whispery sound rises up to its head . . . which it hears . . . and disregards . . . listening for the next sound . . .

JULY MORNING

The day is awake. The bark calls to the rain still in the cloud.
"Never forget the lonely taste of the white dew."
And woolen-robed drummers call on the naked to dance,
all the particles of the body shout together.

Sitting on the disc, the mourning dove coos a porch, then a cathedral,
then the two arms of the cross!

He gives the nose, then the head, then the two ears of this rabbit
hopping along the garden,
then his death . . .

After that we will be alone in the deep blue reaches of the river.

AN EMPTY PLACE

Empty places are white and light-footed. "Taking the road" means
being willing to die, as the pigeon grass clump, that dies so quietly.
There is a joy in emptiness. One day I saw an empty corncob on the
ground, so beautiful, and where each kernel had been, there was a
place to live.

The eyes are drawn to the dusty ground in fall—
pieces of crushed oyster shell,
like doors into the earth made of mother-of-pearl;
slivers of glass,
a white chicken's feather that still seems excited by the warm blood,
and a corncob, all kernels gone, room after room in its endless
 palace . . .
this is the palace, the place of many mansions,
which Christ has gone to prepare for us.

PRAYER SERVICE IN AN ENGLISH CHURCH

Looking at the open page of the psalm book,
I see a ghostly knot floating in the paper!

Circles within circles on the page, floating,
showing that a branch once lived there!

Looking at the knot long and long,
I hear the priest call on the Saviour to come again.

The old around me keep on singing . . .
If the Saviour is a branch, how can he come again?

And the last day . . .
the whispers we will make from the darkening pillow . . .

FISHING ON A LAKE AT NIGHT

Someone has left a light on at the boathouse
to guide the fishermen back after dark.
The light makes no sound as it comes.
It flies over the waves like a bird with one wing.
Its path is a boatful of the dead, trying to return to life
over the broken waters.

 And the light
simply comes, bearing no gifts,
as if the camels had arrived without the Wise Men.
It is steady, holding us to our old mountain home.
Now as we watch the moon rises over the popple forest.
It too arrives without fuss,
it goes between the boards around the pulp-cutter's house—
the same fence we pass through by opening the gate.

NIGHT OF FIRST SNOW

Night of first snow.
I stand, my back against a board fence.
The fir trees are black at the trunk, white out on the edges.
The earth balances all around my feet.

The apple trunk joins the white ground with what is above.
Fir branches balance the snow.
I too am a dark shape vertical to the earth.
All over the sky, the gray color that pleases the snow mother.

A woman wades out toward the wicker basket, floating,
rocking in darkening reeds.
The child and the light are half asleep.
What is human lies in the way the basket is rocking.

Black and white end in the gray color of the sky.
What is human lies in the three hairs, caught,
the rabbit left behind
as he scooted under the granary joist.

MOSES' BASKET

I don't know if we love most the divine
Or the human. The Pharaoh's wife at dawn—
Do you remember?—wades out into the reeds.
The baby and the Pharaoh are about to meet.

Moses' basket floated on Red Sea water.
And the reeds, weren't they beautifully delicate,
Alluvial, bird-filled, and marshy . . .
The sweet hair of the Water Mother?

They were. We cherish nothing more than the reeds.
But it is the basket with the baby in it,
Rocking in darkening reeds, that our eyes love to see,
And the curving lines the basket makes in the river water.

THE CROW'S HEAD

Suppertime. I leave my cabin and start toward the house. Something blowing among the tree trunks . . . our frail impulses go to shelter behind thin trees, or sail with the wind. A day of solitude over . . . the time when after long hours alone, I sit with my children, and feel them near. . . . At what I want to do I fail fifty times a day, and am confused. At last I go to bed.

I wake before dawn hearing strong wind around the north bedroom windows. On the way to the cabin, I see dust of snow lying on yesterday's ice. All morning snow falls.

Snow continues all morning. By noon I give up working, and lie listening to the wind that rises and falls. Sometimes it makes the sound of a woman's skirt pulled swiftly along the floor. . . . At other times it gives a slow growl without anger like the word "Enoch." . . .

I go to the window. The crow's head I found by the bridge this summer, and brought home, rests on the window sash. Feathers edge its Roman beak. It is fierce, decisive, the one black thing among all this white.

FROST STILL ON THE GROUND

I walk out in the fields; the frost is still on the ground.
It's like someone just beginning to write, and nothing has been said!

The shadows that come from another life
gather in folds around his head.

So I am, all at once. What I have
to say I have not said.

The snow water glances up at the new moon. It is
its own pond. In its lake the serpent is asleep.

LATE MOON

The third week moon reaches its light over my father's farm,
half of it dark now, in the west that eats it away.
The earth has rocks in it that hum at early dawn.
As I turn to go in, I see my shadow reach for the latch.

A DREAM OF RETARDED CHILDREN

That afternoon I had been fishing alone,
Far from home. Strong wind,
Some water slopping in the back of the boat.

Geese woke me several times that night.
In my dream retarded children were playing,
 and one came near.
And her teacher, face open, hair light.
For the first time I forgot my distance.
I took her in my arms and held her.

The pale and cold dawn woke me.
I walked on the dock,
Fishing alone in the far north.

THE SEVEN STARS OF THE GREAT BEAR

The teeth of the black and shaggy pony rips grass from its roots.
So the night rips light away from day
Uttering the cry the crystal makes when it regains its twelve sides.

Our earthly house stands between two fierce mountains.
One mountain is a womb filled with black owls,
The other a jagged grave that explodes the soul up into Sirius.

The grave will eat this table, this pen, and these warm fingers.
Yet the grass continues to lift itself into the horse's teeth.
Dragon lines sweep through our bodies as through the chalk hills.

Minerals hidden in our veins feed the ores on Venus.
The Great Bear is seven old men walking.

THE TREE KNOCKED DOWN BY LIGHTNING

After a long walk I come down to the shore,
Where a cottonwood lies stretched out in the grass,
A tree knocked down by lightning—
Hollows the owls made now open to the rain.

Like the two of us, the tree lies stretched out;
It hasn't moved from where it fell in the grass.
It is so mysterious, waters below, waters above,
So little of grief we can ever know!

DREAM OF AN AFTERNOON WITH A WOMAN I DID NOT KNOW

I woke up, and went out. Not yet dawn.
A rooster claimed he was the sickle moon.
The windmill was a ladder that ended at a gray cloud.
A feed grinder was growling at a nearby farm.

Frost has made clouds of the weeds overnight.
In my dream we stopped for coffee, we sat alone
near a fireplace, near delicate cups.
I loved that afternoon, and the rest of my life.

NAILING A DOCK TOGETHER

The dock is done, pulled out on the lake. How I love
putting my wet foot
on the boards I sawed myself!
It is a ladder stretching back to land. . . .

So many secrets are still hidden.
A walker digs up a tin box with secrets
and then joyfully buries it again
so that the night and day will remain fresh.

The horse stands penned, but is also free.
It is a horse whose neck human
beings have longed to touch for centuries.
He stands in a stable of invisible wood.

AN EVENING WHEN THE FULL MOON ROSE
AS THE SUN SET

APRIL 11, 1976

The sun goes down in the dusty April night.
"You know it could be alive!"
The sun is round, massive, compelling, sober, on fire.
It moves swiftly through the tree-stalks of the Lundin grove as
 we drive past . . .
The legs of a bronze god walking at the edge of the world, unseen
 by many,
On his archaic errands, doubled up on his own energy.
He guides his life by his dreams.
When we look again he is gone.

Turning toward Milan, we see the other one, the moon, whole
 and rising.
Three wild geese make dark spots on that part of the sky.
Under the shining moon the pastures leap forward.
Grass fields rolling as in October, the sow-colored fields near the
 river.
The rising one lights the pair of pintails alert in the shallow pond.
It shines on those faithful to each other, alert in the early night.
And the life of faithfulness goes by like a river
With no one noticing it.

OUT PICKING UP CORN

It is late December. I walk through the pasture.
Light on the hillocks, light
On the grassy mounds eaten clean by horse teeth.

Now the plowing—black clods turning up. My shoes
Look for solid home;
I look for ears of corn not discovered by deer.

I am learning; I walk through the plowed fields, with a bag,
Picking up corn for the horses.
Some small pebbles shine in the late sun.

Surely we do not eat only with our mouths, or drink
Only by lifting our hands!
Surely there are essences we absorb from the wild ground.

"My master is up gathering ferns on the mountain." What he picks
Is something respectable people
Do not want to take in, walking in fog near the cliff.

THE MAN
IN THE
BLACK
COAT
TURNS

(1981)

I

SNOWBANKS NORTH OF THE HOUSE

Those great sweeps of snow that stop suddenly six feet from the
 house . . .
Thoughts that go so far.
The boy gets out of high school and reads no more books;
The son stops calling home.
The mother puts down her rolling pin and makes no more bread.
And the wife looks at her husband one night at a party, and loves
 him no more.
The energy leaves the wine, and the minister falls leaving the church.
It will not come closer—
The one inside moves back, and the hands touch nothing, and are safe.

The father grieves for his son, and will not leave the room where the
 coffin stands.
He turns away from his wife, and she sleeps alone.

And the sea lifts and falls all night, the moon goes on through the
 unattached heavens alone.
The toe of the shoe pivots
In the dust . . .
And the man in the black coat turns, and goes back down the hill.
No one knows why he came, or why he turned away, and did not
 climb the hill.

FOR MY SON NOAH, TEN YEARS OLD

Night and day arrive and day after day goes by,
and what is old remains old, and what is young remains young,
and grows old.
The lumber pile does not grow younger, nor the two-by-fours lose
their darkness,
but the old tree goes on, the barn stands without help so many
years;
the advocate of darkness and night is not lost.

The horse steps up, swings on one leg, turns his body,
the chicken flapping claws onto the roost, its wings whelping and
walloping,
but what is primitive is not to be shot out into the night and dark.
And slowly the kind man comes closer, loses his rage, sits down at
table.

So I am proud only of those days that pass in undivided
tenderness,
when you sit drawing, or making books, stapled, with messages to
the world,
or coloring a man with fire coming out of his hair.
Or we sit at a table, with small tea carefully poured.
So we pass our time together, calm and delighted.

THE PRODIGAL SON

The Prodigal Son is kneeling in the husks.
My friend, the steering column in his chest,
Cried: "Don't let me die, doctor!"
The swine go on feeding in the sunlight.

When he folds his hands, his knees
On corncobs, he sees the smoke of ships
Floating off the isles of Tyre and Sidon,
And father beyond father beyond father.

An old man once being dragged across
The floor by his shouting son, cried:
"Don't drag me any farther than that crack on the floor—
I only dragged my father that far!"

So this dragging of father and son goes on
Century after century after century.
There are brothers, some favorites, some
Not. Neither brother gets what he wants.

My father is seventy-five years old.
Looking at his face, I look into water.
How difficult it is! Under the water
There's a door that the pigs have gone through.

THE SENSE OF DECLINE

The Farallones seals clubbed,
Whales gone, tortoises
Taken from islands
To fill the holds; the Empire

Dying in its provincial cities.
No one to repair the baths;
Farms turned over
To soldiers; the judges corrupt.

The wagon behind bouncing,
Breaking on boulders, back
And forth, slowly
Smashed to pieces. This crumb-

Ling darkness is a reality
Too, the feather
On the snow, the rooster's
Half-eaten body nearby.

And other worlds I do not see:
The Old People's Home
At dusk, the slow
Murmur of conversation.

THE CONVICT AND HIS RADIO

The child left alone on the butte calls out to his grandmother in the pine.
She answers, the hide slips off the rack, the hatchet leaps up from the
 ground.
The buffalo gallop, the cliff lies just ahead.
Men shaped like stones lie waiting . . .
 They leap up flapping hides;
the buffalo flow over the cliff, rib
 and leg bones splinter,
a few roll down the pile and stagger off.
The prison opens at last, the convict comes out carrying a cardboard box.
No one can speak to him, his tongue by now is forgotten.
He sits alone by a black radio.
At night he cries, reaching for the small table by his bed.
 He does not stop all night,
he cries until dawn.

MOURNING PABLO NERUDA

Water is practical,
Especially in
August.
Faucet water
That drops
Into the buckets
I carry
To the young
Willow trees
Whose leaves have been eaten
Off by grasshoppers.
Or this jar of water
That lies next to me
On the carseat
As I drive to my shack.
When I look down,
The seat all
Around the jar
Is dark,
For water doesn't intend
To give, it gives
Anyway,
And the jar of water
Lies
There quivering
As I drive
Through a countryside
Of granite quarries,
Stones
Soon to be shaped
Into blocks for the dead,
The only
Thing they have
Left that is theirs.

For the dead remain inside
Us, as water
Remains
Inside granite—
Hardly at all—
For their job is to
Go
Away,
And not come back,
Even when we ask them,
But water
Comes to us—
It doesn't care
About us, it goes
Around us, on the way
To the Minnesota River,
To the Mississippi River,
To the Gulf,
Always closer
To where
It has to be.
No one lays flowers
On the grave
Of water,
For it is not
Here,
It is
Gone.

II

ELEVEN O'CLOCK AT NIGHT

I lie alone in my bed; cooking and stories are over at last, and some peace comes. And what did I do today? I wrote down some thoughts on sacrifice that other people had, but couldn't relate them to my own life. I brought my daughter to the bus—on the way to Minneapolis for a haircut—and I waited twenty minutes with her in the somnolent hotel lobby. I wanted the mail to bring some praise for my ego to eat, and was disappointed. I added up my bank balance, and found only $65, when I need over a thousand to pay the bills for this month alone. So this is how my life is passing before the grave?

The walnut of my brain glows. I feel it irradiate the skull. I am aware of the consciousness I have, and I mourn the consciousness I do not have.

Stubborn things lie and stand around me—the walls, a book-case with its few books, the footboard of the bed, my shoes that lie against the blanket tentatively, as if they were animals sitting at table, my stomach with its curved demand. I see the bedside lamp, and the thumb of my right hand, the pen my fingers hold so trust-ingly. There is no way to escape from these. Many times in poems I have escaped—from myself. I sit for hours and at last see a pin-hole in the top of the pumpkin, and I slip out that pinhole, gone! The genie expands and is gone; no one can get him back in the bottle again; he is hovering around a car cemetery somewhere.

Now more and more I long for what I cannot escape from. The sun shines on the side of the house across the street. Eternity is

near, but it is not *here*. My shoes, my thumbs, my stomach, remain inside the room, and for that there is no solution. Consciousness comes so slowly, half our life passes, we eat and talk asleep—and for that there is no solution. Since Pythagoras died the world has gone down a certain path, and I cannot change that. Someone not in my family invented the microscope, and Western eyes grew the intense will to pierce down through its darkening tunnel. Air itself is willing without pay to lift the 707's wing, and for that there is no solution. Pistons and rings have appeared in the world; valves usher gas vapor in and out of the theater box ten times a second; and for that there is no solution. Something besides my will loves the woman I love. I love my children, though I did not know them before they came. I change every day. For the winter dark of late December there is no solution.

THE WINEMAKER AND THE CAPTAIN

1

When a man like me steps out at dawn, it seems to him that he has lived his whole life to create something dark. All our work is inside the wine barrels in the hold of the ship. The casks roll about when the ship rolls, and no one in the crew knows what is in the casks but the captain.

2

The captain stands looking out over the taffrail in the dark, drawn by what follows in shoals behind him. Behind him, fins sail with intense forward strokes. The ship is going to a harbor the captain has chosen, and the casks are rolling. That is all we know.

3

His ship remained tied to the dock for months as the captain lay ill on his pallet in the seaman's home, imagining the covers were a

Medusa with his mother's face. And one day as he woke he was already on board. It must be that he hired the seamen, and bought the supplies, while still asleep. Now the ship is moving, and what does he know about those men he has hired? What are the islands like, where they were born; whom do they kneel to at night, fanning a fire of pencil shavings? Or was the seaman born in a farmhouse in Montana? Did he then pass into prison, and through it, as the earthworm passes through thoughtless soil?

4

Now the wine and the ship are passing over the Equator. And the winemaker, what of him? How many men and women, before we were born, have labored to produce the vines? First the grapes had to be brought from Europe and a climate found, calm and protective; then ground scouted out, difficult to discover with the unknown acids and mineral traces. And it takes so long for the vines to mature. Finally when they are grown, they are tough, twisted, resembling intense dwarf houses. And the winemaker still has to wait so many years before he can bring four casks to the ship.

5

The captain is still alone on the ship, alone among the ocean-flying terns, the great hooded mergansers flopping at early dusk light over the sparse waves they have never been introduced to . . . Mist suddenly appears at mid-ocean . . . No assurances in the ocean.

6

When someone says, "You are a good captain!" you have only to reply, "I am not the captain!" When another says, "You make good wine," you have to reply, "I am not the winemaker." Who am I? So when a man like me steps out of the house at dawn, and breathes in the air, it seems to him that he has lived his whole life to create something dark!

THE DRIED STURGEON

I climb down the bank at Rock Island, Illinois, and cross some tracks. Westward the black railway bridge makes short hops across the river. The riverbank is confused with drifted leaves, the sand cold in late October.

I see a dried-out fish. It is a sturgeon. It is stiff, all its sudden motion gone. I pick it up. Its speckled nose-bone leads back to the eyesocket, and behind that there is a dark hole where the gills once were.

So just behind the head the darkness enters—the somberness under the bunched leaves, the soothing duskiness ten feet down in sand. The pine tree standing by the roadhouse holds the whole human night in one needle. And the sturgeon holds the sweetness of the hunchback's dreams, where he is straight and whole again, and the earth is flat and crooked. The Virgin brings out four black stones for him from beneath her cloak.

Behind the gill opening the scales go on toward the tail. The dry scales are swift, organized, tubular, straight and humorless as railways schedules or the big clamp of the boxcar, tapering into sleek womanly death.

A BOUQUET OF TEN ROSES

The roses lift from the green strawberry-like leaves, their edges slightly notched, for the rose is also the plum, the apple, the strawberry, and the cherry. Petals are reddish-orange, the color of a robin's breast if it were silk. I look down into the face of one rose: deep down inside there are somber shades, what Tom Thumb experienced so low under chairs, in the carpet-darkness . . . those growing swirls of gathering shadows, which eyes up near lamps do not see. It is the calm fierceness in the aborigine's eye as he holds his spear polished by his own palm.

These inviting lamb-like falmers are also the moist curtains on the part of the woman she cannot see; and the cloud that opens, swarming and parting for Adonis. . . . It is an opening seen by no one, only experienced later as rain. And the rose is also the skin petals around the man's stalk, the soft umber folds that enclose so much longing; and the tip shows violet, blind, longing for company, knowing already of an intimacy the thunderstorm keeps as its secret, understood by the folds of purple curtains, whose edges drag the floor.

And in the center of the nine roses, whose doors are opening, there is one darker rose on a taller stem. It is the rose of the tumbling waters, of the strumming at night, the color of the Ethiopian tumblers who put their heads below their feet on the Egyptian waterfront, wheeling all over the shore. . . . This rose is the man sacrificed yesterday, the silent one wounded under the oak, the man whose dark foot needs to be healed. He experiences the clumsy feeling that can only weep. It is the girl who has gone down to the world below, disobeying her mother, in order to bring calm to the house, traveling alone . . . and the rose windows of Chartres, the umber moss on the stag's antlers . . .

VISITING EMILY DICKINSON'S GRAVE WITH ROBERT FRANCIS

A black iron fence closes the graves in, its ovals delicate as wine stems. They resemble those chapel windows on the main Aran island, made narrow in the fourth century so that not too much rain would drive in . . . It is April, clear and dry. Curls of grass rise around the nearby gravestones.

The Dickinson house is not far off. She arrived here one day, at fifty-six, Robert says, carried over the lots between by six Irish laboring men, when her brother refused to trust her body to a carriage. The coffin was darkened with violets and pine boughs, as she

covered the immense distance between the solid Dickinson house and this plot . . .

The distance *is* immense, the distances through which Satan and his helpers rose and fell, oh vast areas, the distances between stars, between the first time love is felt in the sleeves of the dress, and the death of the person who was in that room . . .

> *Exultation is the going*
> *Of the inland soul to sea,*
> *Past the houses, past the headlands*
> *Into deep Eternity.*

. . . the distance between the feet and head as you lie down, the distance between the mother and father, through which we pass reluctantly.

About her parents and their habit of prayer, Emily wrote to a friend, "My family addresses an Eclipse every morning, which they call their 'Father.'"

As we leave the cemetery, Robert says, "My apartment is small, but I took it because I could see her grave from my window." He has given his life to seeing what is far away. He used to serve a visitor—in a small glass—wine made from his own dandelions. "Can you mistake us? . . . For this I have abandoned all my other lives."

FINDING AN OLD ANT MANSION

The rubbing of the sleeping bag on my ear made me dream a rattlesnake was biting me. I was alone, waking the first morning in the North. I got up; the sky clouded, the floor cold. I dressed and walked out toward the pasture. And how good the unevenness of the pasture feels under tennis shoes! The earth gives little rolls and humps ahead of us . . .

The earth never lies flat, but is always thinking, it finds a new

feeling and curves over it, rising to bury a toad or a great man, it accounts for a fallen meteor, or stones rising from two hundred feet down, giving a little jump for Satan, and a roll near it for Calvin. . . . I turn and cut through a strip of cleared woods; only the hardwoods are still standing. As I come out into the pasture again, I notice something lying on the ground.

It is a wood chunk, but it has open places in it, caves chewed out by something. The bark has fallen off, that was the roof. . . . I lift it up and carry it home kitty-corner over the field.

When I set it on my desk, it stands. The base is an inch or two of solid wood, only a bit eaten by the acids that lie in pastures. The top four or five inches is also solid, a sort of forehead.

In between the forehead and the base there are sixteen floors eaten out by ants. The floors flung out from the central core are light brown, the color of workmen's benches, and old eating tables in Norwegian farmhouses. The open places in between are cave-dark, the heavy brown of barn stalls in November dusk, the dark the cow puts her head into at the bottom of mangers . . . A little light comes in from the sides, as when a woman at forty sees what her mother's silences as she washed clothes meant, and which are the windows in the side of her own life she has not yet opened . . .

And these open places are where the ant legions labored. The antlered layers awaken, as antennae brush the sandy roof ceilings, low and lanterned with the bull heat of their love. Now the lively almsgivers go forth, over the threshold polished by thousands of pintail-like feet, workers with their electricity for the whole day packed into their solid-state joints and carapaces. Caravans go out, climbing, gelid with the confidence of landowners; and soon they are at work, right here, making delicate balconies where their eggs can pass their childhood in embroidered chambers; and the infant ants awaken to old father-worked halls, uncle-loved boards, walls that hold the sighs of the pasture, the moos of confused cows, the sound of oak leaves in November, flocks of grasshoppers passing overhead, some car motors from the road, held in the sane wood, given shape by Osiris's love.

. . .

Now it seems to be a completed soul home. These balconies are good places for souls to sit in the half-dark. If I put it on our altar, souls of the dead in my family can come and sit here, I will keep this place for them. The souls of the dead are no bigger than a grain of wheat when they come, yet they too like to have their back protected from the wind of nothing, from the wind of Descartes, and of all who grew thin in maternal deprivation. Vigleik can come here, with his lame knee, pinned in 1922 under a tree he himself felled, rolling cigarettes with affectionate fingers, patient and protective. And my brother can sit here if he can find the time, he will bring his friend if he comes; my grandmother will come here surely, sometimes, with the ship she gave me. This balcony is like her kitchen to the southwest, its cobstove full of heating caves; and Olai with his favorite horse and buggy, horsehide robe over his knees, ready to start for town with his mustache; the dead of the Civil War, Thomas Nelson, fat as a berry, supported by his daughters: and others I will not name I would like to come. I will set out a drop of water and a grain of rye for them. What the ants have worked out is a place for our destiny, for we too labor, and no one sees our labor. My father's labor who sees? It is in a pasture somewhere not yet found by a walker.

III

THE GRIEF OF MEN

The Buddhist ordered his boy to bring him, New Year's
morning, a message. He
woke; answered;
tore open the message
he himself had written, and signed, "Buddha."

"Busyness has caught you, you have slowed and stopped.
If you start toward me, I
will surely come
to meet you." He wept.
Exhausted by work and travel, I walk.

I hear the coot call his darkening call,
and the dog's doubt far back in his throat.
A porcupine walks
by the water at dusk;
no one sees him, under the low bushes.

Men have died on high slopes, as others watch.
They look around, and do not see
those they love most,
and call out
the sound the porcupine does not make.

And fresh waters wash past the tidal sands,
into the delta, wash past clear
bars and are gone.
Women can die
in childbirth, Bertha, inwardly near me, died,

my father's sister. "No more children, that's it,"
the doctor said. They wanted a child.
The doctor stands
by the bed, but Bertha
dies, her breath ends, her knees quiver and are still.

Her husband will not lie quiet.
He throws himself against the wall.
Men come to hold him down.
My father is there,
sits by the bed long night after night.

KENNEDY'S INAUGURATION

Sister de Chantal hands
Me the sticky pod
Of the Sweet Gum Tree.
New to me, it's the size
Of a cow's eyeball, brown
And prickly. Its seeing
Is all gone, finished,
Exploded out
Through the eyeholes.
I turn it in my palm;
It pricks the tender skin.

The hard-edged eye-
Holes resemble hen
Beaks widening in fear.
Are the dogs coming?
Where an ear
Should be, another
Beak is opening, where
A comb should be, another
Beak is opening. Fear
Of the dogs makes
The cries more hoarse.

And what did I do today?
I drove the long way twice
So as not to pass
The funeral home.
I had three conversations,
All distant. If I know
So well how to live,
Then why am I frightened?
A man's head has been
Broken by a cannonball,
One eye dangles out.

King Leopold's men
Set up rubber plantations,
Bring Bantus in
To bleed the trees. Some
Skip work. "If he's
A father, the best thing
Is to cut off the hands."
A photographer catches
The scene: The son's hands
Lie on the ground
Between the father's feet.

In Nineteen Thirty-Eight,
The Brown Shirts arrive,
Take women away
Into breeding hotels.
Jews and Gypsies
Bleed the trees.
It is all prepared.
Marilyn Monroe is there.
I see her drugged
Arm hanging out
Over the side of the bed.

Out of her back comes the Marine's
Cry for the medic.
His foot is lying a few
Feet away. His
Lips are open, the brain
Is missing—only
The throat and the cry are there.
And the President
In the cold, the back of his head
Still intact, lays
One hand on the Bible.

WRITTEN AT MULE HOLLOW, UTAH

For Robert and Ollie

After three days of talk, I long for silence and come here.
It's called Mule Hollow. I love this granite steep shooting
upward. The base seems to remain
in grief—all the children killed when you return to the cave.

Haven't you ever longed for all these cheerful noises
to end? These hellos and goodbyes? We fall asleep speaking.
Perhaps talking we sleep;
our ability to stay awake stays hidden in rocks we never visit.

This tree I stand beside—a stone wall behind it,
sedimentary, moving in waves—it is neither tree nor pine;
it has half-leaves, half-needles,
and a scaly bark, like someone constantly waking up in the night.

All the failures of the stone are perfectly clear—spoken—
how it gave way to pressures, bent between humps,
as when a man lets his hands
climb over his head, and says, "It's true, it's true, why say it isn't?"

How many failures we hide, talking. When I am too public,
I am a wind chime, ringing, to cheer up the black
Angel Moroni, and feed him
as he comes dancing, prancing, leaving turkey tracks in the mist.

Talking, we do not say what we are! Sensing what others want,
used to hiding from our parents, talking,
not saying what we want,
we sustain the brilliant glass skeleton on which we hang.

THE BEAR'S TAIL

1
Herbs, turtle-faced porcupine babies,
Fur, pawmarks on shore,
The hair in the mouse's ear.

2

This delight is the wheeling of the inexhaustible
Bear, whose tail
Dips again and again into the ocean.

3

We are like those rheumatic pilgrims, stalking
In the night air,
Driving flocks of angel cattle before them.

4

And the molluscs, the mollusc shells, grow large.
Smoke twists up through water,
The moon rockets up from the sea floor.

5

Long seeds drop into November loam.
The mother throws off her clothes, descending—
The Virgin is lost among the other stars.

WORDS RISING

For Richard Eberhart

I open my journal, write a few
Sounds with green ink, and suddenly
Fierceness enters me, stars
Begin to revolve, and pick up
Alligator dust from under the ocean.
The music comes, I feel the bushy
Tail of the Great Bear
Reach down and brush the sea floor.

All those deaths we lived in the sunlit
Shelves of the Dordogne, the tunes we sang
To the newborn and the skeletons
Of Papua, the many times
We died—wounded—under the cloak
Of an animal's sniffing, all of these
Return, and the grassy nights
We ran in the moonlight for hours.

Watery syllables come welling up.
Anger that barked and howled in the cave,
The luminous head of barley
The priest holds up, growls
From under fur, none of that is lost!
The old earth-fragrance remains
In the word "and." We experience
"The" in its lonely suffering.

We are bees then; language is the honey.
Now the honey lies stored in caves
Beneath us, and the sound of words
Carries what we do not.
When a man or woman feeds a few words
With private grief, the shames we knew
Before we could invent
The wheel, then words grow. We slip out

Into farmyards, where rabbits lie
Stretched out on the ground for buyers.
Wicker baskets and hanged men
Come to us as stanzas and vowels.
We see a million hands with dusty
Palms turned up inside each verb,
Lifted. There are eternal vows
Held inside the word "Jericho."

Blessings then on the man who labors
In his tiny room, writing stanzas on the lamb;
Blessings on the woman, who picks the brown
Seeds of solitude in afternoon light
Out of the black seeds of loneliness.
And blessings on the dictionary maker, huddled among
His bearded words, and on the setter of songs
Who sleeps at night inside his violin case.

A SACRIFICE IN THE ORCHARD

The man with the Roman nose sits high
on the roof ridge, longs for it
to be Saturday. And moles
begin crossing the lawn,
thousands of moles,
the grief-stricken parents
come behind in closed cars.
Come with me, we will
sink on this blue raft
down through acres
of continental water. Shaggy
goats bound from the earth.
Over them, men
hang from the branches.
They are all apples. The side
of the apple gleams,
and in that gleam
all the water on the planet
plunges down at once. . . .

MY WIFE'S PAINTING

1

I walk on a gravel path through cut-over
Woods. November's bare light has arrived.
I come at dusk
Where, sheltered by poplars, a low pond lies.
The sun abandons the sky, speaking through cold leaves.

2

This Tang painting is called "The Six Philosophers."
Five Chinamen talk in the open-walled house,
Exchanging poems.
Only one is outdoors, looking over
The cliff, being approached from below by rolling mists.

3

A deer comes down the bare slope toward me,
Sees me, turns away, back up the hill
Into the lone trees.
It is a doe out in the cold and air alone.
It is the woman turned away from the philosopher's house.

4

It's an old, long story. After Heraclitus dies,
The males sink down to a-pathy,
To not-suffering.
When you shout at them, they don't reply.
They turn their face toward the crib wall, and die.

5

My wife showed me yesterday her new
Painting. One bird of hers, a lively one,
Had come.
It was a large bird with big feet,
And stubby wings, arrows lightly stuck in the arms.

MY FATHER'S WEDDING

1924

Today, lonely for my father, I saw
a log, or branch,
long, bent, ragged, bark gone.
I felt lonely for my father when I saw it.
It was the log
that lay near my uncle's old milk wagon.

Some men live with an invisible limp,
stagger, or drag
a leg. Their sons are often angry.
Only recently I thought:
Doing what you want . . .
Is that like limping? Tracks of it show in sand.

Have you seen those giant bird-
men of Bhutan?
Men in bird masks, with pig noses, dancing,
teeth like a dog's, sometimes
dancing on one bad leg!
They do what they want, the dog's teeth say that!

But I grew up without dogs' teeth,
showed a whole body,
left only clear tracks in sand.
I learned to walk swiftly, easily,
no trace of a limp.
I even leaped a little. Guess where my defect is!

Then what? If a man, cautious
hides his limp,
somebody has to limp it! Things

do it; the surroundings limp.
House walls get scars,
the car breaks down; matter, in drudgery, takes it up.

On my father's wedding day,
no one was there
to hold him. Noble loneliness
held him. Since he never asked for pity
his friends thought he
was whole. Walking alone, he could carry it.

He came in limping. It was a simple
wedding, three
or four people. The man in black,
lifting the book, called for order.
And the invisible bride
stepped forward, before his own bride.

He married the invisible bride, not his own.
In her left
breast she carried the three drops
that wound and kill. He already had
his barklike skin then,
made rough especially to repel the sympathy

he longed for, didn't need, and wouldn't accept.
They stopped. So
the words are read. The man in black
speaks the sentence. When the service
is over, I hold him
in my arms for the first time and the last.

After that he was alone
and I was alone.

No friends came; he invited none.
His two-story house he turned
into a forest,
where both he and I are the hunters.

FOUR WAYS OF KNOWLEDGE

1
So many things happen
when no one is watching.
Yesterday Peter and I
arrived on the island
to visit Iolani Luahine,
the old holy dancer.
We couldn't find her.
Later that night, he
dreamt he flew out,
saw her temple ahead,
but grew tired, faltered,
turned back, saw me
standing by the window,
caught the balcony
railing, pulled himself in.
I was not there;
instead a woman with claw
feet and hands met him.
She intended to pull
all that he had
out through his navel.
What to do . . . to stall her.
To fight or to flee—
He didn't know. He wanted
to fight *and* to flee.

His feet in tennis shoes
moved back and forth,
rubbing the carpet.
I awoke at four, hearing
the sound of shoe soles
scuffing the soft rug.
Peter was still asleep
and in his bed. When
I called his name,
the sound of shoe soles
stopped. At breakfast
he mentioned his dream.

2
Now I have gone alone
to write by the ocean,
and watch the fish
between rocks.
I feel my eyes
open below the water.
Some power I cannot see
moves these small fish.
The sunlit ocean approaches
and recedes, rolling in
on its black lava base.
So much happens
when no one is watching,
perhaps *because*
no one is watching.
Pirates bring their ship in
when night has come;
the dancer becomes beautiful
when men see her
no longer; the movie becomes
clear when all

the actors are dead.
Earth is a thicket of thistles
waiting for the Wild Man.
Everything is in motion,
even what is still.
The planet turns, and cows
wait for the grassblades
to come rushing to their mouths.

3
I know there is someone
who tries to teach us.
He has four ways
to do that: First
is Memory, chosen.
I remember that I fell
one Sunday—I was three
or four—from my parents'
car; I saw it leaving
me on the road.
My parents do not recall it.
If we ignore that, he
waits till we are asleep,
opens the images, borrows
faces, turns men into turtles.
I dreamt that I sat
in a chair, and every other
second I disappeared.
That didn't reach me;
I went on with no change.
Then he moves, inter-
feres with matter, books fall
open to a certain passage.
Two strangers in one day
speak the same sentence.

The funeral is over;
the telephone rings;
or tennis shoes
that have no molecules
wake a sleeper.
If we still learn nothing,
then he turns to accidents,
disease, suffering,
lost letters, torpid sleeps,
disasters, catatonia.
We walk, the glass
mountain opens, we fall
in. I usually ignore
the earlier three,
and learn by falling.
This time we live it,
and only awaken years later.

FIFTY MEN SITTING TOGETHER

1
After a long walk in the woods clear cut for lumber,
Lit up by only a few young pines,
I turn home,
Drawn to water. A band of shadow
Softens half the lake,
Draws the shadow
Down from westward hills.
I see in that massive
Masculine shadow
Fifty men sitting together
In hall or crowded room,
Lifting something indistinct
Up into the resonating night.

2

Near shore, reeds stand about in groups
Unevenly as if they might
Finally ascend
To the sky all together!
Each reed has its own
Thin thread
Of darkness inside so
It is relaxed
And rooted in the mud.
So the son who has lived
Protected by the mother lives protected
By reeds in the joy of the half-darkness.

3

The woman stays in the kitchen, and does not want
To waste fuel by lighting a lamp,
As she waits
For the drunk husband to come home.
Then she serves him
Food in silence.
What does the son do?
He cleaves to her,
Looks down,
Goes outdoors to feed with wild
Things, lives in the reeds,
Pulls away from men,
Reaches upward, looks to the sky, ascends.

4

How far he is from working men when he is forty!
From all men! The men singing
Chant far out
On the water grounded in downward shadow.
He cannot go there because

He still hopes
He will not die. He will
Not throw
Himself into the shadow.
The dark comes down slowly,
The way snow falls,
Or herds pass a cave mouth.
I look up at the other shore; it is night.

CRAZY CARLSON'S MEADOW

Crazy Carlson cleared this meadow alone.
Now three blue
jays live in it.
Crazy Carlson cleared it back to the dark firs.
Feminine poplars have stepped out
in front, now
he is dead,
winding their leaves slowly in the motionless October air,

leaves midway between pale green and yellow,
as if a yellow
scarf were floating
six inches down in the Pacific. Old fir branches
above and below make sober
octopus caves,
inviting as the dark-
lidded eyes of those women on islands who live in bark huts.

A blue sky rises over the trees, pure blue,
too pure and blue.
There is no room
for the dark-lidded boys who longed to be Hercules.

There is no room even for Christ.
He broke off
his journey toward the Father,
and leaned back into the Mother's fearful tree.

He sank through the bark. The energies the Sadducees
refused him
turned into nails,
and the wine of Cana turned back to vinegar.
Blessings on you, my king, broken
on the poplar tree.
Your shoulders quivered
like an aspen leaf before the storm of Empire.

You fell off then, and the horse galloped away
into the wind without
you and disappeared
into the blue sky. Did you both reach the Father's house?
But the suffering is over now, all
consequences finished,
the lake closed
again, as before the leaf fell, all forgiven, the path ended.

Now each young man wanders in the sky alone,
ignoring the absent
moon, not knowing
where ground is, longing once more for the learning
of the fierce male who hung for nine days only
on the windy tree.
When he got down,
darkness was there, inside the folds of darkness words hidden.

KNEELING DOWN TO LOOK INTO A CULVERT

I kneel down to peer into a culvert.
The other end seems far away.
One cone of light floats in the shadowed water.
This is how our children will look when we are dead.

I kneel near floating shadowy water.
On my knees, I am half inside the tunnel—
blue sky widens the far end—
darkened by the shadowy insides of the steel.

Are they all born? I walk on farther;
out in the plowing I see a lake newly made.
I have seen this lake before . . . it is a lake
I return to each time my children are grown.

I have fathered so many children and returned
to that lake—grayish flat slate banks,
low arctic bushes. I am a water-serpent, throwing water drops
off my head. My gray loops trail behind me.

How long I stay there alone! For a thousand years
I am alone, with no duties, living as I live.
Then one morning a feathery head pokes from the water.
I fight—it's time—it's right—and am torn to pieces fighting.

LOVING
A WOMAN
IN TWO
WORLDS

(1985)

I

THE INDIGO BUNTING

I go to the door often.
Night and summer. Crickets
Lift their cries.
I know you are out.
You are driving
Late through the summer night.

I do not know what will happen.
I have no claim on you.
I am one star
You have as guide; others
Love you, the night
So dark over the Azores.

You have been working outdoors,
Gone all week. I feel you
In this lamp lit
So late. As I reach for it
I feel myself
Driving through the night.

I love a firmness in you
That disdains the trivial
And regains the difficult.
You become part then

Of the firmness of night,
The granite holding up walls.

There were women in Egypt who
Supported with their firmness the stars
As they revolved,
Hardly aware
Of the passage from night
To day and back to night.

I love you where you go
Through the night, not swerving,
Clear as the indigo
Bunting in her flight,
Passing over two
Thousand miles of ocean.

"OUT OF THE ROLLING OCEAN, THE CROWD . . ."

It is not only the ant that walks on the carpenter's board alone,
Nor the March turtle on his boulder surrounded by March water . . .
I know there are whitecaps that are born and die alone,
And a rocky pasture, and a new one nearby, with a path between.
There are branchy stalks, dropped to the ground last summer,
And tires, half worn-down, lifted to the gas-station-owner's rack.
All of them I saw today, and all of them were dear to me,
And the rough-barked young cottonwood alone on the windy shore.
Behind matter there is some kind of heat, around and behind things,
So what we experience is not the turtle nor the night
Only, nor the rising whirlwind, nor the certainty, nor the steady gaze,
Nor the meeting by the altar, nor the rising sun only.

THE WHOLE MOISTY NIGHT

The Viking ship sails into the full harbor.
The body meets its wife far out at sea.
Its lamp remains lit the whole moisty night.
Water pours down, faint flute notes in the sound of the water.

SECRETS

I walk below the over-bending birches,
birches that arch together in the air.
It is an omen of an open door,
a fear no longer found in the wind.
Are there unions only the earth sees?
The birches live where no one else comes,
deep in the unworried woods . . .
These sand grains looked at by deer bellies.

LETTER TO HER

What I did I did.
I knew that I loved you
and told you that.
Then I lied to you
often so you would love me,
hid the truth,
shammed, lied.

Once human beings
in their way do what they do
they find peakéd

castles ahead, they see
lanterns aloft over
the seal-like masses
where they love at night.

The hurricane carries
off the snail, still
clinging to his pine
tree. At night the o-
possum sees the golden
lion upside
down in his dream.

To do what we do
does not mean joy. The sun
rises, and some-
thing strong guides the sun
over the sky until
it carries its spark down
to the northern forests.

TWO PEOPLE AT DAWN

The sun orange and rose
lights up covers and clouds.
Her head lies in his lap.
And his hand curves round
the bone box of her head.
Odor of candles
floats in the room.

He says, "Our river flows
on a black mud bottom.
Are we walking there?

Are we underwater?"
"We are under the ocean."
"Ah well," he says, "the ocean
is only a slow river."

His hand remains firm.
Her courage shines
the whole length of her body.
The man joins her
in that briny place
where cattle graze
on grass below the water.

WINTER POEM

The quivering wings of the winter ant
Wait for lean winter to end.
I love you in slow, dim-witted ways,
Hardly speaking, one or two words only.

What caused us each to live hidden?
A wound, the wind, a word, a parent.
Sometimes we wait in a helpless way,
Awkwardly, not whole and not healed.

When we hid the wound, we fell back
From a human to a shelled life.
Now we feel the ant's hard chest,
The carapace, the silent tongue.

This must be the way of the ant,
The winter ant, the way of those
Who are wounded and want to live:
To breathe, to sense another, and to wait.

IN RAINY SEPTEMBER

In rainy September, when leaves grow down into the dark,
I put my forehead down to the damp, seaweed-smelling sand.
The time has come. I have put off choosing for years,
Perhaps whole lives. The fern has no choice but to live;
For this crime it receives earth, water, and night.

We close the door. "I have no claim on you." Dusk
Comes. You say, "The love I have had with you is enough."
We know we could live apart from one another.
The sheldrake floats apart from the flock.
The oak tree puts out leaves alone on the lonely hillside.

Men and women before us have accomplished this.
I would see you, and you me, once a year.
We would be two kernels, and not be planted.
We stay in the room, door closed, lights out.
I weep with you without shame and without honor.

THE THIRD BODY

A man and a woman sit near each other, and they do not long
At this moment to be older, or younger, or born
In any other nation, or any other time, or any other place.
They are content to be where they are, talking or not-talking.
Their breaths together feed someone whom we do not know.
The man sees the way his fingers move;
He sees her hands close around a book she hands to him.
They obey a third body that they share in common.
They have promised to love that body.
Age may come; parting may come; death will come!

A man and a woman sit near each other;
As they breathe they feed someone we do not know,
Someone we know of, whom we have never seen.

TWO MIDDLE-AGED LOVERS

An Etching by Dürer

The man and the woman linger under a tree,
Soberly, standing near his horse.
Man and woman hear the low muttering speech
Instinct makes to instinct.
Their canoe shoots down the narrow channel;
The climber goes rock by rock up the mountainside.
The yaks, hair blowing, disappear into the storm.

FINDING SHARKS' TEETH IN A ROCK

The cabin of the early snail swerves and falls
through miles of murky stuff, and the shark, turning,
swerves, one fin working, finally settles,
joins the rock, serves. When I strike it hard,
teeth delicate as black kites fall out!
So it is, has been. Sharks' teeth glitter
in the light of the old moon. It was to her
the Chaldean horns shot out their cry at dawn,
mingling our uneasy cries with the containing rocks.

THE ROOTS

Finally in the bear's cabin I come to earth.
There are limits. Among all the limits
We *know* so few things. How is it that I know
Only one river—its turns—and one woman?
The love of woman is the knowing of grief.
There are no limits to grief. The loving man
Simmers his porcupine stew. Among the tim-
Ber growing on earth grief finds roots.

WHAT FRIGHTENED US

Drops of rain fall into black fields.
Leaves fallen on the highway remain
where they fall, and resist the wind.
A power neither of us knows has spoken to us.

All night rain came in. We had descended
yesterday to some inner, or innermost cave,
and this—as we woke today with faces wet
from overnight rain—frightens us a little.

Smoke of rain lifts from gravel roads.
Rainwater gathers below the barns.

Other waters slowly join in woods.
Silent in the moonlight, no beginning or end.

SEEING YOU CARRY PLANTS IN

How much I love you. The night is moist.
The air is still, as when I love you.
It is not every evening that I love you.
I come back like the stars, sometimes out of clouds.

The night is moist, and nourishing as your mind
that lets everything around you live.
I saw you carry the plants inside tonight
over the grass, to save them from the cold.

Sometimes I slip behind a door, so that
I will not be called on, or walk
hunched on sandbars below earth, not sure
if anyone in my family can love.

Your voice is water open beneath stars,
collected from abundant rain, gone to low places.
The night is moist, the ground wet,
air still, trees silent, and tonight I love you.

THE TWO RIVERS

Inside us there is a river born in the good cold
that longs to give itself to the Gulf of light.
And there is another river more like the Missouri
that carries earth, and earth joys, and the earthly.

COME WITH ME

We walk together in willows, among willows.
The cowrie shell has its rosy mouth;
the tree nods and rises;
the conch returns to the dark waters.

Come with me, we will walk alone,
away from the buildings and the high places.
I love to go with you,
and enter the valley where no one is king.

AT MIDOCEAN

All day I loved you in a fever, holding on to the tail of the horse.
I overflowed whenever I reached out to touch you.
My hand moved over your body, covered
with its dress,
burning, rough, an animal's foot or hand moving over leaves.
The rainstorm retires, clouds open, sunlight
sliding over ocean water a thousand miles from land.

IN THE TIME OF PEONY BLOSSOMING

When I come near the red peony flower
I tremble as water does near thunder,
As the well does when the plates of earth move,
Or the tree when fifty birds leave at once.

The peony says that we have been given a gift,
And it is not the gift of this world.

Behind the leaves of the peony
There is a world still darker, that feeds many.

NIGHT FROGS

I wake and find myself in the woods, far from the castle.
The train hurtles through lonely Louisiana at night.
The sleeper turns to the wall, delicate
aircraft dive toward earth.

A woman whispers to me, urges me to speak truths.
"I am afraid that you won't be honest with me."
Half or more of the moon rolls on in shadow.
Owls talk at night, loons wheel cries through lower waters.

Hoof marks turn up—something with hooves tramples
the grasses while the horses are asleep.
A shape flat and four feet long slips under the door
and lies exhausted on the floor in the morning.

When I look back, there is a blind spot in the car.
What is it in my father I keep not noticing?
I cannot remember years of my childhood.
Some parts of me I cannot find now.

I intended that; I threw some parts of me away
at ten; others at twenty; a lot at twenty-eight.
I wanted to thin myself out as a wire is thinned.
Is there enough left of me now to be honest?

The lizard moves stiffly over November roads.
How much I am drawn toward my parents! I walk back
and forth, looking toward the old landing.
Night frogs give out the croak of the planet turning.

THE MARCH BUDS

They lie on the bed, hearing music.
The perfumed pillow, the lake, a woman's laughter.
Wind blows faintly, touches the March buds.
The young trees sway back and forth.

THE TURTLE

Rain lifts the lake level, washing the reeds.
Slowly the milkweed pods open, the yellow lily pads.
Through the mist man and woman see the far shore.
The turtle's head rises out over the water.

SUCH DIFFERENT WANTS

The board floats on the river.
The board wants nothing
but is pulled from beneath
on into deeper waters.

And the elephant dwelling
on the mountain wants
a trumpet so its dying cry
can be heard by the stars.

The wakeful heron striding
through reeds at dawn wants
the god of sun and moon
to see his long skinny neck.

You must say what you want.
I want to be the man
and I am who will love you
when your hair is white.

FERNS

It was among ferns I learned about eternity.
Below your belly there is a curly place.
Through you I learned to love the ferns on that bank,
and the curve the deer's hoof leaves in sand.

THE HUMMINGBIRD VALLEY

I love to come near the hummingbird valley,
that place where we have played so often.
It is a garden where the night-hummingbirds live,
hovering in the night on fast wings.

Hills on each side close in that garden,
immaculate as the mouse's fur;
there the hummingbirds come to the plum trees,
and the plums lie about on the darkening earth.

Isn't it a house? It has been a house to me.
The cantor waits to enter the synagogue—
more than a garden—and I hear the slow oceany
chanting of the Babylonian masses.

And with what interest I hear the hummingbird listening
to words about to be spoken for the first time.
They bless all the hummingbirds, and they bless this house
where we first exchanged salt and bread together.

LOVE POEM IN TWOS AND THREES

What kind of people
are these? Some stammer
of land, some
want nothing but light—
no house or land
thrown away for a woman,
no ample recklessness.
How much I need
a woman's soul, felt
in my own knees,
shoulders and hands.
I was born sad!
I am a northern goat
of winter light,
up to my knees in snow.
Standing by you, I am
glad as the clams
at high tide, eerily
content as the amorous
ocean owls.

RETURNING POEM

Men bring the boat at night inside its slanted house by the shore;
goats return when the farmer calls them to their earth-barn at night.
Brothers, working on different farms, go home after dark
and sleep together at last in the attic room under its slanting roof.
And the deer returns, finding her way through woods to her
 curving grass.

At night the man goes to the bus to meet the woman he loves—
it has only been a day—and impatiently brings her home.
So what was far out into the air, and the longitudes of the earth
is brought home, taken in, a place prepared in the chest,
and the mountain loon returns, and soon is asleep in the mountain
 lake.

THE RAM

The ram walks over the minty grass.
The hawk ruffles his shoulder feathers.
Two chooks sit with feathers overlapping.
Just before dark big snowflakes fall.

NIGHT WINDS

Night winds sway the lilacs near the abandoned woodshed.
I am alone now; trees dark; the time for heroes is over.
Night winds pull me out; I am pulled away from day;
I float in the current, calm and mad as a sleepy cork.

All afternoon, lying on a hill of kisses and fever,
we felt winds around us, below us, above us,
holding us where we want to be, and I live now
surrounded by those swirls as an island by smoky water.

I sway like the branches, and do not choose the motion.
I am faithful as the ant with his small waist.
What do heroes and Hercules mean to me now?
I will remain here; you will find me where you left me.

ALONE A FEW HOURS

Today I was alone a few hours, and slowly
windows darkened, leaving me alone, naked,
with no father or uncle,
born in no country . . . I was a streak of light
through the sky,
a trail in the snow behind the field mouse,
a thing that has
simple desires, and one
or two needs, like a barn darkened by rain.

Something enters from the open window.
I sense it, and turn slightly
to the left. Then I notice
shadows are dear to me, shadows in the weeds
near the lake,
and under the writing table where I sit
writing this.
"The hermit is not here;
he is up on the mountain picking ferns."

That's what the hermit's boy told the visitor
looking for him. Then I realize that I do love,
at last, that the simple
joy of the field mouse has come to me.
I am no longer
a stone pile visited from below
by the old ones.
"It's misty up there . . .
I don't know where he is . . . I don't think you can find him."

THE MOOSE

The Arctic moose drinks at the tundra's edge,
swirling the watercress with his mouth.
How fresh the water is, the coolness of the far North.
A light wind moves through the deep firs.

MOUNTAIN GRASS

Rain falls on mountain grass; we remain close all day.
The fuchsia lifts its tendrils high.
I need you, to hold you, as mountain grass holds rain.
Dampness falls on dampness; rain on wet earth.
I am the traveler on the mountain who keeps repeating his cry.

WHAT WE PROVIDE

Every breath taken in by the man
who loves, and the woman who loves,
goes to fill the water tank
where the spirit horses drink.

POEM ON SLEEP

"Then the bright being disguised as a seal dove into the deep billows."
I go on loving you after we are asleep.
I know the ledges where we sit all night looking out over the briny sea,
and the open places where we coast in sleekness through the sea.

And where is the hunter who is cunning? The practical part of me?
Oh he is long since gone, dispersed among the bold grasses.
The one he does not know of remains afloat and awake all night;
he lies on luminous boulders, dives, his coat sleek, his eyes open.

THE ARTIST AT FIFTY

The crow nests high in the fir.
Birds leap through the snowy branches
uttering small cries. Clumps fall.
Mice run dragging their tails in the new-fallen snow.

Year after year the artist works,
early and late, studying the old.
What does he gain? Finally he dreams
one night of deer antlers abandoned in the snow.

WORDS BARELY HEARD

The bear in his heavy fur rises from the bed.
The extravagant one he has left behind murmurs . . .
Or is murmured . . . Words barely heard.
Her face shines; and he turns back toward her.

THE CONDITIONS

What we have loved is with us ever,
ever, ever!
So you are with me far into the past,
the oats of Egypt . . .
I was a black hen!
You were the grain of wheat
I insisted on
before I agreed to be born.

A MAN AND A WOMAN AND A BLACKBIRD

A man and a woman
Are one.
A man and a woman and a blackbird
Are one.

—Wallace Stevens

When the two rivers
Join in the cloudy chamber,
So many alien nights
In our twenties, alone

On interior mountains,
Forgotten. Blackbirds
Walk around our feet
As if they shared
In what we know.
We know and we don't know
What the heron feels
With his wing-
Tip feathers stretched
Out in the air above
The flooded lake,
Or the odorous constellations
The pig sees
Past his wild snout.
A man and a woman
Sit near each other. On
The windowpane
Ice.
The man says: "How
Is it
I have never loved
Ice before?
If I have not loved ice,
What have I loved?
Loved the dead
In their Sumerian
Fish-cloaks?
The vultures celebrating?
The soldiers
And the poor?"
And yet
For one or two
Moments,
In our shared grief
And exile,

We hang our harps
On the willows,
And the willows
Join us,
And the man
And the woman
And the blackbird are one.

III

THE MINNOW TURNING

Once I loved you only a few minutes a day.
Now it is smoke rising, the mushroom left by the birch,
and the horse's forefoot, the way the minnow stirs silver
as he turns, carrying his world with him.

FIRMNESS

My fierceness when I hold you belongs
to the fir logs rolling on the shore.
And your affections coming toward me are the Oregon
islands disappearing in surf and mist.

CONVERSATION

I sat beneath maples, reading,
a book in my lap, alone all morning.
You walked past—whom I have loved
for ten years—walked by and were gone.

That was all. When I returned
to reading, not all of me returned.

My sex, or rosy man,
reached on its own and touched the book.

It must be some words have fur.
Or mute things exchange thought.
Or perhaps I am no longer
weary, grieving, and alone.

We know it's true: the bee's foot
knows the anther and its dwarves,
as the castle of women knows
of the rider lost outside in the trees.

SHAME

A man and a woman sit
among firs, looking eastward.
Sun is rising. Wind
from behind them lifts
them and carries them
over the fir needles.
They whirl, and the motion
carries them
down through the narrow
opening at the center.
Through it each must
pass, with toes curled out,
arms thrown back,
all shame gone.

THE HORSE OF DESIRE

"Yesterday I saw a face
that gave off light."
I wrote that the first time
I saw you; now the lines
written that morning
are twenty years old.
What is it that
we see and don't see?

When a horse swings
his head, how easily
his shoulders follow.
When the right thing happens,
the whole body knows.
The road covered with stones
turns to a soft river
moving among reeds.

I love you in those reeds,
and in the bass
quickening there.
My love is in the demons
gobbling the waters,
my desire in their swollen
foreheads poking
earthward out of the trees.

The bear between my legs
has one eye only,
which he offers
to God to see with.
The two beings below with no
eyes at all love you

with the slow persistent
intensity of the blind.

LISTENING TO THE KÖLN CONCERT

After we had loved each other intently,
We heard notes tumbling together,
In late winter, and we heard ice
Falling from the ends of twigs.

The notes abandon so much as they move.
They are the food not eaten, the comfort
Not taken, the lies not spoken.
The music is my attention to you.

And when the music came again,
Later in the day, I saw tears in your eyes.
I saw you turn your face away
So that others would not see.

When men and women come together,
How much they have to abandon! Wrens
Make their nests of fancy threads
And string ends, animals

Abandon all their money each year.
What is that men and women leave?
Harder than wrens' doing, they have
To abandon their longing for the perfect.

The inner nest not made by instinct
Will never be quite round,
And each has to enter the nest
Made by the other imperfect bird.

CONVERSATION WITH A HOLY WOMAN NOT SEEN FOR MANY YEARS

After so many years, I come walking to you.
You say: "You have come after so long?"
I could not come earlier. My shabby mouth,
with its cavernous thirst, ate the seeds of longing
that should have been planted. Awkward and baffled,
dishonest, I slept. And I dreamt of sand.
Your eyes in sorrow do not laugh.
I say, "I have come after so many years."

WHAT MOVES AND DOESN'T MOVE

At night desire and longing enter, and we feel water
hurrying through a grassy place.
By dawn we know
all minglings, things of sorrow,
rings of Saturn, the raccoon's wrist-joints and his smooth tail.

This is not Mozart, but a music more vulgar and grand.
Laughing we see the lizard hurry
to become a mammal,
or go back to the worm, or be a bird.
It is early spring; fronds rise; the frog leaps here and there.

Outdoors the dawn drifts restless with all its odors,
from tree to tree, between the insects,
among the stars,
leaping from twig to twig.
I am with you, held always moving in the night valley.

THE HERON DRINKING

The bird dips to take some water in its bill.
You know we do not drink only with our hands.
We receive what nothing else can give.
We are thirsty for the heron
and the lake, the touch of the bill on the water.

THE GOOD SILENCE

Reading an Anglo-Saxon love poem in its extravagance,
I stand up and walk about the room.
I do not love you in a little way;
oh yes, I do love you in a little way,
the old way, the way of the rowboat alone in the ocean.

The image is a white-washed house, on David's Head, in Wales,
surrounded by flowers, bordered by seashells
and withies. A horse appears at the door
minutes before a storm; the house stands
in a space awakened by salt wind, alone on its cliff.

I take your hand as we work, neither of us speaking.
This is the old union of man and woman,
nothing extraordinary; they both feel a deep
calm in the bones. It is ordinary affection
that our bodies experienced for ten thousand years.

During those years we stroked the hair of the old, brought in
roots, painted prayers, slept, laid hair
on fire, took lives, and the bones
of the dead gleamed from under rocks where the love
the roaming tribe gave made them shine at night.

And we did what we did, made love attentively, then
dove into the river, and our bodies joined as calmly
as the swimmer's shoulders glisten at dawn,
as the pine tree stands in the rain at the edge of the village.
The affection rose on a slope century after century,

And one day my faithfulness to you was born.
We sit together silently at the break of day.
We sit an hour, then tears run down my face.
"What is the matter?" you say, looking over.
I answer, "The ship saileth on the salte foam."

THE HAWK

The hawk sweeps down from his aerie,
dives among swallows,
turns over twice in the air,
flying out of Catal-Huyuk.
Slowly a seeing hawk
frees itself from the fog;
its sleek head sees far off.

And the ocean turns in,
gives birth to herring
oriented to the poles.
Oregon fir needles, pungent
as the proverbs of old men,
ride down the Rogue River,
enter the ocean currents.

Land and sea mingle, so we
mingle with sky and wind. A mole

told me that his mother
had gone into the sky,
and his father lay curled
in a horsechestnut shell.
And my brother is part of the ocean.

Our great-uncles, grandfathers,
great-grandfathers, remain.
While we lie asleep, they see
the grasshopper resting
on the grassblade, and the wolverine
sweeping with his elegant
teeth through the forest.

And they come near. Whenever
we talk with a small
child, the dead help us
to choose words. Choosing words,
courage comes. When a man
encouraged by the dead goes
where he wishes to go,

then he sees the long tongue
of water on which the whale
rides on his journey.
When he finds the way
long intended for him,
he tastes through glacial water
the Labrador ferns and snows.

IN THE MONTH OF MAY

In the month of May when all leaves open,
I see when I walk how well all things
lean on each other, how the bees work,
the fish make their living the first day.
Monarchs fly high; then I understand
I love you with what in me is unfinished.

I love you with what in me is still
changing, what has no head or arms
or legs, what has not found its body.
And why shouldn't the miraculous,
caught on this earth, visit
the old man alone in his hut?

And why shouldn't Gabriel, who loves honey,
be fed with our own radishes and walnuts?
And lovers, tough ones, how many there are
whose holy bodies are not yet born.
Along the roads, I see so many places
I would like us to spend the night.

MEDITATIONS ON THE INSATIABLE SOUL

(1994)

I

MEN AND WOMEN

1

Horses go on eating the Apostle Island ferns,
Also sheep and goats; also the big-nostrilled moose
Who knocks down the common bushes
In his longing for earthly pleasure.
The moose's great cock floats in the lily pads.
That image calms us. His nose calms us.
Slowly, obstinately, we retrieve the pleasures
The Fathers, angry with the Gnostics, threw away.

2

The glad body sings its four-leggéd tunes.
It has its honesty. Lovers know the obstinacy
Of the hippopotamus, the grunts that say to spirit,
Gone, gone. The lover's body leaps at its own
Sweetness, snaps off blossoms with its teeth. Later
He seems good to her eyes, like a waterhole
Muddied by animals. Tristan and Isolde
Love their bawdy lodge, no north, no south.

3

We know that women, some women, want
Heaven and earth joined. Men, some men, want sawn
Boards, roads diverging, and jackdaws flying,

Heaven and earth parted. Women in their wildness
Want storks dancing, daughters roving
On the mountainside, canvases with Venus
And a naked man, doves returning at dusk,
Cloths folded, and giants sitting down at table.

WAITING FOR THE STARS

1

How much I long for the night to come
Again—I am restless all afternoon—
And the huge stars to appear
All over the heavens!—The black spaces between stars—
And the blue to fade away.

2

I worked on things with my back to the window,
Waiting for the darkness that I remember
I saw from my cradle.
When I step over and open the door, I am
A salmon slipping over the gravel into the ocean.

3

One star stands alone in the western darkness:
Arcturus. Caught in their love, the Arabs called it
The Keeper of Heaven. I think
It was in the womb that I received
The thirst for the dark heavens.

THE MAN WHO WALKS TOWARD US

There is so much forgotten rock in the world
And so much blue, glacial ice crowding down to die,
So many overhangs on which no petroglyphs are ever found,
And so many ships that rise up and slip down with no iceberg near.

There are stories long told that have never been understood
And so many metaphors that Valentinus muttered to the frogs
And so much wainscoting that widows have painted over.
There are moments when the gold sun in Lisbon is gone.

We see houses in our dreams that need to be repaired
And horses that no one has fed for three weeks.
There are so many shoulders we have never touched with our fingers,
And there are days when I forget I have a mother.

We drink down so many angers at our mother's breast.
There are so many cries no one makes during the wedding service.
There are so many poets whose poems no one reads
And so many pale bottles that the demons set out for milk.

Certain streams go into a mountain and never come out again.
Boys ride rafts down that dark tunnel, we mustn't wait for them.
Sometimes a twin lives with us in the womb for a while and then
 vanishes at birth.
There is a man who walks toward us for days, for years, for sixty years

And arrives, opens the bed clothes, sleeps with us until dawn,
Leaving behind a piece of ivory from the narwhal's horn, pierced
 with many holes.

THE CHINESE PEAKS

For Donald Hall

I love the mountain peak
but I know also its rolling
foothills
half-invisible
in mist and fog.

The Seafarer gets up
long before dawn to read.
His soul
is a whale feeding
on the Holy Word.

The soul who loves the peak
also inhales the deep
breath rising
from the mountain
buried in mist.

LETTER TO JAMES WRIGHT

My dear James, do you know that nothing has happened
Since you died? Ammons is still writing garbage,
And the *Maximus Poems* are back in print. *"Well, I am tired
Of the lost maples of heaven; I want news
Of the living, of you."* Rexroth is gone. He was one of the
Funniest men in the world, and he got a biographer
With no sense of humor. *"I remember Rexroth saying,
'I'll cold-cock Santa Claus if he comes near.' It's the least
An anarchist can do. Eisenhower couldn't find
The Brazilian flag if it were up his butt."* Roger Hecht died

Along with Morgan Blum; Kenyon fumbled your papers
And lost them; they've named a street after you
In Martins Ferry. *"Do you remember that cliff*
We once imagined—hundreds of swallow holes,
And an old Chinese poem rolled up inside
Each hole? We can't unroll them here. We have
To climb inside." Even butterflies unfold. . . .
"That tenderness . . . By God, I'll try anything."

WALLACE STEVENS AND FLORENCE

Oh Wallace Stevens, dear friend,
You are such a pest. You are so sure.
You think everyone is in *your* family.

It is you and your father and Mozart—
And ladies tasting cold rain in Florence,
Puzzling out inscriptions, studying the gold flake.

As if life were a visit to Florence,
A place where there are no maggots in the flesh,
No one screaming, no one afraid.

Your job, your joy, your morning walk,
As if you walked on the wire of the mind,
High above the elephants; you cry out a little but never fall.

As if we could walk always high above the world,
No bears, no witches, no Macbeth,
No one screaming, no one in pain, no one afraid.

ON THE OREGON COAST

For William Stafford

The waves come—the large fourth wave
Looming up, thinking, crashing down—all
Roll in so prominently that I become small
And write this in a cramped script, hard to read.

Well, all this fury, prominent or not
Is also hard to read, and the ducks don't help,
Settling down in furry water, shaking
Themselves, and then forgetting it within a minute.

Remembering the fury, it is up to us, even
Though we feel small compared to the loose
Ocean, to keep sailing and not land,
And figure out what to say to our children.

WHEN WILLIAM STAFFORD DIED

Well, water goes down the Montana gullies.
"I'll just go around this rock and think
About it later." That's what you said.
When death came, you said, "I'll go there."

There's no sign you'll come back. Sometimes
My father sat up in the coffin and was alive again.
But I think you were born before my father,
And the feet they made in your time were lighter.

One dusk you were gone. Sometimes a fallen tree
Holds onto a rock, if the current is strong.

I won't say my father did that, but I won't
Say he didn't either. I was watching you both.

If all a man does is to watch from the shore,
Then he doesn't have to worry about the current.
But if affection has put us into the stream,
Then we have to agree to where the water goes.

THOMAS AND THE CODFISH'S PSALM

1

The Gaiety of Form
How sweet to weight the line with all these vowels!
Body, Thomas, the codfish's psalm. The gaiety
Of form lies in the labor of its playfulness.
The chosen vowel reappears like the evening star
Westerly, in the solemn return the astronomers love.
It comforts us, says: "I am here, be calm."
When a vowel returns three times, then it becomes
A note; and the whole stanza turns to music.

2

The Turtle's Work
Climbing on shore to give her brood a home,
The turtle gathers each day bits of primitive hay,
Piling her leathery eggs at pale midnight.
Obedient to some other moon, to her longing
And the night, her claws bury the eggs
Gleaming in the moonlight, cover them with sand.
Though she cannot protect them from the gulls on shore,
Some young find their way to the enormous sea.

HONORING SAND

In memory of Joseph Campbell

We know the road the gods take, but we do not know
Who will walk on it. All moves slowly
In the soul. There is so much time
We can stay in grieving another hundred years.
The first harp came from an empty turtle.
The ocean thistle that has given up its flowering
Stays there, and its stem teaches us to go down.
Forget the flower; learn to know the sand.

GRATITUDE TO OLD TEACHERS

When we stride or stroll across the frozen lake,
We place our feet where they have never been.
We walk upon the unwalked. But we are uneasy.
Who is down there but our old teachers?

Water that once could take no human weight—
We were students then—holds up our feet,
And goes on ahead of us for a mile.
Beneath us the teachers, and around us the stillness.

THOUGHTS IN THE CABIN

Why do I suddenly feel free of panic?
Here a summer afternoon, wind-
Blown lake, a cabin of strong logs.

I can live and die with no more
Fame; I'd like ground to walk on,
A few books, occasionally a storm.

I know stories I can tell, and I may
Or may not. There is more
To learn: the wind and the screendoor.

The granary of images, the Norwegian
Lore, the power of Shmat-Razum,
Good or evil, success or failure.

Expect something else from me—
Less—and don't rule out
Misdirection, silence, misinformation.

II

VISITING MY FATHER

1
Your chest, hospital gown
Awry, looks
Girlish today.
It is your bluish
Reptile neck
That has known weather.
I said to you, "Are
You ready to die?"
"I am," you said,
"It's too boring
Around here." He has in mind
Some other place
Less boring. "He's
Not ready to go,"
The doctor said.
There must have been
A fire that nearly
Blew out, or a large
Soul, inadequately
Feathered, that became
Cold and angered.
Some four-year-old boy
In you, chilled by your
Mother, misprized

By your father, said,
"I will defy, I will
Win anyway, I
Will show *them*."
When Alice's well-
Off sister offered to
Take your two boys
During the Depression,
You said it again.
Now you bring that
Defiant mood to death.
The four-year-old
Old man in you does as
He likes: he likes
To stay alive.
Through him you
Get revenge,
Persist, endure,
Overlive, overwhelm,
Get on top.
You gave me
This, and I do
Not refuse it.
It is
In me.

2

My Father at Eighty-Six
You are eighty-
Six, and while we
Talk suddenly
Fall asleep.
Would you have been
Proud of me
If I had lived

More like you?
In this same hospital
Room, drying out
Thirty-five years
Ago, you said to me:
"Are you happy?"
I was twenty-eight.
"Happiness is not one
Of the aims I have
Set for my life."
You were alarmed.
I was bluffing, as
Isolated as you.
Now you have almost
Reached the last station.
Shall I say that you
Misspent your life?
You stood vibrating
On a threshing machine,
Pulleys, choppers, shakers
Beneath you,
And kept your balance
Mostly.
I walked on a rope,
Carrying six
Children on my shoulders,
Felt their love.
A woman had
A message for me
And it arrived.
Now for the first time
I can see your skull
Below your closed
Grape-like eyes.
Some modest,

Luminous
Thing has happened.
Is that all?
What did we expect?

3
The Hard Breathing
Your hard breathing
We all three
Notice. To continue
To live here,
One must take air.
But taking air
Commits you
To sharing it
With wolves and cattle.
When breathing stops
You will be free
Of that company.
You came from the water
World, and do not
Want to change
Again. My mother
Does not remember
The water world.
Nieces are here
In this world, nephews,
Classmates, a son.
She sits with puzzled eyes
Now, as if to say,
"Where is that
Reckless man
For whom I gladly left
My father?
Is it this man

With gaunt cheeks
On the bed?
All those times
I drove into town,
Carefully, over
Packed snow, is this
What it comes to?" Yes,
Yes, it is, my
Dear Mother.
The tablecloths
You saved are all
Gone; the baked
Corn dish you
Made for your boys,
The Christmas Eves,
Opening perfume—
Evening in Paris—
From your husband,
The hope that a man
Would alter his
Habits for you—
They are all gone.
The nurse takes my father
For his bath.
You and I
Wait here for Jacob
To come back.
"What sort of
Flowers are those?"
"Daisies," I say.
A few minutes later,
You ask again.
What can I do but
Feel the invisible
River go through

Me, and sit
Here with you?

4
Something Has Come
My mother and I sit
In the hospital room.
What can we say
To each other?
That we are nothing
When the Man
Leaves the room?
That we are bound
By our breathing
To this troubled place?
That I am a son
And you are a mother,
And that something
Has come
Between us,
So that we forget
What has saved us.

5
The Komodo Dragon
My father and I
Swim a half-mile
Or so apart
In a cold sea.
Each of us senses
The other's strokes,
But we swim far from
The care of women.
I swim on, asking
My shoulders why

My lower half
Feels so heavy.
Only my arms
Lift, the ocean
Pulls the rest
Of me down.
I know that far
Below us, scattered
On the ocean floor,
There are Model A
Engines, spoked wheels
From horse rakes,
Engine blocks
Broken apart,
Snapped plow-
Shares, drive shafts
Sticking from sand,
Useless cutter-bars.
Our failures have
Solidified there,
Rusting
In saline water.
We worked all day
Through till mid-
Night and couldn't
Keep the swather
Going, nothing helps,
Drove a piston
Right through the block.
It won't do.
And behind us
A large beast
Swims—four or
Five miles back,
Spines on his nose,

Fins like the
Komodo dragon,
Spiny whiskers,
Following us.

6
The Pharaoh's Servant
My father's large ears
Hear everything.
A hermit wakes
And sleeps in a hut
Underneath
His gaunt cheeks.
His eyes blue, alert,
Disappointed,
And suspicious,
Complain I
I do not bring him
The same sort of
Jokes the nurses
Do. He is a bird
Waiting to be fed—
Mostly beak—an eagle
Or a vulture,
Or the Pharaoh's servant
Just before death.
My arm on the bedrail
Rests there, relaxed,
With new love. All
I know of the Troubadours
I bring to this bed.
I do not want
Or need to be shamed
By him any longer.
The general of shame

Has discharged
Him, and left him
In this small provincial
Egyptian town.
If I do not wish
To shame him, then
Why not love him?
His long hands,
Large, veined,
Capable, can still
Retain hold of what
He wanted:
Six farms. But
Is that what he
Desired? Some
Powerful engine
Of desire goes on
Turning inside his body.
He never phrased
What he desired,
And I am
His son.

7

Prayer for My Father
Your head is still
Restless, rolling
East and west—
That body in you
Insisting on living
Is the old hawk
For whom the world
Darkens. If I
Am not with you
When you die,

That would be grievous
But just. That part
Of you cleaned
My bones more
Than once. But I
Will meet you
In the young hawk
Whom I see
Inside both
You and me.
This young hawk
Guided you
Into the air—
And will guide
You now to
The Lord of Night,
Who will give
You the tenderness
You wanted here.

DREAM OF MYSELF AT TWELVE

At the start of the dream
It was understood you were working
In the grape fields. But
When I walked
Into the barn, I saw

A leg sticking
From the hay. It was you, hiding,
Not working. "How
Long have you
Been here?" Your head

Rose from the hay.
My mother, your calm wife,
Showed up, spoke
For you, said,
"Jacob, you haven't been

Drinking, have you?"
How often as a child I heard
That and did nothing.
This time I broke
A horse-collar, threw

A gun into
The horse-stall, jabbed
A pitchfork into
Loose hay,
Hit the hired man.

My father said nothing.
My brother said it was clear
I could never be-
Come a man,
Would have to play with toys.

Then I looked
Down at the yellow straw
In the stable, my tongue
Still. As I
Woke, a small boy

Clung to me,
Could not feel safe,
Would not take
His arms
From around my neck.

IN THE FUNERAL HOME

1

I missed the hour of your death.
The coffin lid
Lifted shows some
Fall oak leaves sewn
High above
Your winter face.

I have at last some
Leisure near
Your cream-colored hands.
I write down what you did,
Or did wrong, or did
Not do at all.

The funeral director, a kind
Man, says, "I'll
Go upstairs now
With my family. You sit as long
As you like.
No one is here."

2

Your marriage held in-
Visible mountains, touching
And not touching . . .
Too much isolation. I'm not sure
You married at all,
Or whom you married.

For twenty-five years,
An adult, I lived
A half-mile from you.
Why? Perhaps I couldn't get

Enough, or perhaps
I was your wife.

Weren't you my husband?
A hurtful man,
Reckless, wrathful, solemn,
Able to break a man or a book,
Gentle, un-
Churched, bold.

We had twenty-four
Anniversaries then,
Before I moved again,
At fifty-three,
No longer needing
To be married to you.

As I wrote that down, your head
Turned slowly
In the coffin, your jaw
Opened, the teeth showed
Themselves; then
Your head rolled back.

3
Did I tell you that I regret
Being so agreeable
To you in childhood?
I left at seventeen,
A mother's boy,
Dreamy, smart.

I moved back at twenty-
Eight, with a

Wife, a half-
Mile from you. By then
I had found out
What I wanted.

I said it in a poem:
"I want to have
No wife, build
A house with one door,
Be called
Away by wind."

4
You spoke often of the Prince
Of Wales, whom
You admired.
He too wanted something
More—and
He had to steal it.

An old man said to me:
"Your father was
The only man
In the whole county
Who read books
During the Depression."

5
What good was all that
Seeing we did,
So as to miss
Pheasant nests as we
Mowed or rocks
As we plowed?

I lay my palm on
Your chest. Your chest
Is thin below
The burial suit,
A chicken's breast
Below my hand.

Do we have time for
Each other now?
Do you have
Time for me? Seeing
Is good, as Marvell
Said, but eyes

Are also for weeping.
As I stand next
To you in your long
Coffin, I see we
Have more time
Than we can use.

A DREAM OF THE BLACKSMITH'S ROOM

I dreamt last night you
Lived nearby, not
Dead at all, but safe
In a blacksmith's storage room,
With bolts and nails in bins
From floor to ceiling.

You came and brought me
An ivory jar,
Holding a precious fluid,

Which I took. I knew it meant
The time had come,
But I let you leave.

Later a man pushed open
The door and threw
Your body down, a wizened,
Astonishingly small body—
Rope still tied
Around the neck.

I cried out to my wife,
"He didn't die
That way!" The man who threw
The body said, "It's over. You
Don't have to
Rescue him again."

III

MEDITATIONS ON THE INSATIABLE SOUL

1

The man who sits up late at night cutting
His nails, the backs of black whales, the tip
Of the mink's tail, the tongue that slips out of lips, all of these
Testify to a soul used to eating and being eaten.
Urged on by the inner pressure of teeth,
Some force, animal-born, is slippery, edgy,
Impatient, greedy to pray for new heavens,
Unforgiving, resentful, like a fire in dry wood.

2

Greeks sit by the fire cleaning their bright teeth.
Let Portia grieve in her sorrowing house.
Let blackbirds come. The insatiable soul
Begins to eat shellfish, the Caribbean islands,
The rainforests, Amazon. Who wants to eat the meat
Cooked in the Holocaust? Oh, you know.
The traveler asleep in Charlemagne's cave
Laughs in his murky unshaven dream.

3

Some ill-smelling, libidinous, worm-shouldered
Deep-reaching desirousness rules the countryside.
Let sympathy pass, a stranger, to other shores!
Let the love between men and women be ground up

And fed to the talk shows! Let every female breast
Be photographed! Let the father be hated! Let the son be hated!
Let twelve-year-olds kill the twelve-year-olds!
The Great Lord of Desirousness ruling all.

4
Northern lights illumine the storm-troll's house.
There men murdered by God promenade.
The buffalo woman plays her bony flute calling
The lonely father trampled by the buffalo god.
The foreskins of angels shelter the naked cradle.
The stew of discontents feeds the loose souls.
And the owl husbands the moors, harries the mouse,
Beforehand, behindhand, with his handsome eyes.

ANGER AGAINST CHILDREN

The vet screams, and throws his crutch at a passerby.
"Hey, lady, you want to meet a child-killer?"
African drums play all night for the women
With their heads down on motel tables.
Parents take their children into the deepest Oregon forests,
And leave them there. When the children
Open the lunchbox, there are stones inside, and a note saying,
 "Do your own thing."
And what would the children do if they found their way home in
 the moonlight?
The planes have already landed on Maui, the parents are on
 vacation.
Our children live with a fear at school and in the house.
The mother and father do not protect the younger child from the
 savagery of the others.

What is it like to have stayed this long in civilization—
To have witnessed the grave of Tutankhamun open once more—
What is it like to wear sweatshirts and bluejeans
And wait for hours to see the bracelets of those wasteful death-coddlers,
Who learned to conquer conscious life?
What is it like to have the dynamo, the lightbulb,
 the Parliamentary system,
 the electrical slaves embedded in
 elevator doors,
The body scanners that see sideways, the extravagant and elegant
 fighters,
And still be unconscious? What is that like?

Well, of course there is rage.
The thirty-four-year-old mother
Wants to reject the child still in the womb,
And she asks Senators to pass laws to prevent that.
The husband dreams of killing his wife, and the wife lays plots.
She imagines that he is an Oppressor,
And that she is an Aztec Princess.
In the night she holds an obsidian knife over her husband's sleeping
 body.
He dreams he is a deer being torn apart by female demons.

This is the rage that shouts at children.
This is the rage that cannot be satisfied,
Because each year more ancient Chinese art objects go on display.
So the rage goes inward at last,
It ends in doubt, in self-doubt, dyeing the hair, and love of celebrities.
The rage comes to rest at last in the talk show late at night,
When the celebrities without anger or grief tell us that only the
 famous are good, only they live well.
There are waifs inside us, broken by the Pauline gospels;
We know them,
And those who step on desire as a horse steps on a chick.

No cry comes out, only silence, and the faint whisper of the
 collapsing birdskull.

Here the sleepers sleep, here the Rams and the Bears play.
The old woman weeps at night in her room at the Nursing Facility.
There are no bridges over the ocean.
She sees a short dock, and ahead of that darkness, hostile waters,
 lifting swells,
Fitfully lit, or not lit at all.
Tadpoles drowse in the stagnant holes.
The gecko goes back to his home in the cold rain.

The wife of the Chrysler dealer is in danger of being committed again.
She left the hospital hopeful, she struggles hard,
She reads Laing and Rollo May;
But nothing works, she dreams she is interned in Burma.
Cars go past her house at night, Japanese soldiers at the wheel.
Nothing can be done, the kernel opens, all is swept away;
She is carried out of sight.
The doctor arrives; once more she leaves dry-eyed for the hospital.

I am twenty-eight again. I sleep curled up,
My fingers widen as I sleep, my toes grow immense at night.
Tears flow; I am in some bin apart from him I love.
The ocean king, far at sea, lies alone on his bed.
His interior engine has been catapulted into fragments,
Valves and drive shaft scattered, the engine mount settles to sand.
The saddened king goes about, all night he reaches down,
Picking up bolts from the sand, and piston rings; by morning all is
 scattered again.

We wake, no dream is remembered, the scenes gone into smoke.
We are in some enormous place, abandoned,
Where Adam Kadmon has been forgotten, the luminous man is
 dissolved.

The sarcophagus contains the rotted bones of the monks; so many
lived in the desert.
None are alive, only the bones lie in the dust.
My friend goes to Philadelphia to claim his father's body.
It lies in an uncarpeted room in the ghetto, there was no one else
to claim the body.
The time of manifest destiny is over, the time of grief has come.

IV

ST. GEORGE, THE DRAGON, AND THE VIRGIN

A SCULPTURE MADE BY BERNT NOTKE
IN 1489 FOR STOCKHOLM CATHEDRAL

St. George fights the dragon.
The spiny dragon,
Who lives in the rat-
Filled caves, is losing.
He fights back,
As when a child
Lifts his four
Feet to hold
Off the insane
Parent. The dragon
Hand grasps the wooden
Lance that has
Penetrated his thorny
Chest, but . . .
Too late . . .

And this girlish knight?
Oh I know him.
I read the New
Testament as I lay
Naked on my bed
As a boy.
That solar boy

Rises up radiant
With his forehead-
Eye that sees past
The criminals' gibbet
To the mindful
Towers of the spirit city.
I hate this boy
Whom I have been
Lifting his lance above
The father. Each of us
Has been this marsh
Dragon on his back.
He is Joseph, Grendel,
What we have forgotten,
The great spirit
The alchemists knew of,
Without whom is nothing.

As children, we knew ours
Was a muddy greatness.
How long it took
To break down that horse
So that he would agree
To abet the solar boy.
This earth-handed, disreputable,
Hoarse-voiced one
Is dying, all
Over the world.
And the Virgin?
She prays
On her knees while
This goes on,
As well she might.

I wrote this to bless
The swamp monster
And the marsh hag
Who bore him.

IVAR OAKESON'S FIDDLE

Let it be, let
It be. Let it be!
Portia awakes
In her sorrowing house;
The Orkney serpent
Lies close beside her,
Curls around her arm.

But the sorrowing fiddle
Has stayn awake all night.
The wooden-walled house
Is a resonating box.
The wood gourd that loves
The strings cries out
To those who love to dance.

Lovers and husbands
Whirl round and round.
Men and women
Sweat and shout, kick-
Ing and invit-
Ing their desire.
Oh, let it be.

QUESTION IN THE LOS GATOS HILLS

How often I have
Called to ponderable
Things: these
Eucalyptus-smelling
Sea-fogged
Hills
And chimney-hiding
Gorges;
I have called
Boulders to
Enter my poems,
Black dusty
Earth, rangy
Minnesota grass.
Why do I hesitate
Then to
Call to God?
Years ago I
Sat curled up
Behind a shed,
Saying to myself:
"You are a boy
Who will never
Be heard."
Forget that idea.
You are no
Longer a boy.
Let the sound come
Out of the mouth.
You hear the sitar
Cry, let the poem
Cry, even from
Behind the shed,
Where we all are.

HOW DAVID DID NOT CARE

What does it mean to live
As those before
Have lived? A field
Of boisterous men
And women who lift,
Shouting, singing,
And dancing a sheaf
Of wheat up to the sun.

When David danced for joy,
We guess he did not care.
When David played
The Song of Degrees
On his lute, when he cried,
"My bones call out
From the depths," then we know
He did not care.

For not to care is this:
To love the orphans
And the fatherless,
To dance as we sink
Into the badger's grief,
To let the resonating
Box of the body sound,
Not to ask to be loved.

HOW THE SAINT DID NOT CARE

When we start westward
In Spain, we wander
Through vast expanses;
Among harsh gulleys
We find Roman leg-
Bones, Carthaginian
Spearheads, the bitter
Cross that betrayed so many.

When men and women lifted
The saint's body onto
A wagon, it was a lilac
Bush moving through
The French fields, so that
The reapers paused:
The fragrance shows how much
He did not care.

Who is it that can break
The hold the Cross has on us—
No not the Cross, the wolf
That eats up our desire.
Those who do not care
Retrieve one instant of time.
They dive as the cormorant
Dives after living fish.

HOW JONAH DID NOT CARE

When have we had enough?
When we can turn our head,

Say no to the dog-headed,
Furry-nosed, anus-
Eyed beast of duty,
Give payback to God.
Friends, remember no one
Can see his own ears.

When Jonah sat
Shaded by the spindly
Leaves of a gourd,
Hot in the desert
Sand, he didn't care, nor
Did the worm who that night
Chewed the stalk
So that the gourd fell.

For not to care is this:
To love the sunlight,
As it falls on the table,
To leap out of misery
Once or twice
Like a great fish
Before falling
Back into the ocean.

THE DARK EGG

A man bends over the gunwales,
Gazes into the sea
Hour after hour, sees
A lion rising upward.
If he looks to the sky, he sees
A dark egg perfectly

Visible in the Crow's
Stickly nest.

When the Terrible Nurse
Took Vincentine by the
Waist, and threw her
Into the ocean, a whale
Poured her into
His copious throat,
And there she lived
Without husband or children.

What does it matter,
Suffering or not! Bad
Parents, or good
Parents, luck or none—
Let us agree to climb
The trunk of the Crow's tree,
And steal the Black
Egg from his nest!

HOW MIRABAI DID NOT CARE

My mother gave me body,
My father a black
Overcoat for the soul.
Now it is time to
Love the third power,
The black sun that shines
On bones and leaves
From beneath the earth.

Mirabai, night after night,
Let herself down castle
Walls on saris to visit
Her low-born teacher.
When she washed his old
Feet and drank the water,
Any idiot would know
She did not care.

Glimpsing the grave ahead,
The body leaps up,
Cries, "What if death
Comes, what if it all ends!"
Let it end—let the sand
And the ocean part,
Let it be, let
Heaven and earth go their ways.

TIME RUNS BACKWARD AFTER DEATH

1

Samson, grinding bread for widows and orphans,
Forgets he is wronged, and the answers
The Philistines wrangled out of him go back
Into the lion. The bitter and the sweet marry.
He himself wronged the lion. Now the wheat
Caresses the wind with its wifely tail; the donkey
Runs in the long grass; and having glimpsed heaven,
The fox's body saunters the tawny earth.

2

After death the soul returns to drinking milk
And honey in its sparse home. Broken lintels

Rejoin the sunrise gates, and bees sing
In the sour meat. Once more in the cradle his
Hair grows long and golden; Delilah's scissors
Turn back into two tiny and playful swords.
Samson, no longer haunted by sunset and shadows,
Sinks down in the Eastern ocean and is born.

MORNING

POEMS

(1997)

I

EARLY MORNING IN YOUR ROOM

It's morning. The brown scoops of coffee, the wasplike
Coffee grinder, the neighbors still asleep.
The gray light as you pour gleaming water—
It seems you've traveled years to get here.

Finally you deserve a house. If not deserve
It, have it; no one can get you out. Misery
Had its way, poverty, no money at least.
Or maybe it was confusion. But that's over.

Now you have a room. Those light-hearted books:
The Anatomy of Melancholy, Kafka's *Letter
To His Father*, are all here. You can dance
With only one leg, and see the snowflake falling

With only one eye. Even the blind man
Can see. That's what they say. If you had
A sad childhood, so what? When Robert Burton
Said he was melancholy, he meant he was home.

THE SHOCKS WE PUT OUR PITCHFORKS INTO

The shocks said that winter
Was coming. Each stood there,
Said, "I've given myself away.
Take me. It's over."

And we did. With the shiny tips
Of our forks, their handles so
Healthy and elegant,
We slipped each bundle free,

Gave it to the load.
Each bundle was like
A soul, tucked back
Into the cloud of souls.

That's how it will be
After death—such an abundance
Of souls, all together—
None tired, in the heavy wagon.

WHY WE DON'T DIE

In late September many voices
Tell you you will die.
That leaf says it. That coolness.
All of them are right.

Our many souls—what
Can they do about it?
Nothing. They're already
Part of the invisible.

Our souls have been
Longing to go home
Anyway. "It's late," they say.
"Lock the door, let's go."

The body doesn't agree. It says,
"We buried a little iron
Ball under that tree.
Let's go get it."

HAWTHORNE AND THE ELEPHANT

Hawthorne's walking stick—very short—lay
Under glass at the Customs House. On the wharf,
A crab shell, emptied by a gull, lies alone.
His walking sticks lie near . . . but the crab is gone,
Like Hawthorne. Bedrooms were low;
You were taxed for high ceilings in those days.
Ships brought licorice and peppers. Hawthorne's father
Died of a fever off the coast of Sumatra,
Guides say, and *America*, his ship, brought
The first elephant here in 1794.
Water got short on the way; to save the elephant
They gave her thirty bottles of beer a day.
She—Bette—died in Maine, an alcoholic.
How alert we were at the House of Seven Gables!
Clifford's room is the little one up the secret stairs.

THE OLD WOMAN FRYING PERCH

For Donald Hall

Have you heard about the boy who walked by
The black water? I won't say much more.
Let's wait a few years. It wanted to be entered.
Sometimes a man walks by a pond, and a hand
Reaches out and pulls him in.
 There was no
Malice, exactly. The pond was lonely, or needed
Calcium. Bones would do. What happened then?

It was a little like the night wind, which is soft,
And moves slowly, sighing like an old woman
In her kitchen late at night, moving pans
About, lighting a fire, frying some perch for the cat.

CONVERSATION WITH THE SOUL

The soul said, "Give me something to look at."
So I gave her a farm. She said,
"It's too large." So I gave her a field.
The two of us sat down.

Sometimes I would fall in love with a lake
Or a pinecone. But I liked her
Most. She knew it.
"Keep writing," she said.

So I did. Each time the new snow fell,
We would be married again.
The holy dead sat down by our bed.
This went on for years.

"This field is getting too small," she said.
"Don't you know anyone else
To fall in love with?"
What would you have said to Her?

HE WANTED TO LIVE HIS LIFE OVER

What? You want to live your life over again?
"Well, I suppose, yes . . . That time in Grand Rapids . . .
My life—as I lived it—was a series of shynesses."

Being bolder—what good would that do?
"I'd open my door again. I've felt abashed,
You see. Now I'd go out and say, 'All right,

I'll go with you to Alaska.' Just opening the door
From inside would have altered me—a little.
I'm too shy . . ." *And so, a bolder life*

Is what you want? "We could begin now.
Just walk with me—down to the river.
I'll pretend this boat is my life . . . I'll climb in."

THE GLIMPSE OF SOMETHING IN THE OVEN

Childhood is like a kitchen. It is dangerous
To the mice, but the husband gets fed; he's
An old giant, grumbling and smelling children.
The kitchen is a place where you get smaller

And smaller, or you lose track. In general
You become preoccupied with this old lady
In the kitchen. . . . She putters about, opens oven doors.
The thing is the old woman won't *discuss* anything.

The giant will. He's always been a fan of Aristotle,
Knew him at school. It is no surprise to him
That the Trojan War lasted ten years, or how it
Ended. He knows something you don't.

Your sister says, "Say, what's that in the oven?"

BAD PEOPLE

A man told me once that all the bad people
Were needed. Maybe not all, but your fingernails
You need; they are really claws, and we know
Claws. The sharks—what about them?
They make other fish swim faster. The hard-faced men
In black coats who chase you for hours
In dreams—that's the only way to get you
To the shore. Sometimes those hard women
Who abandon you get you to say, "You."
A lazy part of us is like a tumbleweed.
It doesn't move on its own. Sometimes it takes
A lot of Depression to get tumbleweeds moving.
Then they blow across three or four States.
This man told me that things work together.
Bad handwriting sometimes leads to new ideas;
And a careless god—who refuses to let people
Eat from the Tree of Knowledge—can lead
To books, and eventually to us. We write
Poems with lies in them, but they help a little.

THINGS TO THINK

Think in ways you've never thought before.
If the phone rings, think of it as carrying a message
Larger than anything you've ever heard,
Vaster than a hundred lines of Yeats.

Think that someone may bring a bear to your door,
Maybe wounded and deranged; or think that a moose
Has risen out of the lake, and he's carrying on his antlers
A child of your own whom you've never seen.

When someone knocks on the door, think that he's about
To give you something large: tell you you're forgiven,
Or that it's not necessary to work all the time, or that it's
Been decided that if you lie down no one will die.

TWO WAYS TO WRITE POEMS

"I am who I am." I wonder what one has to pay
To say that. I couldn't do it. For years
I thought, "You are who you are." But maybe
You weren't. Maybe you were someone else.

Sam's friend, who loved poetry, played football
In school even though he didn't want to.
He got hit. Later he said to me, "I write poems.
I am who I am . . . but my neck hurts."

How many times I have begun a poem
Before I knew what the main sounds
Would be. We find out. Toward the end
The poem is just beginning to be who it is.

That's all right, but there's another way as well.
One picks the rhyme words, and so the main
Sounds, before one begins. I wonder what
Yeats had to pay in order to do that.

THE BARN AT ELABUGA

What is it like to "get killed"? Getting killed
Happens during a war a lot to horses and people.
This time there's no long struggle in the bedroom,
No hoarse cries and confessions after which the clock
Stops, and the priest needs some coffee in the kitchen.
Just being killed leaves you small and unattached.
The boy aiming the mortar makes a mistake
And horses crazed by the noise kill your father
While he is feeding geese. Those times our family
Died that way hasn't left any mark on us.
But I could ask why my thumb keeps moving
Around my forefinger when I read, or why that line
Comes down from my mouth. We do know that people
At the end of a war tend to hang themselves
In the nearest barn, without telling anyone.

THE RUSSIAN

"The Russians had few doctors on the front line.
My father's job was this: after the battle
Was over, he'd walk among the men hit,
Sit down and ask: 'Would you like to die on your
Own in a few hours, or should I finish it?'

Most said, 'Don't leave me.' The two would have
A cigarette. He'd take out his small notebook—
We had no dogtags, you know—and write the man's
Name down, his wife's, his children, his address, and what
He wanted to say. When the cigarette was done,
The soldier would turn his head to the side. My father
Finished off four hundred men that way during the war.
He never went crazy. They were his people.

He came to Toronto. My father in the summers
Would stand on the lawn with a hose, watering
The grass that way. It took a long time. He'd talk
To the moon, to the wind. 'I can hear you growing'—
He'd say to the grass. 'We come and go.
We're no different from each other. We are all
Part of something. We have a home.' When I was thirteen,
I said, 'Dad, do you know they've invented sprinklers
Now?' He went on watering the grass.
'This is my life. Just shut up if you don't understand it.'"

II

SOME MEN FIND IT HARD TO FINISH SENTENCES

Sometimes a man can't say
What he . . . A wind comes
And his doors don't rattle. Rain
Comes and his hair is dry.

"There's a lot to keep inside
And a lot to . . ." "Sometimes shame
Means we . . ." Children are cruel.
"He's six and his hands . . ."

Even Hamlet kept passing
The King praying
And the King said,
"There was something . . ."

VISITING THE EIGHTY-FIVE-YEAR-OLD POET

The eighty-five-year-old man stands up,
And walks to the bookcase, his hair tousled,
His legs thin, to fetch a book, then pulls
It down and says, "No doubt you've already read this?"

He has. He paddles among these ice floes,
These enormous fat books, like a great Eskimo
Hunter, for there are seals below in the sea,
Offering their hides, their fat, their great lonesome eyes.

"*Oh* yes!" he says, "*Oh* yes." Some truths have been
Said. Someone in China or Hardanger has written great
Poems. "*Oh* yes." He stands again, goes to the wall.
"Emerson was a *keen* reader. *Oh* yes!"

He has lived his whole life on three acres
Of apple trees, chopping wood, visiting
The madhouse, throwing plates against the wall,
Translating, packing apples, writing poems.

I am proud to know him, this old man late in life
Who stands up and says, "No doubt you've already lived this?"

For the Norwegian poet Olav H. Hauge

ALL THESE STORIES

There are so many stories. In one, a bear
Marries a sailing ship, and they have children
Who are islands (covered with low brush).
In another an obstinate woman floats upstream.

Or the child wailing on a rock, set ashore
By her seal mother (her real mother), waits
And wails, and faces appear at windows until
Charlotte Brontë agrees to begin her novel.

You know stories like that. The Terrible Nurse
Throws the Daughter into the sea. A whale
Swallows her, and she is free from husband
And children long enough to be herself.

Something in us wants things to happen.
We twist our ankle and end up reading Gibbon.
In some dreams a wolf pursues us until we
Turn into swallows, and agree to live in longing.

THE RESEMBLANCE BETWEEN YOUR LIFE AND A DOG

I never intended to have this life, believe me—
It just happened. You know how dogs turn up
At a farm, and they wag but can't explain.

It's good if you can accept your life—you'll notice
Your face has become deranged trying to adjust
To it. Your face thought your life would look

Like your bedroom mirror when you were ten.
That was a clear river touched by mountain wind.
Even your parents can't believe how much you've changed.

Sparrows in winter, if you've ever held one, all feathers,
Burst out of your hand with a fiery glee.
You see them later in hedges. Teachers praise you,

But you can't quite get back to the winter sparrow.
Your life is a dog. He's been hungry for miles,
Doesn't particularly like you, but gives up, and comes in.

READING IN A BOAT

I was glad to be in that boat, floating
Under oak leaves that had been
Carved by crafty light.

How many times during the night
I laughed, because She
Came near, and stayed, or returned.

The boat stopped, and I woke.
But the pages kept turning. I jumped
Back in the book, and caught up.

I was not in pain, not hungry,
Friend, I was alive, sleeping,
And all that time reading a book.

WAKING ON THE FARM

I can remember the early mornings—how the stubble,
A little proud with frost, snapped as we walked.

How the John Deere tractor hood pulled heat
Away from our hands when we filled it with gas.

And the way the sun brought light right out of the ground.
It turned on a whole hill of stubble as easily as a single stone.

Breathing seemed frail and daring in the morning.
To pull in air was like reading a whole novel.

———

The angleworms, turned up by the plow, looked
Uneasy like shy people trying to avoid praise.

For a while we had goats. They were like turkeys
Only more reckless. One butted a red Chevrolet.

When we washed up at noon, we were more ordinary.
But the water kept something in it of the early morning.

WHEN THRESHING TIME ENDS

There is a time. Things end.
All the fields are clean.
Belts are put away.
And the horses go home.

What is left endures
In the minds of boys
Who wanted this joy
Never to end.

The splashing of hands,
Jokes and oats:
It was a music
Touching and fervent.

The Bible was right.
Presences come and go.
Wash in cold water.
The fire has moved.

A FAMILY PHOTOGRAPH, SUNDAY MORNING, 1940

They've gathered on the farm lawn, ten people, all ages.
Esther Berg's hair has waves like Clara Bow's;
The women look as if they have too much to do.
One boy smiles—it is me—and looks down. He seems glad,
But his sweater sleeve is too short. The men's hands,
None placed in pockets, all hang down.
They look as if they wanted to grasp something.
The men smile, but their eyes say hard things.
"The world pulls at me—it tore my father
Away already. That forty-acre farm he bought
By Marietta is still black. I have to go now."
It was nineteen-forty, grasshoppers, hard times.
Two old women who guard the group on both sides
Take nothing on trust. "I trust my hands, and that's all."

A FARM IN WESTERN MINNESOTA

When I look at childhood, I see the yellow rose bush
Grandma planted near her door, the gravel
Beneath the bicycle tires, and the new legs pumping
As we raced along; and the roads that invited us
West—only a mile from home the land began to rise.

We tried those wind chargers. My father
Was open to any new idea, and one day
A thousand sheep—starving—arrived in cattle cars
From Montana—almost free. We took four
Hundred. How thin they were! Some lived for years.

Many rooms were cold at night, and the hired men
Didn't have much of a life. Sometimes they'd just leave.
I remember my father throwing dead ewes over
The edge of the gravel pit. It was efficient. There
Was work to do, but no one learned how to say goodbye.

FOR A CHILDHOOD FRIEND, MARIE

She knew a lot about life on a farm: wagon
Poles that sometimes broke, and grown men
Pinned against the fencepost by a bull.
Sometimes you tie a favorite lamb
To a tree so that the old bucks will not kill him,
And he hangs himself from the rope.
Movies Saturday night—girls laughed
Behind their sleeves, at men or boys.
Marie, thirty years old, still loved
The high school, the tall boys, gossip
About the teachers, the proms. She also
Loved our lives that were not going
So well. She married the hired man—
My grandmother told her not to—and he drank.

WHAT THE ANIMALS PAID

The Hampshire ewes standing in their wooden pens,
Their shiny black hooves close to each other,

Had to pay with their wool, with their wombs,
With their eating, with their fear of the dogs.

Every animal had to pay. Horses paid all day;
They pulled stone-boats and the ground pulled back.

And the pigs? They paid with their squealing
When the knife entered the throat and the blood

Followed it out. The blood, steaming and personal,
Paid it. Any debt left over the intestines paid.

"I am what I am." The pig could not say that.
The women paid with their bowed heads, and the men,

My father among them, paid with their drinking.
Demons shouted: "Pay to the last drop!"

THE BEAR AND THE MAN

Suppose there were a bear and a man. The bear
Knows his kin—old pebbles, fifty-five-
Gallon barrels, big pine trees in the moonlight,
Abandoned down jackets; and the man approaches warily—

He's read Tolstoy, knows a few symphonies.
That's about it. Each has lost a son. The bear's
killed by a trap, the man's killed by a bear.
That boy was partly drunk, alone in the woods.

The bear puts out black claws firmly on earth.
He's not dumb. Skinned, he's like a man. People
Say that both bears and men receive a signal
Coming from far up there, near the North Pole.

WHEN MY DEAD FATHER CALLED

Last night I dreamt my father called to us.
He was stuck somewhere. It took us
A long time to dress, I don't know why.
The night was snowy; there were long black roads.

Finally, we reached the little town, Bellingham.
There he stood, by a streetlamp in cold wind,
Snow blowing along the sidewalk. I noticed
The uneven sort of shoes that men wore

In the early Forties. And overalls. He was smoking.
Why did it take us so long to get going? Perhaps
He left us somewhere once, or did I simply
Forget he was alone in winter in some town?

III

THE GREEN COOKSTOVE

A lonely man once sat on a large flat stone.
When he lifted it, he saw a kitchen: a green
Enamel range with big claw feet, familiar.
Someone lives in that room, cooking and cackling.

"I saw her once," Virgil said. "She and Helen
Were sisters." Menelaus
Sits by the window, peeling garlic cloves,
And throwing bread crusts to the chickens.

We'll never understand this. Somewhere below
The flat stone of the skull, a carnivorous couple
Lives and plans future wars. Are we innocent?
These wars don't happen by accident—they occur

Too regularly. How often do we lift the plate
At the bottom of our brain and throw some garlic
And grain down to the kitchen? "Keep cooking,
My dears," we say. "Something good will come of this."

THE PLAYFUL DEEDS OF THE WIND

Sometimes there's the wind. Sometimes the wind
Takes a certain scrap of paper, and blows
It back into the Bible. Then your family line
Is whole, and your great-great-grandparents
Stretch out in the coffin, and rest. That's something
Wind can do. Sometimes wind blows
A skirt up an inch or two, and the body
Signs a contract for its novel; then babies
Come, and people sit at breakfast, and the old
Words get spoken. Or the wind blows an ash
Into the anarchist's eye, and he pulls
The trigger too soon, and kills the King instead of
The fat factory owner, and then
A lot of men get on motorcycles. They
Dig trenches, and the wind blows the gas
Here and there, and you and I get nothing
Out of that wind except blind uncles
And a boy at the table who can't say "Please."

IT IS SO EASY TO GIVE IN

I have been thinking about the man who gives in.
Have you heard about him? In his story
A twenty-eight-foot pine meets a small wind
And the pine bends all the way over to the ground.

"I was persuaded," the pine says. "It was convincing."
A mouse visits a cat, and the cat agrees
To drown all her children. "What could I do?"
The cat said. "The mouse *needed* that."

It's strange. I've heard that some people conspire
In their own ruin. A fool says, "You don't
Deserve to live." The man says, "I'll string this rope
Over that branch, maybe you can find a box."

The Great One with her necklace of skulls says,
"I need twenty thousand corpses." "Tell you what,"
The General says, "we have an extra battalion
Over there on the hill. We don't need all these men."

WANTING MORE APPLAUSE AT A CONFERENCE

It's something about envy. I won't say I'm envious,
But I did have certain moods when I was two.
Now of course I can't remember any of that.
I'm happy if another receives some praise or attention

That's really mine. I talk, and the man next to me
Talks, and he gets the applause. Or I am confused
And she makes sense. This is hard to bear.
I bear it, but it causes trouble inside the den.

Is it a mammal problem then? Six teats are palpable
Far inside the wiry fur, and I want more
Than one? Is that it? It is, but such greed
Is mainly a problem for small mammals,

And I am no longer small. Let's call it a mood
When we can't remember. Let's call it a habit
Of opening the mouth when we, who have
Much, want more, even what belongs to the poor.

CALLING YOUR FATHER

There was a boy who never got enough.
You know what I mean. Something
In him longed to find the big
Mother, and he leaped into the sea.

It took a while, but a whale
Agreed to swallow him.
He knew it was wrong, but once
Past the baleen, it was too late.

It's OK. There's a curved library
Inside, and those high
Ladders. People take requests.
It's like the British Museum.

One needs a fire to get out.
Maybe it was the romance
Novels he burned. Smoke curls
Up the whale's gorge. She coughs.

And that's it. The boy swims to shore;
It's a fishing town in Alaska.
He calls his father. "I'm here.
Let me tell you a story."

THINKING ABOUT OLD JOBS

Well, let's say this morning is all of life there is—
Let's suppose the weather (rainy), the room
(Creamy-walled), the bed (soft), your cells (calm,
Excitable and dense) are it. Don't expect more.

Then what? Does it matter how you chose
To live at twenty? You felt detached, let's say,
So you blew your legs and arms off.
Why feel bad? It helped in some ways.

You had more solitude, because friends avoid stumps.
Of course you had to live. You started picking
Other people's cucumbers with your teeth,
As you lay flat on a board. Don't be ashamed.

It was a deal. It worked. The boss's children
Later sent you back the canceled contract.
Then remember the job you had lying about
Your health to life insurance companies?

Or performing as a Santa in Depression wards?
All those jobs were all right. But that time is over.
Am I content? I am. But we don't
Have to live in the way we did then: Let's talk.

CONVERSATION WITH A MONSTER

A man I knew could never say who he was.
You know people like that. When he met a monster,
He'd encourage the monster to talk about eating
But failed to say that he objected to being prey.

A day goes by; a week; a month; it's summer.
The adolescent wolverines go out scouting;
Crabs lift their claws; the praying mantises
Get religious. This man keeps trying to adapt.

Adopt? Be adopted? It's funny, but those born
From eggs seem not to feel homeless. Something
Pushes them out, and they fly to sea, or swim
Up from the gravel, milkily transparent, and they're gone.

This man went up to monsters and asked to be
Adopted. I've done that often. Reader, are you
Fond of the Jonah story? Say to a monster,
"I may have something for you, but I can't promise."

THE BLACK FIGURE BELOW THE BOAT

We hear phrases: "He made me do it."
"I never wanted that." The boy's boat gets
Pushed out on the sea, and before long the tidal
Currents guide it from beneath. He goes to sleep.

Then he meets a woman, and marries her even though
He doesn't want to. He says, "It was the current."
But some tiny black figure swims below the boat,
Pushing it. This man or god works all night.

Then what? Months go by, years, twenty years.
A lot of water. The boat hits gravel.
It's an island—the kind where giants live.
"Don't say you didn't want it. Just get ready."

THE MAN WHO DIDN'T KNOW WHAT WAS HIS

There was a man who didn't know what was his.
He thought as a boy that some demon forced him
To wear "his" clothes and live in "his" room
And sit on "his" chair and be a child of "his" parents.

Each time he sat down to dinner, it happened again.
His own birthday party belonged to someone else.
And—was it sweet potatoes that he liked?—
He should resist them. Whose plate is this?

This man will be like a lean-to attached
To a house. It doesn't *have* a foundation.
This man is helpful and hostile in each moment.
This man leans toward you and leans away.

Maybe you've met this man who doesn't know what is his.

THE MOUSE

It's good to have poems
That begin with tea,
And end with God.

A man is drinking tea,
Let's say, and a mouse
Runs across the floor.

It makes him think
Of all hidden things.
A mouse is a furry

Cruelty with paws.
It's a secret with ears,
A shame the man

Thought he could tell
No one of, a shame
That searches quietly

For kernels of grain
Below that awful
Cat of Augustine.

THE STORM

A sadness comes when we think back.
The car says, "I will bring you home."
Confusion says, "Is it all clear?"
The driver says, "A storm is coming."

The car was still warming up
When the storm came. Like all storms,
It lacked subtlety and obeyed
Something or someone irresistible.

The people stood looking out at the car.
There wasn't room for everyone.
Someone would be left behind
In the cold house. Human longing

Says, "I know there's a better place."
The car says, "Let's stop talking and go."
Confusion says that we're quite clear about it.
And the storm says, "Here I come."

THE YELLOW DOT

In memory of Jane Kenyon

God does what she wants. She has very large
Tractors. She lives at night in the sewing room
Doing stitchery. Then chunks of land at mid-
Sea disappear. The husband knows that his wife
Is still breathing. God has arranged the open
Grave. That grave is not what we want,
But to God it's a tiny hole, and he has
The needle, draws thread through it, and soon
A nice pattern appears. The husband cries,
"Don't let her die!" But God says, "I
Need a yellow dot here, near the mailbox."

I V

IT'S AS IF SOMEONE ELSE IS WITH ME

1

It's as if someone else is here with me, here in this room
In which I lie. The longing the ear feels for sound
Has given me the sweetness that I confuse with Her.

The joy of being alone, eating the honey of words.
The white-walled room, and Stevens, and the sun.
This is the joy of the soul that has preserved
Itself despite fleas and soap in the light-hearted sun.

One is not alone when one is alone, if She
Is here. It is a She that no one loves, a She
That one loves when one loves what one does love.

2

November is gone, bare trees, winter.
At nightfall the lonely streets fill with
Ice and cars. Loneliness fills my chest,
As if I walked all night by the North Sea.

I am here, somewhere near the edge of life,
A warm room, lamps, some poems I love—
To nudge a poem along toward its beauty—
Is that selfishness? Is it something silly?

Do others love doing this? Longing
To find her in a phrase, and be close
There, kissing the walls and the doorframe.
Happy in the change of a single word.

3

A lamp pours light into the room, and it's your
Room, and you write poems there. You never
Tire of the curving lines, and the freedom of the sounds,
And the demons peering around the molding.

The beauty that six or seven words can bring
Together makes the whole brain sing.
And I feel like a single-souled cook in the Middle
Ages praising God in the kitchen pans.

But our praise is more like humming of bees.
What if a beehive were run this way? Who would
Eat up all the honey? Don't worry about it.
The workers say, "I'll fly out and be religious."

4

It's morning and it's calm. And the man
Writes along, inviting this detail
And that—looking toward some playful life.
What life? Oh never mind—the life of language.

And thinking. Longing waves one arm,
And the woman inside us looks out
From her eternal indolences, feeding
The hummingbirds with her flowery thoughts.

I lie here with a cover and coffee and a pen,
Feeling delight in being a child of language,

Neither man nor woman exactly, but a young monk
In a skin boat, bobbing among the seals of sound.

5

I've been thinking about these little adventures
In morning longing—these embarkations,
Excursions in round hideboats on the sea,
Passing over the beings far below.

The deep vowels—perhaps whales—mourn
And sing at their stone table five miles down
On the ocean floor. They mourn some loss.
But the small finny sounds, the *er*s and *in*s

And *or*s and *ing*s, mourn as well—we don't
Know what. Perhaps vowels were all created
In a moment of sorrow before creation—
A grief they've not been able to sing in this life.

6

It's good to remain in bed a while, and listen
For the *ay* slyly hidden in sequacious,
And scent in summer world the two *er*s.
I especially love the *in* hidden in woodbins.

Am I like the hog snuffling for truffles,
Followed by skimpy lords in oversized furs?
For this gaiety do I need forgiveness?
Does the lark need forgiveness for its blue eggs?

So it's a bird-like thing then, this hiding
And warming of sounds. They are the little low
Heavens in the nest; now my chest feathers
Widen, now I'm an old hen, now I am satisfied.

7

The world is its usual rich self. Disturbed news
Came before sleep, then hours below light, finally
A return to coffee and the joy of unfinished poems.
It is early October, bright leaves falling everywhere.

What could it mean that such sharp leaves fall?
Does it imply that the best are called first?
Do we long to think that when a baby
Dies early it nevertheless blesses the stars?

I don't want to imply such abundance of meaning
Exists in me. A lamppost shines over
The ocean. The waves take what they want of the light.
The rest they give back, to the hospitals and the poor.

8

The dawn comes. Leaves feel it's time
To say something, and I feel myself drawn
To You. I know this is wrong.

To be drawn to You can cause trouble,
I do so against all advice, from that one
In me who saved me by keeping me alone.

I've lived in so many houses, where
You were not. If You became a dock
I became a boat and pushed away.

Those who are drawn to You become land
If You are land, or water if You are water.
I want nothing from You but to see You.

A WEEK OF POEMS AT BENNINGTON

SUNDAY
THE DOG'S EARS

A little snow. Coffee. The bowled-over branches,
The wind; it is cold outdoors; but in the bed
It's warm, in the early lamplight, reading poems.

These fingers, so rosy, so alive, move about
This book. Here is my wide-traveling palm,
The thumb that looks like my father's, the wedding ring.

It's time to prepare myself, as a friend suggested,
"Not to be here." It will happen. People will say,
"That day the dish lay empty on the brown table.

"The gold knob shone alone in the dark.
The light came in, and no eyes received it,
And bits of ice hung on the dog's ears."

MONDAY
WHEN THE CAT STOLE THE MILK

Well there it is. There's nothing to do.
The cat steals the milk and it's gone.
Then the cat steals you, and you're found
Days later, with milk on your face.

That implies that you become whoever
Steals you. The trees steal a man,
And an old birch becomes his wife
And they live together in the woods.

Some of us have always wanted
God to steal us. Then our friends
Would call each other, and print
Posters, and we would never be found.

BEING HAPPY ALL NIGHT

It's as if the mice stayed warm inside the snow,
As if my cells heard laughing from the Roman vineyards.
Mice slept despite the cruel songs of the stars.
We laughed and woke and sniffed and slept again.

Some people inside my body last night
Married each other just in order to dance.
And Sara Grethe smiled so proudly the men
Kicked their heels on the planks, but kept the beat.

Oh I think it was the books I read long ago.
It's as if I joined other readers on a long road.
We found dead men hanging in a meadow.
We took dew from the grass and washed our eyes.

For S. B.

THE WIDOWED FRIEND

I hear rustlings from the next room; and he is ready
To leave. "See you tomorrow." A long line
Of feeling follows him out the door. He carries
On his shoulders—which slope a little—a divorce,

Prosody, marital love as pertinacious
As a bulldog's mouth, a grandfather, grand-
Mother. Land and death weigh him down, so he
Becomes a large man on a thin bridge walking.

If, now, he lives alone, who will hear
The thin cough in the morning, who will hear
The milk hitting the pail when the old man sings?
Who will notice the forty drafts on yellow paper?

It's up to us to see him, call him, and say,
"Stay, friend, be with us, tell me what happened."

For D. H.

THURSDAY

WE ONLY SAY THAT

"There are so many things to love around here."
We only say that when we want to hint
Something—the day after we notice a woman,
Who waves a hand with her female bravery.

We say, "The icicles are really brilliant today!"
Or, "Let's make fun of other people."
That would bring us closer. Or "Martha brought
Her dog out into the morning snow."

Her hand reaches up to brush her neck,
Or she puts on her boots. A voice inside us
Says, "Oh a woman! Let's close the door.
Let's flirt and not flirt. Let's play cards and laugh."

FRIDAY

WOUNDING OTHERS

Well I do it, and it's done.
And it can't be taken back.
There's a wound in my chest
Where I wounded others.

But it will knit, or heal, in time.
That's what you say.
And some that I wounded
Claim: "I am the better for it."

Was it truth-telling or
A thin man with a knife?
The wound will close, or heal
In time. That's what you say.

SATURDAY

WHAT THE BUTTOCKS THINK

Don't tell me that nothing can be done.
The tongue says, "I know I can change things."
The toe says, "I have my ways."
The heart is weeping and remembering Eden.

Legs think that a good run will do it.
Tongue has free tickets; he'll fly to heaven.
But the buttocks see everything upside down:
They want you to put your head down there,

Remind the heart it was upside down
In the womb, so that when your mother,
Knowing exactly where she was going,
Walked upstairs, you weren't going anywhere.

WHAT BILL STAFFORD WAS LIKE

With small steps he climbed very high mountains
And offered distinctions to persuasive storms,
Delicacies at the edge of something larger,
A comfort in walking on ground close to water.

Something large, but it wasn't an animal snorting
In a cave, more like the rustling of a thousand
Small-winged birds, all together, comfortable,
In a field, feeding. One felt at home nearby.

There are many possible ways to see the world
(To whom we should be fair). When someone
Spoke, his face thought, and his eyebrow
Said it. The words weren't always comforting,

But calculated to nudge us along to that place
—Just over there—where we would be safe for the night.

A POEM IS SOME REMEMBERING

It's morning; there's lamplight, and the room is still.
All night as we slept, memory flowed
Onto the brain shore. Memories rise and fall
And leave behind a delicate openness to death,

Almost a longing to die. That longing
Is like rain on canyon ground, only droplets.
And the brain is like brown sand, it stretches
On and on, and it absorbs the rain.

What is a poem? "Oh it is some remembering,"
A woman said to me. "Thousands of years ago,
When I stood by a grave, a woman handed
Me a small bone made red with ochre.

"It was a poem about heaven, and I wept so."

RETHINKING WALLACE STEVENS

What can I say? You have this funny
Idea that the gods are dead.

You were so rash. I'd *play* saying
The gods have died, but I'd never *say* it.

If they're gone, only Imagination
Can replace them. That's you.

We'll have to come to you, where
You stand in your Hartford garden,

Looking and lolling and longing
Like a girl in a white dress.

TASTING HEAVEN

Some people say that every poem should have
God in it somewhere. But of course Wallace Stevens
Wasn't one of those. We live, he said, "in a world
Without heaven to follow." Shall we agree

That we taste heaven only once, when we see
Her at fifteen walking among falling leaves?
It's possible. And yet as Stevens lay dying
He invited the priest in. There, I've said it.

The priest is not an argument, only an instance.
But our gusty emotions say to me that we have
Tasted heaven many times: these delicacies
Are left over from some larger party.

URTH GRADE

—Wallace Stevens

In the fourth grade he sat on his school bench
Daydreaming. He was already admiring his voice
That he hadn't found. And later on the lawn

He spent hours standing at the edge of Hartford
Looking at the moon. That is where his voice was,
Far up there, in air, near the rounded moon.

He knew the moon was made of clogged magma,
And volcanic rinsings, and punk and dog poop.
That was all right. That was better. It was more

Like us. The rogue moon couldn't hold God
Any longer; we'll have to make do with waltzes,
And Florida and those prancing white horses.

There is no Divine; there are only Viennese horses,
And ordinary evenings and houses. Things have changed.
The boy on the bench can become in poems a god.

THE WALTZ

One man I know keeps saying that we don't need
Heaven. He thinks embroidered Russian
Wedding blouses will take the place of angels,
Or windy nights when the crows fly up in front
Of your car will replace all the Psalmists.

He wants us to dance high-hearted, like the Bacchae,
Even if it's a waltz. It's a little awkward;
But if you practice, he says, you can do it.
The hard thing is to try to figure out how
To say goodbye—even just going to the grocery.

V

THE NEURONS WHO WATCH BIRDS

We have to think now what it would be like
To be old. Some funny little neurons,
Developed for high-speed runners, and quick-
Handed bowmen, begin to get tired. They fire

But then lay down their bows and watch birds.
The kidney cells—"Too much thinking!" the Chinese
Say—look around for help, but the kids have
All gone to the city. Your friends get hit by lightning,

And your enemies live on. This isn't going to get
Better. Crows yelling from the telephone wires
Don't include you in the stories they tell, and they seem
To remember some story that you haven't heard.

What can you do? We'll have to round up
All those little people wandering about
In the body, get them to sit up straight, and study
This problem: How *do* we die?

A QUESTION THE BUNDLE HAD

When summer was nearly over,
The bundles would stand in the stubble
Whispering. One said: "For a while,
It looked like I might get away.

"I could have done it—
No one would have noticed.
But it was hard to know
If I should go singly, or with others."

Each of us resembles that
Bundle. For years we waited
For the right moment to escape.
Perhaps it was that moment in July

When the thunder came. But the next
Day it was too late. And we
Ended up in the thresher.
Were we right to wait?

SEEING THE ECLIPSE IN MAINE

It started about noon. On top of Mount Batte,
We were all exclaiming. Someone had a cardboard
And a pin, and we all cried out when the sun
Appeared in tiny form on the notebook cover.

It was hard to believe. The high school teacher
We'd met called it a camera obscura,
People in the Renaissance loved to make them.
Later, when only a sliver was left of the sun,

Light passing through the branches of a fir
Made dozens of crescents all by itself,
Thousands! Even our straw hats produced a few
As we moved them over the bare granite.

We shared chocolate, and one man from Maine
Told a joke. Suns were everywhere at our feet.

CLOTHESPINS

I'd like to have spent my life making
Clothespins. Nothing would be harmed,
Except some pines, probably on land
I owned and would replant. I'd see
My work on clotheslines near some lake,
Up north on a day in October,
Perhaps twelve clothespins, the pine
Still fresh, and the fall wind blowing.

THE FACE IN THE TOYOTA

Suppose you see a face in a Toyota
One day, and you fall in love with that face,
And it is Her, and the world rushes by
Like dust blown down a Montana street.

And you fall upward into some deep hole,
And you can't tell God from a grain of sand.
And your life is changed, except that now you
Overlook even more than you did before;

And these ignored things come to bury you,
And you are crushed, and your parents
Can't help anymore, and the woman in the Toyota
Becomes a part of the world that you don't see.

And now the grain of sand becomes sand again,
And you stand on some mountain road weeping.

THE SCANDAL

The day the minister ran off with the choir director
The bindlestiffs felt some gaiety in their arms.
Spike-pitchers threw their bundles higher on the load
And the County Assessor drove with a tiny smile.

Actually the minister's wife felt relieved that morning,
Though afraid too. She walked out by the slough,
And admired the beaver's house, partly above
Water, partly beneath. That seemed right.

The minister felt dizzy as the two of them drove
For hours: country music and the loose ribbon
Mingled in his mind with the *Song of Songs*.
They stopped at a small motel near Bismarck.

For the threshers, the stubble was still dry,
The oat dust itchy, the big belt needed grease,
The loads pulled up to the machine. This story happens
Over and over, and it's a good story.

LOOKING AT THE STARS

I still think about the shepherds, how many stars
They saw. We owe our love of God to these sheep
That had to be followed, or companioned, all night.
One can't just let them run. By midnight

The stars had already become huge talkers.
The Parent sits in her proud Chair, and is punished.
The Dog follows the Hunter. Each time a story ends
There is such a long pause before another begins.

Those of us who are parents, and getting older,
Long, as tonight, for our children to stand
With us, looking at the stars. Here it is,
Eight thousand years later, and I still remember.

AFTER A FRIEND'S DEATH
For Orrin

It must be summer. Push the dock out,
Bring the canoe down, find your old
Books—bird books, Hawthorne. Drive
To Gooseberry. Even in the Swedish islands,

Summer comes. They pull the linen off chairs,
Bring out the blue dishes, write some poems.
Say again: "It must be summer."
Even though people die, it must be summer.

THE PARCEL

It's a parcel of some sort. The exchange
Takes place at night. Sometimes
Dark spots show on the brown wrapping paper,
Because rain was falling.

It happened. The two had met each other only
Yesterday. Neither had read many novels;
They didn't plot this. It had something to do with the planets,
With destiny, with rain.

Because it happened, certain gates were shut;
A door opened. Children were born; one died.
How could we call it innocent? The rain
Was innocent.

Do you remember the night of that exchange?
Some forces wanted this to happen.
The rain didn't care, but no one else
Was innocent.

MY DOUBTS ON GOING TO VISIT
A NEW FRIEND

I'm glad that a white horse grazes in that meadow
Outside your kitchen window; even when it rains
There's still someone there. And it rains often
In the mountains.

I have to ask myself what kind of friend I can be.
You'll want to know whether I do dishes,

Or know my share of stories, or any Wallace
Stevens poems by heart.

I know that I won't talk all the time, or steal
Money, or complain about my room,
Or undermine you, or speak disparagingly
Of your family.

I am afraid there'll be a moment when
I fail you, friend; I will turn slightly
Away, our eyes will not meet, and out in the field
There will be no one.

For John

ONE SOURCE OF BAD INFORMATION

There's a boy in you about three
Years old who hasn't learned a thing for thirty
Thousand years. Sometimes it's a girl.

This child had to make up its mind
How to save you from death. He said things like:
"Stay home. Avoid elevators. Eat only elk."

You live with this child, but you don't know it.
You're in the office, yes, but live with this boy
At night. He's uninformed, but he does want

To save your life. And he has. Because of this boy
You survived a lot. He's got six big ideas.
Five don't work. Right now he's repeating them to you.

THOUGHTS

There's something dangerous
In being with good talkers.

The fly's stories of his ancestors
Don't mean much to the frog.

I can't be the noisy person I am
If you don't stop talking.

Some people talk so brilliantly
That we get small and vanish.

The shadows near that Dutch woman
Tell you that Rembrandt is a good listener.

THE GRANDPARENT AND THE
GRANDDAUGHTER

"Will you rescue her?" We have dreams like that
When a grandchild is about to be born.
We're called upon and we have to help.
I dreamt that a baby had fallen off a cliff

Into the water. The baby's mouth was opening
And closing. I climbed fast, hand over
Hand down to the shore and pulled her in.
She was all right! That's how I did my part.

THE OCEAN RISING AND FALLING

Each fall it rains a lot in the northern woods.
Many parts of our brain hear the rain;
And one part says, "Oh good. Let's sleep."
Another says, "A visitor is coming. It's
A sign!" The oldest brain says: "If that person
Doesn't look like us, we'll stone him." I guess
It's family. The cedar trees mutter,
"About time." Some forest streams
Are amazed to be noticed. Rivers, the big ones, are sure
They deserve it. Only the ocean pays no
Attention, being past all that. The ocean just
Goes up and down saying, "I need no more."

OCEAN RAIN AND MUSIC

Rain falls on the shore bushes and the pawky sea
Lettuce, as if it were rain from some other century,
Rain that arrived with the sailing ships,
A steady rain that came out of the Indian Ocean
Along with so much music. Well then, since I speak
So affectionately, is it music that has saved me?

Did music become my mother? Music cannot
Close doors, nor keep murderers out.
Some children need to be safe, but most aren't.
Children get born in our world, but who protects them?
A few find gypsy wagons and hide there.
The tribe steals them away, and they are gone, for now.

I thought to leave with a gypsy troupe in my twenties.
Someone did take me away. I had heard
Rumors of heroism. Yeats stole me away.
We leave family and community and never
Get back. But one has to get used to being stolen.
And there are certain secrets that stolen children know.

VI

LOOKING AT AGING FACES

Some faces get older and remain who they are. Oh
You can see disappointment there, where parent-teacher
Meetings have affected the chin; or the nose got pushed
To one side by deaths. So many things happen:
People move away, or your mother becomes crazy
And bites the nurse.

Each face had a long time in the womb to decide
How much it would let worldly things affect it,
How often it would turn toward the wall or the woods,
So it didn't have to be seen, how much
It would give in, how stubbornly it would
Hold its own.

Some faces remain whole and radiant. We study them
To find a clue. Aunt Nettie said, "My father
Put on cufflinks every day." Memories like that
Help. One face, as firmly profiled as a hawk,
Used to say: "The world is fair, and if it's not,
I think it is."

For some of us, insults sink in, or the feet
Inherit two roads and lose the way; for others, cold
And hunger come. Some faces change. It's not wrong.

And if you look carefully, you can see,
By glimpsing us just after we wake,
Who we are.

For Bill and Nancy

NOVEMBER

Some aggravations include the whole world.
What can you do? An old pulp-cutter
Longs to die, imagines
The Easter nails.

On his Icelandic farm, Guttorm hears
The news: his two sons
Dead. He pulls the covers
Up over his head.

Some oak leaves hang, others fall.
The body says, "It's all right
To die. It's not an insult
To the world."

THREE-DAY FALL RAIN

The three-day
October rain blows
Leaves down. We knew
That life wouldn't last long.

The dock gleams
With oak leaves, cold
Leaves in the boat, leaves
Spotted in the old man grass.

Hardy warned
Us. Jesus in his boat,
Standing, his back turned,
Being rowed to the other shore.

WINTER AFTERNOON BY THE LAKE
For Owen

Black trunks, black branches, and white snow.
No one nearby, five o'clock, below zero,
Late January. No birds. No wind.
You look, and your life seems stopped. Perhaps

You died suddenly earlier today. But the thin
Moon says no. The trees say, "It's been this way
Before, often. It's cold, but it's quiet." We've experienced
This before, among the messy Saxons putting back

The hide flap. A voice says: "It's old. You'll never
See this again, the way it is now, because
Just today you sensed that someone gave you
Life and said, 'Stay as long as you like.'"

The snow and the black trees pause, to see if we're
Ready to re-enter that stillness. "Not yet."

ISAAC BASHEVIS AND PASTERNAK

Old literary privacies are in danger.
Eudora Welty is eighty, and Hannah Arendt
Is gone. The coelacanth is found more rarely
In the coral off Madagascar. Many of us long

For them. The Kabbalist who sat in Poland,
Eating dry biscuits, the shy painter
Sleeping in his studio, watching the light, in love
With green and orange, who has replaced them?

Is a flavor, once in the water, a gift from fallen
Oak leaves, gone? This water stained with old
Privacies that once stood in barrels from Sicily
To Norway—tell me where I can find it.

PEOPLE LIKE US

For James Wright

There are more like us. All over the world
There are confused people, who can't remember
The name of their dog when they wake up, and people
Who love God but can't remember where

He was when they went to sleep. It's
All right. The world cleanses itself this way.
A wrong number occurs to you in the middle
Of the night, you dial it, it rings just in time

To save the house. And the second-story man
Gets the wrong address, where the insomniac lives,

And he's lonely, and they talk, and the thief
Goes back to college. Even in graduate school,

You can wander into the wrong classroom,
And hear great poems lovingly spoken
By the wrong professor. And you find your soul,
And greatness has a defender, and even in death you're safe.

A CHRISTMAS POEM

Christmas is a place, like Jackson Hole. We all agree
To meet there once a year. It has water, and grass for horses;
All the fur traders can come in. We visited the place
As children, but we never heard the good stories.

Those stories only get told in the big tents, late
At night, when a trapper who has been caught
In his own trap, held down in icy water, talks, and a man
With a ponytail and a limp comes in from the edge of the fire.

As children, we knew there was more to it—
Why some men got drunk on Christmas Eve
Wasn't explained, nor why we were so often
Near tears or why the stars came down so close,

Why so much was lost. Those men and women
Who had died in wars for a thousand years,
Did they come that night? Is that why the Christmas tree
Trembled just before we opened the presents?

There was something about angels. *Angels we have
Heard on high Sweetly singing o'er the plains.*

The angels were certain. But we were not
Certain if our family tonight was worthy.

READING *SILENCE IN THE SNOWY FIELDS*

A word I love comes—snow; then fencepost
And dust and grass and night and barn door,
Also lightpole and cottonwood, but seldom *you*.
That's how the words flowed when I was thirty,

Or even forty. It's as if some furtive men said,
"This word *you* is not right. It would lead you
To imagine closeness. We know that
Won't happen. We have your best interests in mind."

The bitter ones—the old ones—lived
Inside the Shirley Temple creamers of blue glass
That stood on our kitchen table; they blessed us,
We thought, along with the County Extension Agent,

The movies, and the *Philip Morris Mystery Theater.*
Some mornings I close my ears to these voices—
I abandon all the blue glass in the world to them—
Then I too speak this beautiful word *you*.

WORDS THE DREAMER SPOKE TO MY FATHER
IN MAINE

Ocean light as we wake reminds us how dark
Our old house is. That's home. Like Hamlet,
One visit to Wittenberg is enough, and we'll soon be
Back in crazy Denmark. I dreamt I stood

In a machine shop; my dead father stands beside me.
We talk, but his eyes remain on my chest.
I say to him for the first time: "Oh look at me
When we talk." I could see cubbyholes

With dark tools, and a rough floor stained with oil.
Clotted windows, cobwebs, a black vise.
But sunlight outside our windows speaks of ocean
Light, bone light, Labrador light, prairie light.

It's the same light that glints off swords, and shines
From Idaho rivers some days, and from the thin
Face just before death. I say to my father,
"We could be there if we could lift our eyes."

VISITING SAND ISLAND

Somebody showed off and tried to tell the truth
And drank wine and went to bed. Someone
Woke in the night and wanted his children
To walk in the grass on this island under the stars.

Someone was lucky. Someone had eyes and found
Stars. Someone had feet and found grass.

Someone loved thought, and knew things to learn.
Someone could turn in the river and go up or down.

Someone thought he was unlucky, thought he didn't try
To tell the truth. Someone thought his head was dark.
Someone tried to feel as bad as others did; someone
Flapped along the ground to draw the fox to him.

Tell him, friends, that the nest is now gone;
Tell him the little twigs are all dispersed.
Tell him all he has to do is walk under stars.
Tell him the fox has long since eaten his dinner.

A POEM FOR GIAMBATTISTA VICO WRITTEN BY THE PACIFIC

A rephrasing of Vico:
All cultures go through three stages.
Culture moves from the sacred world to the
aristocratic realm to the democratic place,
and back again.

1

We were sitting there, badly blessed, and brooding
On aristocracies near the trouserless ocean.
We knew we were pure prose; the ocean stretched
Out, blown by wind, but we remained where we were.
The sand shifted; all of us walked on flat boards.
We were no one in particular, in our messy lives.
We tended to stay who we were. Our minds stay in this
Particular room with Nils and Judy and Tom.
If death is the mother of fashion, we don't mind.
I am myself; I am what is around me.

Pinecones fall and stick where they fall.
That is what it's like when we are born
Not from wind or spirit, but from things.

2
Spirit moves where it moves; that is what
People are like who are born of the Spirit.
For in high air there burns a furious spirit.
It rises out of ground like Milton's mind
That meets all furies high above the sea.
It wants to rise. "If music be the food of love,
Play on." So notes, inspired not by our toes
But by th'inspired intellect, take us
Out of the dark soul-house, upward through turns
And spiral stairs, fighting the darken'd air.
The Spirit carries us, and in our minds
We know if we are high or not. It is
Something like this for those still in the Spirit.

3
The wind blows where it likes: that is what
Everyone is like who is born from the wind.
Oh now it's getting serious. We want to be those
Born from the wind that blows along the plains
And over the sea where no one has a home.
And that Upsetting Rabbi, didn't he say:
"Take nothing with you, no blanket, no bread.
When evening comes, sleep wherever you are.
And if the owners say no, shake out the dust
From your sandals; leave the dust on their doorstep."
Don't hope for what will never come. Give up hope,
Dear friends, the joists of life are laid on the winds.

FOR RUTH

There's a graceful way of doing things. Birch branches
Curve slightly upward; or the wind brings a few
Snowflakes down, and then joins the night;
Or you leave me a sprig of chervil and no more.

Each morning we have this new chance. We can walk
A few steps behind the others down the mountain;
We can enter a conversation as if we were blessed,
Not insisting on our old way of gaining pity.

There's a way you have of knowing what another
May need ahead of time, before the party
Begins, as smoke sometimes disappears
Downward among branches. And I've learned

From you this new way of letting a poem be.

A CONVERSATION WITH A MOUSE

One day a mouse called to me from his curly nest:
"How do you sleep? I love curliness."

"Well, I like to be stretched out—I like the bones to be
All lined up. I like to see my toes way off over there."

"I suppose that's one way," he said, "but I don't like it.
The planets don't act that way—nor the Milky Way."

What could I say? You know you're near the end
Of the century when a sleepy mouse brings in the Milky Way.

THE
NIGHT
ABRAHAM
CALLED
TO THE
STARS

(2001)

THE
NIGHT
ABRAHAM
CALLED
TO THE
STARS

(2001)

I

THE NIGHT ABRAHAM CALLED TO THE STARS

Do you remember the night Abraham first saw
The stars? He cried to Saturn: "You are my Lord!"
How happy he was! When he saw the Dawn Star,

He cried, "You are my Lord!" How destroyed he was
When he watched them set. Friends, he is like us:
We take as our Lord the stars that go down.

We are faithful companions to the unfaithful stars.
We are diggers, like badgers; we love to feel
The dirt flying out from behind our back claws.

And no one can convince us that mud is not
Beautiful. It is our badger soul that thinks so.
We are ready to spend the rest of our life

Walking with muddy shoes in the wet fields.
We resemble exiles in the kingdom of the serpent.
We stand in the onion fields looking up at the night.

My heart is a calm potato by day, and a weeping
Abandoned woman by night. Friend, tell me what to do,
Since I am a man in love with the setting stars.

THE WILDEBEEST

Once more the murky world is becoming confused. Oh
The essence of Reason's House *is* confusion,
So this development is like the owl becoming owlish.

Arithmetic has failed to bring order to our sorrow.
Newton is not guilty, because the man who
Invents the knife is not responsible for the murder.

Bees, abandoned by their Queen, clump
Together in the dusty light of the hemlocks.
Even programmers don't know when she will return.

The Herd Girl and the Shepherd Boy spend all year
At the opposite shores of the Milky Way.
In spring the lovers receive one night together.

The wildebeest leaps into the river spread-legged
Among the crocodiles; and the wolf packs are sad
Chasing the caribou endlessly over the steppes.

The beaver make their dens over and over. Grandmother
After grandmother dies, and nothing changes.
The Moses of the beaver does not see the Promised Land.

JEREZ AT EASTER

Please tell me why the lamb is in love with the wolf
And why the child's finger calls the hammer down
And why at dusk Alexander walks toward his enemies.

Tell me why the gazelle grazes so close to the lion
And why the rat makes up games on the snake's tail
And why the student bends his head when he's attacked.

One meadow in the redwoods can contain a thousand ferns.
By this we deduce we are living in the serpent's home.
Each curly fern is his tongue unfolding.

The poet makes a meadow from each leaf.
Each curve of language turns into a lamb's ear,
Because a genius is a child in the house of suffering.

None of us is free from a certain bend in the knee.
The caws from the oak-bound ravens in the trees
Around our house guide Alexander toward the night.

The old man's voice breaks as he sings at Easter.
In between the clapping, there's always a voice breaking.
Last night in Jerez some people lived, some people died.

GIORDANO BRUNO AND THE MUDDY
FOOTPRINT

Furry demons come to the door offering separations.
The crane's foot in the mud is the map of our life.
That sucking sound of the farm boot is the planet's cry.

Curly hair guards the opening to the womb.
Because there is heaven inside the womb, we will not allow
Our eyes to turn away from a single black hair.

———

There is so much glory in the great hooves
Of the stag that Tristan tracks through the glen,
And so much fear in the naked footprint near the river.

It's all right to praise the raven's dark feet,
And the crows settling down at dusk in the oak,
For setting stars always predict the stars that rise.

The web in the morning speaks of the origin of all dew.
The lovers look at each other's bodies so carefully,
And they need no more, and see all India there.

What relaxes us comes from God. It was when
He first saw the print of the sparrow's foot in the mud
That Giordano Bruno knew that the world was on fire.

MOSES' CRADLE

The Pharaoh's wives touch the mud with their toes.
You and I float in Moses' cradle. Dear friends, you and I
Are parted by a thin skin from the ignorance of the Nile.

Ghosts compose themselves from ground mist.
Friends, our souls are moist. "Dry souls are best."
Plotinus thought so, but he was nursing at eleven.

Some children hear the thin words spoken by the dead.
Men piece out secrets hidden in prime numbers.
Women report what Eternity has told them to say.

Our cradle, like Moses', is porous to the Nile.
You and I will never have one whole day of light.
At three o'clock, a wall will creak, or a hare will die.

Beauty has reached us drenched in birth blood.
As our eyes open, bright blood splashes on the floor.
The baby's descent gives us a taste for war.

Some souls remember well, climb so high
They are remembered forever. But Macbeth fell
A thousand miles when the feathers touched his face.

THE DEAD OF SHILOH

"A drowsy numbness pains my sense." Keats heard
The nightingale cry out from the place of war.
It was the thud of the buffalo-killer's gun.

The slant soul loves to play cards in the serpent's house.
The crow arrived only yesterday on Noah's boat
With the mud of Abraham's earth between his toes.

Shiloh was like a drug that hid secretly
Among the rough leaves on the Natchez Trace.
All the drinkers wanted it, and fell asleep.

We value addition and subtraction too much.
Ten thousand Newtons wrapping their equations
Around the serpent's tail can't replace a single lover.

The sunfish flashes light to the reeds below.
Moonlight slips inside the oyster's closed eyes.
The Light of Heaven widens the frog's mouth.

The bobber floats in the shadowy weeds.
But a dark Hook hangs farther down.
There is nothing on that hook but "Farewell."

WHEN WE BECAME LOVERS

Do you laugh or cry when you hear the poet sing?
"Out of the first warmth of the spring, and out
Of the shine of the hemlocks . . ." It's the hemlocks then,

Swaying above the grasses in the cemetery,
That encourage us in our affair with the world.
We have secret meetings with moss at night.

When the night-singer sang, did you notice the mice
Going by? They leave tracks like the setting stars.
Haven't you heard the grunting of the hollyhocks,

Bringing forth their hairy life by the widow's door?
Gravestones gather up the stray tufts of time
That wind would otherwise scatter in the fields.

You and I have been in love with the moon
Rising for a long time, ever since the day
Our mothers took our hands in the spring field.

That was the day we heard the cry of the hemlocks.
We became lovers then; and our road was decided.
We laughed and cried over the warmth of the spring.

MONET'S HAYSTACKS

It's strange that our love of Beauty should lead us to hell.
I caught one glimpse of you, and a moment later
My house and books were all thrown into the fire.

Plato wrote by the light from sharks' teeth.
There is always terror near the Quiet Garden.
If we have come to a bad end, let's blame beauty.

The horses of sorrow are always restless, breaking
Out of fences, trampling the neighbors' garden.
The best odes are written by pirates in the moonlight.

When Monet glimpsed the haystack shining in fall dawn,
Knowing that despair and reason live in the same house,
He cried out: "I have loved God!" And he had.

I walked down the aisles of the grocery weeping.
Gleams of light came off my hair when I saw you
And I found myself instantly under the horses' hooves.

My improvidence was to have been too hopeful.
My improvidence was not to see the fall.
I apologize to those in hell for my disturbances.

WHAT KEPT HORACE ALIVE

Men and women spend only a moment in Paradise.
The two lovers watch Charlie Chaplin eat his shoe,
And a moment later find themselves barefooted in the grave.

I know that I wanted more than two years with you.
If my wife had been able to absorb more cruelty,
Perhaps I could have paid the fiery angels to go away.

The dead man lies in bed with his great toe
Sticking up; it is because of his toe
That he could carry the burden of marriage so long.

Sometimes I frighten that boy who sleeps on the ground.
He keeps his head in his arms; all he smells is the hair
That is left behind when the groundhog is eaten.

There are as many groundhogs as there are stars.
Wherever there is a lot of anything, we are in trouble.
It is the generosity of snowflakes that leads us to suicide.

The bats' wings are the Saviours of the mosquitoes;
And the cod long for the net. It was only the certainty
Of death that kept Horace alive so long.

THE LOVE FROM FAR AWAY

We have a longing for the mud on riverbanks,
And for the wet earth around growing carrots.
When Jaufre Rudel spoke of the love from far away,

He was already bathing his head in lion's blood.
He wasn't that crazy about freedom! He cried out,
"I want to be held prisoner by the Arabs!"

The mourning dove is so well named; its brief call
Rises out of Eternity on a thin ash branch;
And the mother reaches for her son in the silence.

The moment the dove caught one glimpse of the Face,
The hollyhocks rooted themselves in the ground.
Only rooted oysters are able to produce pearls.

Swimmers, when they dive to the pool-floor,
Turn sometimes and look up toward the sky;
They see sunlight killing its bulls in the water.

"Cry out when your feet touch the bottom! We'll
Follow the bubbles down to where you are." Even
Underwater we can hear the mourning dove.

EUDALIA AND PLATO

The Dutch have been growing tulips since 1500.
There are eight thousand tulips in one Dutch field.
Every century is full of lovers; so it's not to worry.

Clouds drift over the sea when the wind blows.
Dickens knew there are lovers even in the Law Courts—
The lovers without lawyers receive vast settlements.

The lovers' books are always open to Inspection.
We can see Romeo and Juliet in the tomb,
And paintings of tiny ships in Divine Waters.

Always the lover's body is saving and spending.
During the day its donkey gathers thousands of pearls.
Then at night it spends all that the earth has saved.

Eudalia will not allow Plato to come near
The Garden of Lovers because Eudalia knows
He, being lofty, is afraid of the glory of ruin.

I know how much ruin love can bring.
But at night I hang around the orchard
Hoping to catch one breath from the lovers' tree.

THE TRAP-DOOR

Men and women spend only a moment in Paradise.
Then a trap-door sends them down to the Lords of Misreason,
Where baby kangaroos carry us all off in their small pouches.

Let's all praise the saints who never mention God!
Why should the Leghorn family praise the Knife-Grinder?
I don't think it's right for water to assist the grindstone, either.

The walls of my poetry house are splashed with blood.
I don't want to be inward. Every day a thousand mice
Run out of my door heading for Tennyson's house.

Arabs with big eyes studied all night for years
And translated the Tablets of the Alchemists.
They could pull Mercury from the knees of the wind.

Jabir the Brilliant at fourteen could arrange
Sounds so they became holy. Friends, each day
I crawl over and kiss some of the books I love.

It is because the lovers have been exiled
To the nonexistence of the onion fields
That the pauper wakes up playing the flute of gratitude.

HANNIBAL AND ROBESPIERRE

We saw new ice in the ruts on the way to school.
Once I saw through the ice, even dying sheep
Could not convince me that the world is not right.

Sometimes ears of corn were left hanging
On the stalks. The picker had missed them. Those ears
Lay touching the ground the whole winter.

The dove's drunken call rising from the orchard
Where the young lambs stood near their mothers
Convinced me to throw in my lot with the dust.

I hope you've stopped saying that people
Are bad and animals good. Bees have their hives.
Every old frog is a son of Robespierre.

Our joy was ruined anyway long ago
For the sake of order; the boy's and girl's Delight
Would still be bound even if Rousseau got his way.

Hannibal's elephants never got back to Africa.
We know that the world loses many things. But
Even wars don't mean that the world is wrong.

WALKING BACKWARD

Friends, there is only one joy and hundreds of sorrows.
We live down here in the Abode of Smelly Bones
Near the widow's door, near Whitman's retarded brother.

Even though it's dawn on the rooftops, it's still night
Here, among cabbages and shoats, among
Glints from the wings of the mice-seeking owls.

Sometimes milk makes us afraid. Savonarola
Was uncomfortable in a strawberry patch,
And Aristotle was uneasy beside the generous sea.

Mother's milk is what frightened both
The Italians and the Greeks. A drop of milk
Creates a crown when it falls back into milk.

The Sumerians, pressing their stylus into wet clay,
Found their way to the sites of their great
White-walled cities by the smell of milk.

In our messy world, we all walk backward,
Each holding a potato that points to the grave.
The night of infidelity and longing goes on forever.

WANTING TO STEAL TIME

People are moving big milk cans around in
The storeroom, and I am there. Each day I move
Barrels full of nothing to a different spot.

I want to charge you for the rust marks on my pants.
When greed comes by, I hitch a ride on the truck.
You'll see nothing but my backside for miles.

Every noon as the clock hands arrive at twelve,
I want to tie the two arms together,
And walk out of the bank carrying time in bags.

Don't bother to associate poets with saints
Or extraordinary beings. People like us have already
Hired someone to weep for our parents.

We have a taste for ignorance, and a fondness
For the mediocre dressed up as fame. We love
To go with Gogol looking for dead souls.

Counting up the twelve syllables in a line
Could make us allies of the stern Egyptians
Whose armies were swallowed by the Red Sea.

CALDERÓN

Each mole and shoat is a shadow thrown by the sun.
Each muskrat, each badger, each hedgehog is a shadow.
That's why they can hide so well in the leaves.

Don't comfort me by putting flowers in my room.
Don't quote me the secret poems of Calderón.
Don't mention freedom in the execution room.

Each day I awake, the Lord of Greed senses
A new way to put my head down on the desk.
At a wedding I envy even the minister.

Whichever room I am in, he wants me to be
First, and I agree. So many injustices
Have come into the world through me.

The burning of monasteries is built into
Our world. In every great city you'll find
A Roman general living near Lucretia's house.

There are so many different designs of the snowflake.
There are so many halibut caught in the net.
There are so many salmon tails touching in the dark.

THE WAGON AND THE CLIFF

The pin fails, and the wagon goes over the cliff.
The doctor steps out a moment and the boy dies.
We might question Emerson about this moment.

Please don't imagine that only people are greedy.
When a crow lifts off, its ungainly wings
Can carry a thousand Mandelas to the Island.

Hippolytus resisted women a little too much
And the Lady of the Sea decided against him.
His horses agreed to drag him along the stones.

Mourning doves singing from the fenceposts
When I was a boy woke the whole countryside.
But a dove's breastbone is a cathedral of desire.

Sometimes the saints make us seem better than we are.
Our ancestors, on their passport photos, knew
The sound of a bird being pushed out of its nest.

Because I've become accustomed to failure,
Some smoke of sadness blows off these poems.
These poems are windows blown open by winter wind.

FORGIVING THE MAILMAN

Let's celebrate another day lost to Eternity.
Minute by minute we eke out the story.
But the spider is on his way from night to night.

The mailman is not the one who ruins our life.
Wind has an affair with a million grains of sand.
Each sand grain has more power than Xerxes.

During those months while we slept in the womb,
The Demiurge gave us a taste for war
So that we were born mortgaged and howling.

Madame Bovary could not endure the good life.
She was like us: she wanted disgraceful nights,
Torn clothes, and the inconstant heart.

Our impoverishment follows naturally from our wealth.
The pain that man and wife feel at breakfast
Each day goes back to decisions in Heaven.

What will you say to Mahler about his daughter
Who died young? There were closed carriages in Vienna.
Freud tried to cure the insufficiency of our sorrow.

THE WAY THE PARROT LEARNS

I'm afraid to talk to you about my little toe,
Because I know that it will never agree to fasting.
The only ally I have is the sole of my foot.

We all live close to our greedy souls.
We have inherited so many longings
That in the other world our name is "So Many."

One teaspoon of envy was enough for me
To attack Robert Lowell; with a tablespoon
I could have taken on Henry James and Abelard.

Trainers once placed a parrot before a mirror,
And a man behind. The parrot, assuming
A parrot was speaking, would learn to talk.

Perhaps if God would put up a mirror
And sit behind it, and talk, I could believe
That those words of mercy were coming from me.

Why should the rooster go over every detail
Of his beheading? Let's leave some darkness
Around those days when we danced in the road.

REMBRANDT'S PORTRAIT OF TITUS WITH A RED HAT

It's enough for light to fall on one half of a face.
Let the other half belong to the restful shadow,
The shadow the bowl of bread throws on the altar.

Some paintings are like a horse's eating place
At the back of the barn where a single beam
Of light comes down from a crack in the ceiling.

Painting bright colors may lie about the world.
Too many windows cause the artist to hide.
Too many well-lit necks call for the axe.

Beneath his red hat, Titus's eyes hint to us
How puzzled he is by the sweetness of the world—
The way the dragonfly hurries to its death.

So many forces want to kill the young
Male who has been blessed. The Holy Family
Has to hide many times on the way to Egypt.

Titus receives a scattering of darkness.
He's baptized by water soaked in onions;
The father protects his son by washing him in the night.

III

NIKOS AND HIS DONKEY

Let's tell the sweet story about the day Nikos,
Wandering around with his donkey and saddlebags,
Turned up one day at a farm of Godseekers.

The Godseekers all came out when he knocked.
They welcomed him, gave him tea, brought
His donkey to the stable for oats and water.

"Stay for supper," they said. How glad he was!
They drank tea for hours. Dinner came.
They all ate happily and began to dance.

The Godseekers sang two lines over and over:
"Compared to God's, our song is only a bray;
How beautiful is the scent of a thousand hairs!"

In the morning, he said, "Could I have my donkey?"
They said: "What do you mean, your donkey?
You ate the meal! You danced. You sang the songs!"

The donkey we have loved for years may be killed
And cooked one day while we go on singing.
So don't write a single poem without gratitude.

PITZEEM AND THE MARE

Let's tell the other story about Pitzeem and his horse.
When the One He Loved moved to the mountains,
He bought a mare and a saddle and started out.

He rode all day with fire coming out of his ears,
And all night. When the reins fell, the mare knew it right
Away. She turned and headed straight for the barn.

No one had told Pitzeem, but his horse had left
A new foal back in the stable. She thought of nothing
All day but his sweet face with its long nose.

Pitzeem! Pitzeem! How much time you've lost!
He put the mountain between the mare's ears again.
He slapped his own face; he was a good lover.

And every night he fell asleep once more. Friends,
Our desire to reach our true wife is great,
But the mare's love for her child is also great. Please

Understand this. The journey was a three-day trip,
But it took Pitzeem thirty years. You and I have been
Riding for years, but we're still only a day from home.

THE COUNTRY ROADS

Last night in my dream, I drank tea steeped
In iron that had failed; at the bottom
I saw ruined tines of an old pitchfork.

Everything we leave behind is testimony,
Even our nail-clippings. Then my old clothes
Are testimony of my love of nakedness.

During the months everyone spoke badly of us,
Then I had the fiercest love for you.
People still try to encourage us by speaking badly.

So many times this week I've felt like weeping.
It's natural, like the cry of Canada Geese
Who call to each other over the darkening reeds.

In my early poems I praised so many lost things.
The way the crickets' cries in October carried
Them into the night sky felt right to me.

Every way of knowing is blessed by bootleggers.
Because the government does not allow delight
To be sold, you have to find it on the country roads.

ISEULT AND THE BADGER

The ink we write with seeps in through our fingers.
What we call reason is the way the parasite
Learns to live in the saint's intestinal tract.

Even the finest reason still contains the darkness
From feathers packed together; General Patton
Was a salmon who grew large in the Etruscan pool.

All our language is woven from animal hair.
The badgers and the thrushes soak up the stain of separation,
Just as lanolin makes the shearer's hands soft.

The old thinkers of quiddity remind us
Of the fear the hogs feel hanging by their hind legs;
For we know our throats are open to the unfaithful.

"I was climbing on the sounds of my lover's
Name toward God," Iseult said. "Then a badger ran past.
When I said, 'Oh badger,' I fell to earth."

Perhaps if we used no words at all in poems
We could continue to climb, but things seep in.
We are porous to the piled leaves on the ground.

IN PRAISE OF SCHOLARS

Furry shadows are bringing gifts to our door.
We have nowhere to live but with the moles.
We'll have to pay the mortgage on the house of sorrow.

This world is roofed with the shingles of parting.
Children slide off their mothers' knees;
The door leads inward to silent wives and husbands.

My father wrote numbers down all his life
With a short, blunt pencil. Even Aristotle
Found himself caught in his dark reason.

It's too late to move now, Friends. We'll have to pay
For years—yes!—and the interest rate is fixed.
It will require our lives, as it did our parents.

Hundreds of scholars work in the basement.
They are good students of the ten thousand things.
Without them we would be at war forever.

There is only one mortgage and so many forms of payment!
There is one peace and so many forms of war.
The furry shadows are bringing gifts to the door.

THE FISH IN THE WINDOW

"The fish are in the fishman's window," the grain
Is in the hall, "the hunter shouts as the pheasant falls."
That shout rises from deep in Adam's chest.

The great trawlers pull in the shining bodies.
Horses' teeth rip night from sleepy day.
We are all like Nebuchadnezzar on his knees.

Because the greedy soul gained its teeth in the womb,
More than one twin died in the safest place;
We fell into the doctor's hands with haunted eyes.

We inherited much when we inherited teeth.
We will never have one whole day of peace.
An old horse will die or a house will burn.

Each evening we reach for our neighbor's food.
Each night we crawl into imaginary beds;
Each midnight we visit the darkness with Saturn.

We can go on sitting in the Meeting House,
But the greedy one in us will still survive.
One cry from the crow contains a thousand more.

MONTSERRAT

Why God allowed Montserrat to fall
Is not explained, nor why the Queen of Cattle
Drove my one calf into the slaughterhouse.

My poems are sad. How could it be otherwise?
The judge and the criminal live in my own house.
I come constantly upon secret court proceedings.

Why do we achieve organization only in wartime?
I want to know why so many plays of Sophocles were lost,
And why God becomes an ox and eats the grass each night.

When I was twenty-six, I sent the words that fed me
To be killed, along with vowels that joined me to others;
My calf of language was cut up and thrown into the ditch.

My small talent was weighted down beneath the water,
And the lungs I breathed with were filled with lies.
If I had been human, it would have been worse.

That is what separation is like: I know it now.
I had only will to save me from drowning.
I was unfaithful even to Infidelity.

THE FRENCH GENERALS

Whenever Jesus appears at the murky well,
I am there with my five hundred husbands.
It takes Jesus all day to mention their names.

The growing soul longs for mastery, but
The small men inside pull it into misery.
It is the nature of shame to have many children.

Earth's name is "Abundance of Desires." The serpent
Sends out his split tongue and waves it
In the air scented with many dark Napoleons.

The general ends his life in a small cottage
With damp sheets and useless French franc notes;
He keeps his old plans of attack under the mattress.

I say to the serpent: "This is your house."
I bring in newspapers to make his nest cozy.
It's the nature of wanting to have many wives.

So many rafters in lifejackets are pulled down
Till their toes touch the bottom of the Rogue River.
Wherever there is water there is someone drowning.

THE BATTLE AT YPRES, 1915

Tammuz, bright with feathers, goes to the Underworld.
The peat-bog man sleeps on his slanted face.
Not to worry; it means that spring has come.

Naked men crawl into tunnels to retrieve the giant
Snakes. They don't resist if pulled out backwards.
Ah, friends, the world pulls us out backwards.

Some say that every bit of iron we pull
Out of the earth, and shape, we have to pay for.
At Ypres we paid dearly for the Bentley car.

Some greedy part hankers for disaster, for things
To go wrong, for the war to start. Many people
Are disappointed when the bombing is canceled.

Events at times turn out exactly wrong with us.
The Magi are misled by a satellite in the night;
And a rabbit sacrifices people during our Easter.

How happy the Europeans were in 1914!
It seemed as though spring had come at last!
Our gaiety the morning of war is momentary.

For Martín Prechtel

THE RAFT OF GREEN LOGS

Poetry is an occupation fit for slaughterers
And knife-wielders. Life on earth needs many kills
To engender the soft leaps of the cheetah.

God made me tender; but writing poetry,
With its furry herd of images that have
To be saved or murdered, has made me fierce.

The Lord of this World condemns half his friends
To death. Music testifies to that. Notes
Wave their arms and sink into the cold Atlantic.

During the years I called to Rilke and Boehme,
I hung onto small branches; I went over
The waterfall still holding the twig of reason.

It's all right if we tumble down the falls.
I remember how many lambs died on the farm.
Our desires reform themselves overnight anyway.

My affections were stuffed into the giant's mouth.
Some marriages are rafts. I saw water between
The green logs. You could not have saved me.

I V

THE FIVE INNS

When I cry, I want everyone else to cry.
I wanted to live at the edge of things as a boy.
A thousand geese gawping were just right for me.

A thousand red-eyed dragons live in a drop
Of clear water, all guarding the same treasure.
A hundred Jesuses are walking near Emmaus.

What are the five inns of the Dark One?
Smoke, fire, wind, mud, and darkness.
Each of these casinos is delicious to the gambler.

My greedy soul and I share the same room.
When I see a book written two thousand years
Ago, I check to see if my name is mentioned.

Men and women like me who put their trust
In the dusky footsteps of the setting stars
Have secret accomplices in the world of night.

Yesterday's Caribbean storm rose when a gnat
Lifted its wing; and there are hundreds of Platos
And Ibn Arabis teaching the pupil of the eye.

THE BAAL SHEM AND FRANCIS BACON

"The Five Ways of Knowing the World" worries me.
The thrush has so many tiny feathers around its bill
That a thousand ways of knowing might be closer.

Some old souls living in the Divine House felt
Such fear at the amount of darkness God
Left inside man during the Second Creation,

That they hid themselves away in an inner room,
And never looked down at those tall grasses
Where Adam sat killing rabbits by the first fire.

When the Baal Shem was about to be born,
His soul was chosen from among that group of souls
Who had turned their eyes away from the window.

That's why the Baal Shem could travel a hundred
Miles in two hours and arrive just in time
To give the poor daughter money for her marriage.

That's why Francis Bacon could never understand
How the world allows itself to be loved, nor how
Joseph's shirt could come back from Egypt.

NATCHEZ INNS

Let's just stay here weeping over old grain.
We've spent hours asleep, and other hours,
Dozens of them, hitched to the black horse.

We love most those hours that carry the burnt flavor
Of the stars; but we have to have praised God
For hours before the burnt minute appears.

Whenever we set a foot down, it is caught.
The steps we take resemble those Natchez inns
Where each pillow covers an open knife.

The bird can sing for hours through its beak!
It picks its grain carefully. But we, the sons
Of forgetfulness, eat the flesh that died shouting.

We have to fight the Agent of Disappointment a year
To love one disappearing star for a moment, because
Any star may carry us close to Orion's belt.

Be frank with me: Tell me how many dead hours
You have eaten, whom you have killed
While waiting for the Lord of this planet to fall asleep.

THE CABBAGES OF CHEKHOV

Some gamblers abandon carefully built houses
In order to live near water. It's all right. One day
On the river is worth a thousand nights on land.

It is our attraction to ruin that saves us;
And disaster, friends, brings us health. Chekhov
Shocks the heavens with his dark cabbages.

William Blake knew that fierce old man,
Irritable, chained, and majestic, who bends over
To measure with his calipers the ruin of the world.

It takes so little to make me happy tonight!
Four hours of singing will do it, if we remember
How much of our life is a ruin, and agree to that.

Butterflies spend all afternoon concentrating
On the buddleia bush; human beings take in
The fragrance of a thousand nights of ruin.

We planted fields of sorrow near the Tigris.
The Harvesters will come in at the end of time
And tell us that the crop of ruin has been great.

THE EEL IN THE CAVE

Our veins are open to shadow, and our fingertips
Porous to murder. It's only the inattention
Of the prosecutors that lets us go to lunch.

Reading my old letters I notice a secret will.
It's as if another person had planned my life.
Even in the dark, someone is hitching the horses.

That doesn't mean I have done things well.
I have found so many ways to disgrace
Myself, and throw a dark cloth over my head.

Why is it our fault if we fall into desire?
The eel poking his head from his undersea cave
Entices the tiny soul falling out of Heaven.

So many invisible angels work to keep
Us from drowning; so many hands reach
Down to pull the swimmer from the water.

Even though the District Attorney keeps me
Well in mind, grace allows me sometimes
To slip into the Alhambra by night.

REMBRANDT'S ETCHINGS

The cross-hatching brings the night into the day,
Just as the donkey brings its cargo into Egypt.
I am a beggar reaching out my hand for darkness.

The cat can't explain how much the mouse loves
Its teaspoon of darkness; nor we why we sip
So thirstily from the pond made with a sharp stylus.

What is this? A monk and a girl in the corn?
He can no more keep his seed from rising
Than the kernel prevent the corn from coming up.

The resting hog is content, tied by one leg,
At least for now. She is far down on the earth;
And no longer remembers small boys or boiling water.

Joseph needs a lantern as he and Mary
Travel silently through the night. The donkey
Is about to put its hoof down in that darkness.

The hatching and shadowiness are everywhere.
The lion, standing by the pollarded willow,
Protects the old St. Jerome while he reads.

THE CARDINAL'S CRY

The cardinal's cry could be heard at Gettysburg.
Some stars have no choice but to set in the west.
It's always night in the grain-bin of birth.

Vintners made strong red wine from the battlefields
Where the Romans died; and we know that hundreds
Of mothers loved the buffalo-killers' hands.

Every poem is a cover over something naked.
Emily Dickinson's poems are shawls woven
From the lengthened hair of the ignorant and insane.

Ducks are swimming in and out of the reeds
In the marshy lakes of the amygdala.
A hunter shoots at everything that flies by.

The tumbling of clowns is part of the abundance
That gives birth to death, along with bitter
Berries, charcoal, and the first snow.

The muddler you are reading has lied to you
Often because he didn't want to see how many
Things cannot be saved even if Abraham returns.

THE OLD ST. PETER BY REMBRANDT

Noah's ship does not sail with its elephants forever.
The crying of the monkeys breaks off and starts again.
Even shame does not last a whole lifetime.

———

"It was dark," Peter said. "We were alone. We had
A single candle which shone on the steel breastplate
Of the Roman soldier. The whole town was asleep."

We are bubbles on the lips of our friends.
Each time they turn their heads, we drift toward the Pole;
We pass into the Many and return.

Who can say, "With God, the rest is nothing"?
Who can say, "I am a grandchild of the unfaithful"?
Who is able to wait one month to drink water?

We fell into weeping yesterday at five o'clock.
We wept because slavery has returned; we wept
Because the whole century has been a defeat.

Oh Peter! Peter! The night behind you is black.
A beam of light falls on your outworn face.
What can you do but lift up your hand for forgiveness?

CHICAGO MUSEUM OF ART

WHY IS IT THE SPARK'S FAULT?

The soul is in love with marshy ground and snails,
With mud, darkness, wind, smoke and fire.
The cucumber and melon lead us back toward Heaven.

Why is it the spark's fault if the moment a hammer
Hits hot iron the spark curves toward earth?
In July even lightning cannot help itself.

———

Italian fiddlers are always ready to play
Near the enclosed bed of the Prodigal Son
While a plump woman cuts a pear with a small knife.

Let's keep disaster remembered in our poems.
Our memory feeds on ruin just as cows
Stand around drinking from river water.

Who stands for the melon? Seth, Abraham,
And Shem. The lightness of grasshoppers suggests
They are taking in some fiddle music from the grass.

Please forgive me if I know so many words
And say so little. The Word catches in my throat,
Because some force does not want me to follow Abraham.

AUGUSTINE ON HIS SHIP

Each time we lower a violin near the Nile River,
The low G string cries; it's like the cry a ribbon
Makes when a raven carries it into his nest.

No one knows what the jaguar's whisker feels
Immersed in the bathwater of St. Francis.
We each have to be careful talking of our betters.

How can the literalists with their heavy voices
Speak through the thin bill of the thrush, or the spark,
Alone in wet cow dung, call to its friends?

So much flesh muffles the slow bones
Of the beaver that it's difficult for light
To pass from the tip of the tail to the skull.

Perhaps that's why Rimbaud whose gold tooth
Was so delicately tuned to the Milky Way
Of language could still die as a slave trader.

Every fall the Kraken comes up and brushes
With his Gnostic arms the hull of the ship
On whose planks Augustine walks at night.

V

THE DIFFICULT WORD

The oaks reluctantly let their leaves fall,
And hesitatingly allow their branches to be bare;
And the bear spends all winter in separation.

The beauty of marriage is such that it dissolves
All earlier unions, and leads man and wife
To walk together on the road of separation.

The word is a difficult one. The thought frightens us
That this planet with all its darkening geese
Was created not for union but for separation.

Suppose there were a dragon curled inside each drop
Of water, defending its gold. It's possible
That abundance has the same effect as separation.

We all knew nothing of this when we floated
In the joy of the womb; but when our lips touched
Our mother's breast, we said, "This is separation."

It is my longing to smooth the feathers
Of brown birds, and to touch the sides of horses
That has led me to spend my life in separation.

TESTIFYING TO THE NIGHT

Perhaps the turtle loves his sturdy back too much.
So much happens when no one is watching.
Our hopes for the universe did not include last night.

Last night I met Her again. In my dream I
Took a room in a German inn; and she was
There. No one else knew about it that night.

When the Queen of Hearts shows up, we throw
The rest of the cards down, and stand up.
We know that the game is over for that night.

We won't have to worry about waking each other
Up at dawn. And we won't bother about sleep.
Good ants carry us around the room all night.

When she comes, why not bet everything?
Sometimes we bet and we lose; and the dealer
Goes away with our head that night.

When one sings, it's best to light candles
All around the singers' feet. The candle is not lit
To give light, but to testify to the night.

THE STORYTELLER'S WAY

It's because the storytellers have been so faithful
That all these tales of infidelity come to light.
It's the job of the faithful to evoke the unfaithful.

Our task is to eat sand, our task is to be sad,
Our task is to cook ashes, our task is to die.
The grasshopper's way is the way of the faithful.

Even though you are a literalist, accept
The invitation to go to Pluto's wedding.
Haven't you learned yet that the stars are faithful?

For every planet, there are a million jellyfish
Shooting along who don't know night from morning.
So is the sea full of the unfaithful or the faithful?

A storyteller has to remember every turn
Of language so that we all know the moment
When the King decides to betray the faithful.

Every story I tell reveals how many tokens
Of loyalty I have forgotten, how often
I have exchanged places with the unfaithful.

For Gioia Timpanelli

HOW THIS WEALTH CAME TO BE

It's hard to know how all this wealth came to the world.
Ishmael was not created from a fight with a whale.
The ocean is not deep enough to have created Melville's soul.

The hungry one in us did not come from our seed.
Our old enemy is one of Adam's grandfathers.
He stood around looking at the shadow of the first soul.

The Ark landed on Ararat; but all those
Who came off the Ark know that the voyage
Was not long enough to produce Abraham's soul.

Oaks once darkened almost all of Great Britain,
Covering it with leaves. But squirrels rummaging
In a million acorns could not find Chaucer's soul.

How many boulders had to be ground down
To produce one square inch of the Sahara?
Maybe the moon gave birth to Mandela's soul.

There is a mystery about the birth of Jesus.
All the snow that fell to earth on Christmas Eve
Finally did shift the weight of Rome's soul.

NOAH WATCHING THE RAIN

I never understood that abundance leads to war,
Nor that manyness is gasoline on the fire.
I never knew that the horseshoe longs for night.

All through my twenties I worked in the opal mines.
No one could open the door to Saturn's house.
I had no choice but to live in my father's night.

I am still a mouse nibbling the chocolate of sadness.
I am an Albigensian reading Bulgarian script.
I am a boy walking across England by night.

Each time we fold in the fingers of our left hand
We bring our ancestors close to each other again,
So they can lie on top of each other in the bed at night.

Soon our grandfather and grandmother will kiss
Once more. Then death will come in his Jewish hat,
And tell Noah to start praising the rainy night.

Even though I know that whenever I say the word
"Abundance," I am laying up trouble for ourselves,
I have no other way to express my love for the night.

LISTENING

The goose cries, and there is no way to save her.
So many cheeps come from the nest by the river.
If God doesn't listen, why are we listening?

Very deep water covers most of the globe.
Whenever I see it, I think of St. John.
There is no remedy for deep water but listening.

The King and Queen already know about love;
They search for each other through the whole deck.
While we play our hands, they are listening.

The day we die, we'll each be like the fish
Abruptly jerked out of the water.
For him, it is the end of all listening.

Like thousands of others, I'm eating beet soup
In some Russian inn. People write letters
To me from heaven, but I'm not listening.

The hermit said: "Because the world is mad,
The only way through the world is to learn
The arts and double the madness. Are you listening?"

SO BE IT. AMEN.

There are people who don't want Kierkegaard to be
A humpback, and they're looking for a wife for Cézanne.
It's hard for them to say, "So be it. Amen."

When a dead dog turned up on the road, the disciples
Held their noses. Jesus walked over and said:
"What beautiful teeth!" It's a way to say "Amen."

If a young boy leaps over seven hurdles in a row,
And an instant later is an old man reaching for his cane,
To the swiftness of it all we have to say "Amen."

We always want to intervene when we hear
That the badger is marrying the wrong person,
But the best thing to say at a wedding is "Amen."

The grapes of our ruin were planted centuries
Before Caedmon ever praised the Milky Way.
"Praise God," "Damn God" are all synonyms for "Amen."

Women in Crete loved the young men, but when
"The Son of the Deep Waters" dies in the bath,
And they show the rose-colored water, Mary says "Amen."

DAWN

Some love to watch the sea bushes appearing at dawn,
To see night fall from the goose wings, and to hear
The conversations the night sea has with the dawn.

If we can't find Heaven, there are always bluejays.
Now you know why I spent my twenties crying.
Cries are required from those who wake disturbed at dawn.

Adam was called in to name the Red-Winged
Blackbirds, the Diamond Rattlers, and the Ring-Tailed
Raccoons washing God in the streams at dawn.

Centuries later, the Mesopotamian gods,
All curls and ears, showed up; behind them the Generals
With their blue-coated sons who will die at dawn.

Those grasshopper-eating hermits were so good
To stay all day in the cave; but it is also sweet
To see the fenceposts gradually appear at dawn.

People in love with the setting stars are right
To adore the baby who smells of the stable, but we know
That even the setting stars will disappear at dawn.

MY
SENTENCE
WAS A
THOUSAND
YEARS
OF JOY

(2005)

I

THE DARK AUTUMN NIGHTS

Imagination is the door to the raven's house, so we are
Already blessed! The one nail that fell from the shoe
Lit the way for Newton to get home from the Fair.

Last night I heard a thousand holy women
And a thousand holy men apologize at midnight
Because there was too much triumph in their voices.

Those lovers, skinny and badly dressed, hated
By parents, did the work; all through the Middle Ages,
It was the lovers who kept the door open to heaven.

Walking home, we become distracted whenever
We pass apple orchards. We are still eating fruit
Left on the ground the night Adam was born.

St. John of the Cross heard an Arab love poem
Through the bars and began his poem. In Nevada it was
Always the falling horse that discovered the mine.

Robert, you know well how much substance can be
Wasted by lovers, but I say, Blessings on those
Who go home through the dark autumn nights.

A POEM FOR ANDREW MARVELL

Tell Tristan the tip of his tongue is beautiful.
Tell the lovers they are blessed. Tell me my poems
Are promises made a thousand years ago.

People who adore literature often say that fall
Is the best of all seasons. Erasmus loved Latin, heavy
Seas, masts breaking, ships going down.

Twice this morning I've kissed Marvell's book.
He's glad for the mourners—whose eyes are blessed
By grief, who "weep the more and see the less."

I know that these poems mean that I am beginning
To get rid of the traces. But at this rate, I'll
Still be washing the floor when the flood comes.

Every drop of water has inside it the strange, mad
Longing to be the ocean. I don't need
To say why every grassblade is so thin.

Robert, your take on the fall is right. Those studying
The Kabbalah gained so much from the story
Of Ruth gleaning barley stalks in the dusk.

LISTENING TO THE SITAR BEFORE DAWN

It is not yet dawn, and the sitar is playing.
Where are the footsteps that were so clear yesterday?
Sometimes stones have no weight at all, and clouds are heavy.

To those who want me to change, I say, "I will
Never stop traveling that road which connects
Socrates to the turtle, and Falstaff to the Baal Shem."

Every sitar note strikes a bargain with the one
Who arranges things. One note says, "A year in heaven."
The turgid silence says, "Two years under the earth."

The sitar players are already pulling heaven down,
While we have hardly learned to carry earth.
Perhaps they remember all their errors in loving.

Some say that Ganesha and Catherine do the work
For us all, but I see a great deal of faithfulness
In the dragonfly with her long, skinny body.

It was still dark when the fingers began to play.
Now we who have listened so hard have nothing to say.
The wavering sitar note is the early dawn.

For David Whetstone

LOAFING WITH FRIENDS AT OJO CALIENTE

Mineral pools remember a lot about history.
Here we are at Ojo Caliente, sitting together,
Soaking up the rumble of earth's forgetfulness.

Why should we worry if *Anna Karenina* ends badly?
The world is reborn each time a mouse
Puts her foot down on the dusty barn floor.

Sometimes *oh*s and *ah*s bring us joy. When
You place your life inside the vowels, the music
Opens the doors to a hundred closed nights.

People say that even in the highest heaven
If you managed to keep your ears open
You would hear angels weeping night and day.

The culture of the Etruscans has disappeared.
So many things are over. A thousand hopes
F. Scott Fitzgerald had for himself are gone.

No one is as lucky as those who live on earth.
Even the Pope finds himself longing for darkness.
The sun catches on fire in the lonely heavens.

For Hanna and Martín

WHEN I AM WITH YOU

When I am with you, two notes of the sarod
Carry me into a place where I am not.
All the farms have disappeared into air.

Those wooden fenceposts I loved as a boy—
I can see my father's face through their wood,
And through his face the sky as threshing ends.

It is such a blessing to hear that we will die.
Ten thousand barks become a hundred thousand;
I knew this friendship with myself couldn't last forever.

Touch the sarod's string once more, so that the finger
That touched my skin a moment ago
Can become a lightning bolt that closes the door.

Now I know why I keep hinting at the word *you*—
The sound of you carries me over the border.
We disappear the same way a baby is born.

Some foolish boy with my name has been trying
To peer all afternoon between the thick boards
Of the fence. Tell that boy it isn't time.

THERE ARE SO MANY PLATOS

The mourning dove insists there is only one morning.
The nail remains faithful to its first board.
The hoarse crow cries out to a thousand planets.

The sun goes down through ghettos of clouds.
There is one Burning Mind and so many Platos.
The Morning Star rises over a flutter of wings.

To those who make up music, and write poems,
I say: Our task is to become a moist tongue
By which subtle ideas slip into the world.

Probably we *were* born too near the potato bin.
Like the potato, we have many closed eyes.
A touch on the thigh displaces all the heavens.

There are more planets than have ever been found.
They rise and set again. Some people say
A painting is a pitcher full of the invisible.

Robert, some images in this poem are just right.
It is probably as good as anyone can do
Who is still living in the old inn of desire.

BACH'S B MINOR MASS

The old Germans step inside Trinity Church.
The tenors, and sopranos, and altos and the horns
Say: "Do not be troubled. Death will come."

The basses reach down into their long coats
And give bits of dark bread to the poor, saying,
"Eat, eat, in the shadow of Jethro's garden."

We all know about the old promise
That the orphans will be fed. The oboes say,
"Oh, that promise is too wonderful for us!"

Don't worry about the sea. The tidal wave that
Wipes out whole cities is merely the wood thrush
Lifting her wings to catch the morning sun.

We know that God gobbles up the Faithful.
The Harvesters on the sea floor are feeding
All of those ruined by the depth of the sea.

Our oak will break and fall. Even after their tree
Has splintered and fallen in the night, once
Dawn has come, the birds can do nothing but sing.

THE BLIND TOBIT

Why does the prophet climb on the same ship so many times?
Why does the sleeper visit other continents by night?
The ship breaks up, and Kafka is lost so many times.

The high school teacher's ghost waits by the stone wall.
Why does the ear always stretch toward the storm?
The Pharaoh imprisons and releases Joseph so many times.

Tobit! Tobit! Your eyes are milky white! Every
Father is blind when his son knocks on the door.
The blind Tobit fumbles for the door so many times.

Why do those who died by the stone wall at Gettysburg
Throw themselves against the Germans at Stalingrad?
The novelist writes and rewrites his novel so many times.

The general fights the same war again and again.
The violinist plays the same toccata over and over.
The conductor conducts the same piece so many times.

Why do some love affairs resemble a blow of lightning?
Are you surprised how often Zoroaster is reborn?
The snow blocks the country roads so many times.

THE GREEK SHIPS

When the waterholes go, and the fish flop about
In the mud, they can moisten each other faintly,
But it's best if they lose themselves in the river.

You know how many Greek ships went down
With their cargoes of wine. If we can't get
To port, perhaps it's best to head for the bottom.

I've heard that the mourning dove never says
What she means. Those of us who make up poems
Have agreed not to say what the pain is.

Eliot wrote his poems for years standing under
A bare lightbulb. He knew he was a murderer,
And he accepted his punishment at birth.

The sitar player is searching: now in the backyard,
Now in the old dishes left behind on the table,
Now for the suffering on the underside of a leaf.

Go ahead, throw your good name into the water.
All those who have ruined their lives for love
Are calling to us from a hundred sunken ships.

VISITING THE TEACHER

I am the grandchild of Norwegian forgetters.
I am a nephew of those who stole the onions.
We are all guests at the criminal's wedding.

Each time we pick up a fallen wren's nest,
We sense despair and injustice, but we love to feel
The little crackling of the abandoned eggshells.

To drink a drop of water increases our thirst.
Black-and-white movies intensify our longing
That night will come and simply take over from day.

The shadowy cave we live in extends far out
Over the world. It's dark there. Even Amundsen
And all his dogs couldn't find the end of it.

Stars have set so often in the woods without
Bringing the Magi, that the badger drinks
Sadness each time his nose touches the water.

Last night I brought my grief to my teacher.
I asked him what he could do about it.
He said, "I thought you came because you liked me!"

For Dr. Nurbakhsh

GROWING WINGS

It's all right if Cézanne goes on painting the same picture.
It's all right if juice tastes bitter in our mouths.
It's all right if the old man drags one useless foot.

The apple on the Tree of Paradise hangs there for months.
We wait for years and years on the lip of the falls;
The blue-gray mountain keeps rising behind the black trees.

It's all right if I feel this same pain until I die.
A pain that we have earned gives more nourishment
Than the joy we won at the lottery last night.

It's all right if the partridge's nest fills with snow.
Why should the hunter complain if his bag is empty
At dusk? It only means the bird will live another night.

It's all right if we turn in all our keys tonight.
It's all right if we give up our longing for the spiral.
It's all right if the boat I love never reaches shore.

If we're already so close to death, why should we complain?
Robert, you've climbed so many trees to reach the nests.
It's all right if you grow your wings on the way down.

TIGHTENING THE CINCH

Hurry, for the horses are galloping along the road.
Our death is being saddled now. They are tightening the cinch.
Just keep shouting, "My heart is never bitter!"

Come, only a moment is left, the sun is touching
The sea at Point Lobos; those waves that Jeffers knew
Will soon wear the Lincolnish coats of night!

You've waited so long for me. And where was I?
Whatever pleases the greedy soul is like a drop
Of burning oil to the heart. What shall we do?

While they saddle the horses, just keep shouting,
"My grief is a horse; I am the missing rider!"
The grief of absence is the only bread I eat.

Whatever pleases the heart is like a drop of burning
Oil to the greedy soul, which can't bear one moment
When men and women are tender with each other.

You know the writer of this poem has a thin
Hold on the reins, and is about to fall off.
Hold on. The horses are galloping toward the night.

CALL AND ANSWER

AUGUST 2002

Tell me why it is we don't lift our voices these days
And cry over what is happening. Have you noticed
The plans are made for Iraq and the ice cap is melting?

I say to myself: "Go on, cry. What's the sense
Of being an adult and having no voice? Cry out!
See who will answer! This is *Call and Answer*!"

We will have to call especially loud to reach
Our angels, who are hard of hearing; they are hiding
In the jugs of silence filled during our wars.

Have we agreed to so many wars that we can't
Escape from silence? If we don't lift our voices, we allow
Others (who are ourselves) to rob the house.

How come we've listened to the great criers—Neruda,
Akhmatova, Thoreau, Frederick Douglass—and now
We're silent as sparrows in the little bushes?

Some masters say our life lasts only seven days.
Where are we in the week? Is it Thursday yet?
Hurry, cry now! Soon Sunday night will come.

ADVICE FROM THE GEESE

Hurry! The world is not going to get better!
Do what you want to do now. The prologue is over.
Soon actors will come on stage carrying the coffin.

I don't want to frighten you, but not a stitch can be taken
On your quilt unless you study. The geese will tell you—
A lot of crying goes on before dawn comes.

Do you have a friend who has studied prisons?
Does a friend say: "I love the twelve houses"?
The word "houses" suggests prison all by itself.

So much suffering goes on among prisoners.
There is so much grief in the cells. So many bolts
Of lightning keep coming down from the unborn.

Please don't expect that the next President
Will be better than this one. Four o'clock
In the morning is the time to read Basilides.

Every seed spends many nights in the earth.
Robert, you've always been too cheerful; you too
Will not be forgiven if you refuse to study.

THE BLINDING OF SAMSON

Don't you see them? They are coming to blind Samson!
But some of us don't want the day to end!
If Samson goes blind, what will happen to the sea?

Isn't it bad enough that the sun goes down
Each night, while children throw shoes at the moon?
I remember my mother's grief at sunset.

Now I remember my father. I remember
Every father when he is wrestling with his son.
Oh Lord of the Four Quarters—he is destined to lose!

You gypsy singers, make some raw cries!
Call in the crows to fly over the plowed fields.
I want the beating palms to cry out for Samson.

I want rough voices and shouting women
To cry out against the blinding of Samson.
I will always cry—take away those knives!

Isn't it enough that the Evening Star sets every night
And lovemaking ends at dawn? Please, God, help
The human beings, for men are coming to blind Samson.

THE NEST IN WHICH WE WERE BORN

Have we forgotten the nest in which we were born?
Have we forgotten the scrawny heads and the stickly floor?
Have we forgotten the cries and the wide-open beaks?

How old were we before we forgave those
Other ones in the nest? Probably it is our own
Necks that should be swinging in the wind.

Last night I dreamt my brother drowned. His body
Did not come in, and he had a wife and children.
Waves kept arriving. At last I saw his shirt.

We are in a rowboat halfway over the ocean
With the oars broken. Water is coming in through cracks.
A blind old man is guiding our route by the stars.

What shall we do with the stories old men tell?
Some say a shaggy being older than Adam
Established a prison inside the grain of rice.

One hair left on the goat's chin will be enough
To bring down lightning on a stormy night
If we have forgotten the nest in which we were born.

REMBRANDT'S BROWN INK

The sorrow of an old horse standing in the rain
Goes on and on. The plane that crashes in the desert
Holds shadows under its wings for thirty years.

Each time Rembrandt touches his pen to the page,
So many barns and fences fly up. Perhaps that happens
Because earth has pulled so many nights down.

When we hear a Drupad singer with his low voice
Patiently waiting for the next breath, we know
The universe can easily get along without us.

So much suffering has been stored in the amygdala
That we know it won't be long before we put
Our heads down on the chopping block again.

Our thighs still remember all those smoky nights
When we crouched for hours on the dusty plains
Holding small-boned mammals into the fire.

How is it possible that so many nights of suffering
Could be summed up by a sketch in brown ink
Of Christ sitting at the table with Judas near?

THE PELICANS AT WHITE HORSE KEY

Occasionally spreading their wings to the sun, pelicans
Dive for fish from dawn to dusk. The Lord of This World
Is a painter working at night in a dark room.

Earth is the place where we've agreed to throw
Away the gifts that Adam's grandfather gave us
During the Dark Time before eternity was born.

The lover's body belongs to ruined earth.
The scattered stars belong to the Milky Way.
The potato field belongs to early night.

The Monitor Lizard is a child of the Mother,
And a favorite child. The Monitor holds a snake
Immobile for an hour and then eats.

We know it's good not to have sharp opinions;
But would you still think so much of Noah
If he had thrown away his bag of nails?

Four times this month I have dreamt I am
A murderer; and I am. These lines are paper boats
Set out to float on the sea of repentance.

FLAMENCO SINGERS IN GRANADA

The singers will never stop protesting against the rain.
The singers will never stop complaining about the sea.
A thousand oak leaves fall on the embezzler's grave.

All of us crying out in Granada are calling
In the Macedonians whose sons and daughters
Died during the night when God was born.

The Mother and son have lived and died for centuries
Before us; some suffering has been steady since Noah.
It is our Babylonian hands that are clapping tonight.

I want the ant to bury the church tower tonight!
I want the church wall to stagger tonight!
I want the ant to gobble the black sugar down!

If you're still alive, tell us again how Jesus
Forgave Judas, and how Judas buried his coins
In a barnyard trampled by sacrificial goats.

We will never end the crying deep in the throat.
Whatever happened the night when God was born,
We will never stop complaining about the sea.

THE HORSES COMING UP BEHIND

Have you noticed the horses galloping past us?
Perhaps they are horses with no riders at all.
Perhaps they are riders who have turned into horses.

A world without horses coming up behind us
Seems absurd to me now. Ride faster!
Why did I let so many centuries go by?

You know how difficult it is to receive a human
Body these days at birth! Don't lose this chance!
Clamp your legs tight against the saddle.

You've given me a bridle and a saddle and a horse
That can go on for miles. But it's always possible
That I am the rider destined to lose the race.

It doesn't matter now. We don't care whether
Anna and Vronsky find their way home or not,
Because there is so much joy in losing the race.

So many superb riders have already run this course!
Look at all these riders on fast horses
Going by with their thin cheekbones in the night!

III

BRAHMS

It must be that my early friendship with defeat
Has given me affection for the month of August.
The potato fields belong to early night.

So many times as a boy I sat in the dirt
Among dry cornstalks that gave assurances
Every hour that Francis has his ear to the night.

Columbus's letters tell us that we will receive
The gifts that mariners all receive at the end—
Memories of gold and a grave in the sand.

The shadow of a friend's hand gives us
Promises similar to those we received from
The light under the door as our mother came near.

Each of us is a Jacob weeping for Joseph.
We are the sparrow that flies through the warrior's
Hall and back out into the falling snow.

I don't know why these images should please me
So much; an angel said: "In the last moment before night
Brahms will show you how loyal the notes are."

JACOB AND RACHEL

The harsh bark on the calendar oaks and the bowl
Of milk spilled on the floor tell us that the lover
Long-parted will arrive too late for the funeral.

We'll never be able to remedy the wounds
That Columbus made in the sea; how could we keep
All the promises we've made to the dark angels?

The Egyptian teacher keeps asking why the dead man
Reaches for the wrong Bible, why the pelican
Mistakes her nest on the morning of Easter.

Jacob will fly once more for seven years toward
Rachel's shawl; once more he'll set spotted twigs
At the spring where the ewes drink at nightfall.

Put more sugar into the watercolorer's tea!
Don't forbid the horses to gallop into the storm!
Please keep all frogs alive in the hill pond!

There are so many mistakes in creation we cannot
Correct. As parents, we may never be able to say
The true blessing we want to give to our children.

For Bridget and Ben

WHAT TO DO WITH THE GARDEN

I'll just stay here. You go on. Leave me behind
In this wrecked garden that Joseph forgot to tend.
I have been here since my mother first laid out my clothes.

A group of women keep reminding me whom I love.
They stand with lifted arms in the orchard. They say,
"Leave this ruined garden you love so much."

I believe repentance no larger than a county
Can become a continent of forgiveness.
I believe the Seal has not been set on this door.

Perhaps even my feeble faith may gain me
Mercy. I do believe a pebble on the road
Can throw a shadow a hundred miles long at dusk.

Because I'm absent when I'm present, and present
When I'm absent, because I drop my eyes to the floor,
I've had seventy years living in this ruined garden.

Robert, give up your longing for a different childhood.
You'll recall that Fabre when he was seventy
Found for his insects one acre of stony ground.

THE SHOEHORN

It's odd that the shoehorn has been able to preserve
Its shape over centuries. At dusk my ignorance
Slips away and hides its eggs in the woods.

Everyone knows when a great man or woman
Is about to die, and fights that. Many of the Jews
Wanted to speak privately to Pilate.

Our parents' faces at dawn have so much grief
That they resemble those stone faces on Easter
Island, gazing toward some missing Friday.

After every one of our wars, the newly dead
Hold out a cup to us. What can we do
But testify to a thousand years of darkness?

Iron keeps calling to earth, and earth to iron.
If you throw a knife high in the air,
The knife soon curves over and sticks in the soil.

I guessed how difficult my selfishness would
Be when I heard the sound the hitch makes
When it slides off the drawbar onto the ground.

SINGING THE SAME THROATY NOTE

I cannot stop weeping over the thousand nights
When I was unable to weep. I am a farm boy
Who follows tracks that lead away from the tractor.

My life failed on the very day I was born.
The long woolen coats of the Dark Angels
Brushed out the words in the snow as they walked past.

The tabla player must have lived through and abandoned
So many lives for the music to sound like this.
His hands are bailing tons of water from the sea.

Women with their newly washed hair, bodies
Born again and again with new souls, boards
Leaning against the fence, what does it all mean?

And women suffer the most—between every boy child,
So many rugs are woven, and then taken apart.
The wine of a hundred bowls is poured out on the ground.

Robert, you keep insisting on the same throaty note.
I don't know how you get permission for that.
You are like an old man gone mad on a ship.

For Marcus Wise

THE PISTACHIO NUT

God crouches at night over a single pistachio.
The vastness of the Wind River Range in Wyoming
Has no more grandeur than the waist of a child.

Haydn tells us that we've inherited a mansion
On one of the Georgia sea islands. Then the last
Note burns down the courthouse and all the records.

Everyone who presses down the strings with his own fingers
Is on his way to Heaven; the pain in the fingertips
Goes toward healing the crimes the hands have done.

Let's give up the notion that great music is a way
Of praising human beings. It's good to agree that one drop
Of ocean water holds all of Kierkegaard's prayers.

When I hear the sitar give out the story of its life,
I know it is telling me how to behave—while kissing
The dear one's feet, to weep over my wasted life.

Robert, this poem will soon be over; and you
Are like a twig trembling on the lip of the falls.
Like a note of music, you are about to become nothing.

LISTENING TO OLD MUSIC

THE RUDRA VINA

I don't know what would bring me closer to you.
Maybe slowing down this music, maybe waking
In the middle of the night, maybe diving for the bottom.

Maybe silence. The speed of the soul leaping over fences
Brings the toe forward. At other times, a book resting
On my chest takes me backward into my mother's arms.

The ache in the fold of my arm must be the old
Sadness that the newborn feels when he senses
That his father has come to claim him for this world.

Don't ask me whether to take Plato's side
Or Freud's. Just come over here and help me
Burn my books so we can move to Argentina.

The drum insists that the night we die
Will be a long night. The Rudra Vina goes on
Insisting that there is not enough suffering.

Well, music, go on growling about God.
I am rubbing my big face against my little face,
I am a blackbird flying through the night.

For Wesley and Sunil

HIDING IN A DROP OF WATER

It is early morning, and death has forgotten us for
A while. Darkness owns the house, but I am alive.
I am ready to praise all the great musicians.

Whatever happens to me will also happen to you.
Surely you must have realized this from hearing
The way the strings cry out no matter who hits them.

From the great oak trees in the yard in October,
Leaves fall for hours every morning. Every night
A thousand wrinkled faces look up at the stars.

When Rabia's donkey fell dead in the desert, she shouted
To God, "Is that the way you treat an old woman?"
The donkey stood up, and they went on to the Meeting.

It is this reaching toward the Kaaba that keeps us glad.
It is this way of hiding inside a drop of water
That lets the hidden face become visible to everyone.

Gautama said that when the Great Ferris Wheel
Stops turning, you will still be way up
There, swinging in your seat and laughing.

FOR ROBERT MOTHERWELL

Hunter, give me my horse. I am going into sorrow again.
I'm looking for the dead people hidden in the grass.
Help me up. I am crazy about suffering again.

I see that I am walking in a dead man's shoes.
I have been born so many times as an orphan. The thin fiddle
Strings stretched tight have saved me from suicide.

When Robert Motherwell lifts up his two black clouds
So that they float a few feet from each other,
I know grief is the one who tells me what to do.

The soul can never get enough of the taste of its sorrow.
I am a horse throwing his head sideways, galloping
Away from the place where the happy people live.

I don't care anymore whether I am educated or not.
We have learned so much pain by not going to school.
Our lines suggest the luck lost between heartbeats.

We who love Motherwell's black clouds may be insane,
But at least we know where to feed. We are close
Relatives of the birds that followed Jesus to Egypt.

LISTENING TO SHAHRAM NAZERI

I know the horses keep galloping for miles.
I know the ants keep lifting their feelers to heaven
And planning new triumphs, but it's already too late!

When Nazeri sings, I don't care if the Second
Adam comes down or not; I don't care if my words
Get you to cry or not—it's already too late.

The smell of coffee spreads out from the fire.
The wild-haired old women sing over the coffin.
Go on complaining and praying. It's already too late!

I know sweet vowels and inescapable rhythms.
I know how sweet it is when a young woman is here
And the old men think of God; but it's already too late.

My tongue never becomes bitter because my mouth
Keeps holding the grief pipe between my teeth.
Go on and conquer bitterness; it's already too late.

Here I am; I am all alone. It's early morning.
I am so happy. How can so much grandeur
Live beneath my skin? Go on asking; it's already too late!

IV

MAILING EVIDENCE TO THE PROSECUTORS

Every leaf in a storm points in the same direction.
The story of an affair is the story of our life.
The lover's body always tilts toward earth.

Lovers sometimes hide things under their pillows.
During our first year, we saved maps of Bali,
The Boundary Waters, and the Maltese lowlands.

We didn't know enough to move into a house.
We slept out in the barley fields night after night,
Watching the stars go over the edge of the world.

We know that lovers travel to distant countries,
Sometimes before they meet. We have agreed
We knew each other a hundred years ago.

When we had mailed evidence to the prosecutors
Three times, they understood that we were destined
For prison. When judges saw us coming, they clapped.

The two of us were blind, but we did drive our horses
Over the endless prairie. You judges, tell me
If you've ever seen wagons that traveled so far.

WAKING IN THE MIDDLE OF THE NIGHT

I want to be true to what I have heard. It was
So sweet to hear music last night. There is so
Much joy in being afraid of the world together.

The snow in the branches, the sadness in your hands,
The foot tracks in the mud, the old Inca faces,
The trout who wait all year for the acorns to descend.

The sitar player is so much like the crow, who rises
Each morning in the sky above the black branches
And cries six cries with no memory of the light.

Every musician wants his fingers to play faster
So that he can go deeper into the kingdom of pain.
Each note on the string calls for one note more.

The hand that has written all these sounds down
Is like a bird who wakes in the middle of the night
And starts out toward its old nest on the mountain.

Robert, I don't know why you would have such
Good luck these days. Those lines about the crows
Crying are better than a whole night of sleep.

A WEEK IN FLORENCE

The donkey has led us through so many cultures!
Virgin after virgin has been born! Fra Lippi's voice
Is one ray of light coming down on the suffering.

Clams have survived so many long nights alone.
Why shouldn't Giotto stand for hours in his workshop?
Go ahead; fast in the night, and weep at dawn.

The green Arno carries the green blood of insects.
Angry men in the Baptistry have stabbed each
Other long before Dante went away weeping.

Mary's face shines so sweetly. Why? The hair
Of the paleolithic elephants falls only once over
Their girlish eyes; then they enter eternal darkness.

The young woman is studying and praying in a room
Open to the Tuscan air. But the wide wings
Of the angel do not fit all the way inside the house.

Robert, if you've seen even one brown donkey's ear
That Giotto painted, that's enough. You don't need to gaze
Through the window at the fields planted for Jesus to see.

For Mary and Alessandro

RAMEAU'S MUSIC

It is such a joy to hear Rameau's music when the night
Is just retreating from the oaky branches,
And the sun's enemy is throwing down his gloves.

Last night I wept so long and deeply in my dream
Because the fish were not returning to that bend
In the river where I swam so often as a boy.

Seeing that Jacob and Esau were both standing
By their father's bed, the old fisherman sent hooks down
And pulled the reckless boy up into the heavens.

Some music is as beautiful as snow on twigs.
I don't really see much distinction between
Words and the bow being drawn over the cello.

Well, how shall we complain after that?
We've been warned that what we receive on earth
Is smoke, fire, wind, mud, and darkness.

It's all right to balance on top of a pole! People
Say if you want the magic thing hidden from all
Others, you'll have to have a life full of exultation!

LOSING THE HOUSE IN A CARD GAME

We have gambled, we've staked our house on a throw,
Lost a thousand times. Each time we finish the course,
We ride our horse back to the loser's circle.

We will never get tired of longing for good things
For each other. We are each, as we make love,
Like the mother bringing her child to the door of the school.

We were only fourteen when I saw you in Geometry
Class. We gobbled ecstasy; but we knew so little
About the skirts of glory stirring up the night.

This lovers' grief must be something the ancients
Worried about, because they knew that light
Of any kind can easily get lost in the dark clouds.

Oh Seth and Shem! Are you still grieving over
The seed of light that descended with no
Defender near into the Egypt of Mary's womb?

It's possible that we have nothing to mourn for,
Nothing to grieve over. We too, with every
Defeat, have gone a little farther into Egypt.

A HISTORY OF MOURNING

It's odd that evening is so speckled with grief.
Birds start singing when the branch reddens.
But we write our poems when the sun goes down.

Our ancestors knew how to cry at death; but they
Had enough to do finding big stones to cover
The dead, and begetting new souls to replace them.

We slept on the limestone plains, and woke
Night after night, tracing the route the dead take
Through holes in limestone and on into the stars.

Some hands outlined with blown powder
On the walls of the cave have missing fingers.
We drew maps of the night sky in the dust.

How slowly it all went! One day a woman wept
When she saw a bone reddened with ochre.
A thousand years later, we put a bead in a grave.

Some graves stand among woods. We still don't understand
Why a pine coffin is so beautiful. We don't know.
We are still brooding over why the sun rises.

A WEEK ON THE OREGON COAST

Being born amounts to peering out from a cliff
Over the sea. The great jellyfish who spread their arms
Out on the sea tell us how deep our ignorance is.

The acts we take resemble ink soaking through a page.
Men and women we cannot see have written on the page
Just before us. It was death who folded over the page.

Why do we assume that we are responsible for
The pain of those near to us? The albatross that lands
On the mast began flying a thousand years ago.

We are floating in an open boat near the Bermudas
Watching drops of seawater fall off the oars.
Soon Melville's ship will come by singing.

All those times we've been born, and died, including
Those times when we were never born at all,
Require Cassiopeia to sit upright in her chair.

Robert, you've become a watcher of the night sky—
You sit up half the night looking at Orion. Be glad
That so many jellyfish spread their arms on the sea.

SAND HEAPS

Last night we took off our wolf skins, and danced
For hours, stomping our feet on the old rug. We were
Sand heaps breaking up in someone else's hands.

It was when we sang the same four bars over
And over that we gradually went mad
On one precious foot that was never put down.

We couldn't tell for a while where the door was
Or where the corners were. We didn't know if it was
Our crying or someone else's that filled the room.

What good will all this dancing do for anyone?
Oh, it's nothing; it will never do any good.
It's as precious as a hundred hours of prayer.

We have no idea why our bodies are jumping
Up and down, nor why our throats are full of sound.
All our years of everything have come to nothing.

We couldn't tell where the walls and floor were.
We lost all our coolness as we danced in the heat.
All our years of everything have come to this.

THE DINGY PLAYING CARDS

Friends, it's time to give up our hope for Rapture.
Saucers will not carry us away. Raskolnikov
Had to depend on the police to help him sleep.

Our soul loves the dingy cards that have been dealt
To the ne'er-do-wells. The old men put the old
Queens down with their smoke-stained fingers.

In the Cirque du Soleil, when the acrobats
Sweep out over the crowd, babies are being
Born who know much more than we ever did.

The yellow teeth of old jackrabbits explains a lot
About the shortage of mercy; the caterpillar's walk
Reminds us of the Mongols galloping toward Khorakhan.

After the funeral, once they are safe, the dead begin
To miss losing at cards. We know that Cain and Abel
Want to meet each other again on the plowed field.

Robert, there's not a single humiliation we could
Have done without. We are still perched on a pole.
What will happen to us depends a lot on the wind.

THE FAT OLD COUPLE WHIRLING AROUND

The drum says that the night we die will be a long night.
It says the children have time to play. Tell the grownups
They can pull the curtains around the bed tonight.

The old man wants to know how the war ended.
The young girl wants her breasts to cause the sun to rise.
The thinker wants to keep misunderstanding alive.

It's all right if the earthly monk is buried near the altar.
It's all right if the singer fails to turn up for her concert.
It's good if the fat old couple keeps whirling around.

Let the parents sing over the cradle every night.
Let the pelicans go on living in their stickly nests.
Let the duck go on loving the mud around her feet.

It's all right if the ant always remembers his way home.
It's all right if Bach keeps reaching for the same note.
It's all right if we knock the ladder away from the house.

Even if you are a puritan it would be all right
If you join the lovers in their ruined house tonight.
It's good if you become a soul and then disappear.

V

SHABISTARI AND *THE SECRET GARDEN*

I can't stop praising Shabistari for bringing
The gnat's and the elephant's legs close to each other.
Next I want Sunday to be brought closer to Monday.

Suppose a bit of straw were able to marry the wind.
Haven't you noticed those good marriages when
The wind and the chaff go down the road together?

When a poem takes me to that place where
No story ever happens twice, all I want
Is a warm room, and a thousand years of thought.

Conrad said the dark swimmer did reach his ship.
If we sink into the suffering that's right for us,
Our dreams will have all that Adam and Eve wept for.

Amazing things do happen. One morning Kierkegaard
Explains exactly what *ressentiment* is
And the mouse agrees to marry everyone in the room.

Robert, those high spirits don't prove you are
A close friend of truth; but you have learned to drive
Your buggy over the prairies of human sorrow.

THE NIGHT THE CITIES BURNED

It must have been Saturn and the other old men
Who arranged this night of darkness for us.
So much of our life goes by in the murky dark.

When you open an apple in order to take in
Its sweet fruit, be sure to eat the tiny black seeds
So you can taste the tartness that Swift knew.

I'm never tired of despair and desperation,
And I won't be quiet. I keep crying out that the house
Is being robbed. I want even the thieves to know.

We'll have to help each other to hear, because
It was in the middle of the night during a storm
That Sophocles and all the weepers were born.

We've tried to go straight for a hundred years
With the help of reason. Friends, we are tufted
Nuthatches blown for miles in the dawn wind.

I don't know why these poems keep veering off
Toward darkness. Robert, you are actually a daughter
Of Lot, fleeing from the ruins of the Enlightenment.

For Michael Ventura

THE BRIDEGROOM

The bridegroom wanted to reach the Norwegian Church.
But the roads were made impassable by huge snows.
We are each the Bridegroom longing for existence.

Marriage brings the moth close to the candleflame.
With their frail wings, men and women
Are constantly flying into the fire of existence.

Some say that each drop of groundwater in Kansas
Knows about the ocean. How can this be?
Every drop of water longs like us for existence.

Abu Said fasted in the desert for twenty years.
Later when he came back, his dragon friend
Wept. "Your suffering gave me a hint of existence."

When the pianist's fingers strike all the notes
In the Tenth Prelude, it's clear Bach's soul has been
Leaping about like a hare in the field of existence.

Robert, you're close to joy but not quite there.
You are a hunchback standing in an Italian
Square, looking in at the festival of existence.

THE HEAD OF BARLEY

I don't know if you've ever met a head of barley
In late August, protected by its spiky beards.
It sticks to your clothes from pure faithfulness.

When a farm girl picks up a Leghorn feather
And waves it in an empty barn, the storm it
Raises is as subtle as the wind of faithfulness.

The last maple leaf hanging on its tree against
The blue sky is like that angel who brought
His wing-tips in near Mary's faithfulness.

The sitar player keeps track of twelve notes
For each raga, five up and seven down. Even
With twelve brides, he maintains faithfulness.

You know a needle sticks up for itself; it's
Not a generous thing, but, joining with the hand,
It starts out on the road to faithfulness.

It's hard to know what to say about the marvels
Inside the soul. Even those of us who have broken
Many promises can still hope for faithfulness.

ADAM'S UNDERSTANDING

Adam agreed the ocean would be the home of salt.
We all understood our souls would hang by a thread.
God agreed the pearl would be out of our hands.

What did the Prodigal Son find inside his room?
His boots and sword, a tiny monkey chained
To an iron ball, a bed, and forgetfulness.

I have written poems lying in so many small beds.
Sometimes a cross hangs on the inside of the door.
Mostly the dark of early dawn is in the room.

Some say farmers have taken on themselves the crime
Of saving and sowing wheat; and bakers have taken
On themselves the crime of baking the bread!

This is what I say, "I want what's owed to me."
A voice says, "We have our inheritance."
Whose voice is that? Is that my old teacher?

Oh what a glory it is that the winter snow
Should be so deep, that we know so little,
And the future should be out of our hands!

EATING BLACKBERRY JAM

When I hear that we all belong to nonexistence,
I drop my eyes, but then I raise them out
Of love for the little creatures of nonexistence.

Some say that perch became like each other
To keep the shark from zeroing in. But staying alive
Doesn't mean they are free from nonexistence.

The cries of the infant barn-swallows rising from
The mud-nests fastened ingeniously to the rafters
Taught me to love the skinny birds of nonexistence.

Taoists with their thin beards fishing all day
With a straight hook tell us they have learned
Not to expect a whole lot from nonexistence.

Blackberries have so many faces that their jam
Is a kind of thickening of nothing; each of us
Loves to eat the thick syrup of nonexistence.

When each stanza closes with the same word,
I am glad. A friend says, "If you're proud of that,
You must be one of the secretaries of nonexistence!"

THE BUFF-CHESTED GROUSE

I have spent my whole life doing what I love.
Let's honor the quail who searches so hard for food.
Here I am, playing flute in a cistern like Joseph.

My genius amounts to persistence in following
Elephants through the wind. Sometimes the long vowels
Go on ahead and show us where the road is.

Thank God for Jaufre Rudel who taught even
The Vikings the road of love. We are incompetent, hopeless
Lovers, but we do play the shawm in the wind.

It was only when I was out in the fields, hiding
From the winds, that I understood that what fell
To pieces last night could be whole this morning.

I don't know if you've heard the buff-chested grouse
When he drums on an old log. He is like Hafez
Repeating something he has heard from his teacher.

Robert, I hope you're not bragging in this poem.
Don't drag out the comparison to Joseph.
We're just talking here of feathers blown in the wind.

STEALING SUGAR FROM THE CASTLE

We are poor students who stay after school to study joy.
We are like those birds in the India mountains.
I am a widow whose child is her only joy.

The only thing I hold in my ant-like head
Is the builder's plan of the castle of sugar.
Just to steal one grain of sugar is a joy!

Like a bird, we fly out of darkness into the hall,
Which is lit with singing, then fly out again.
Being shut out of the warm hall is also a joy.

I am a laggard, a loafer, and an idiot. But I love
To read about those who caught one glimpse
Of the Face, and died twenty years later in joy.

I don't mind your saying I will die soon.
Even in the sound of the word *soon*, I hear
The word *you* which begins every sentence of joy.

"You're a thief!" the judge said. "Let's see
Your hands!" I showed my callused hands in court.
My sentence was a thousand years of joy.

TALKING
INTO
THE EAR
OF A
DONKEY

(2011)

I

RAVENS HIDING IN A SHOE

There is something men and women living in houses
Don't understand. The old alchemists standing
Near their stoves hinted at it a thousand times.

Ravens at night hide in an old woman's shoe.
A four-year-old speaks some ancient language.
We have lived our own death a thousand times.

Each sentence we speak to friends means the opposite
As well. Each time we say, "I trust in God," it means
God has already abandoned us a thousand times.

Mothers again and again have knelt in church
In wartime asking God to protect their sons,
And their prayers were refused a thousand times.

The baby loon follows the mother's sleek
Body for months. By the end of summer, she
Has dipped her head into Rainy Lake a thousand times.

Robert, you've wasted so much of your life
Sitting indoors to write poems. Would you
Do that again? I would, a thousand times.

COURTING FORGETFULNESS

It's hard to know what sort of rough music
Could send our forgetfulness back into the ground,
From which the gravediggers pulled it years ago.

The first moment of the day we court forgetfulness.
Even when we are fully awake, a century can
Go by in the space of a single heartbeat.

The life we lose through forgetfulness resembles
The earth that sticks to the sides of plowshares
And the eggs the hen has abandoned in the woods.

A thousand gifts were given to us in the womb.
We lost hundreds during the forgetfulness of birth,
And we lost the old heaven on the first day of school.

Forgetfulness resembles the snow that weighs down
The fir boughs; behind our house you'll find
A forest going on for hundreds of miles.

It's to our credit that we can remember
So many lines of Rilke, but the purpose of forgetfulness
Is to remember the last time we left this world.

KEEPING OUR SMALL BOAT AFLOAT

So many blessings have been given to us
During the first distribution of light, that we are
Admired in a thousand galaxies for our grief.

Don't expect us to appreciate creation or to
Avoid mistakes. Each of us is a latecomer
To the earth, picking up wood for the fire.

Every night another beam of light slips out
From the oyster's closed eye. So don't give up hope
That the door of mercy may still be open.

Seth and Shem, tell me, are you still grieving
Over the spark of light that descended with no
Defender near into the Egypt of Mary's womb?

It's hard to grasp how much generosity
Is involved in letting us go on breathing,
When we contribute nothing valuable but our grief.

Each of us deserves to be forgiven, if only for
Our persistence in keeping our small boat afloat
When so many have gone down in the storm.

PAYING ATTENTION TO THE MELODY

All right. I know that each of us will die alone.
It doesn't matter how loud or soft the sitar plays.
Sooner or later the melody will say it all.

The prologue is so long! At last the theme comes.
It says the soul will rise above all these notes.
It says the dust will be swept up from the floor.

It doesn't matter if we say our prayers or not.
We know the canoe is heading straight for the falls,
And no one will pick us up from the water this time.

One day the mice will carry our ragged impulses
All the way to Egypt, and at home the cows
Will graze on a thousand acres of thought.

Everyone goes on hoping for a good death.
The old rope hangs down from the hangman's nail.
The forty-nine robbers are climbing into their boots.

Robert, don't expect too much. You've put yourself
Ahead of others for years, a hundred years.
It will take a long time for you to hear the melody.

LONGING FOR THE ACROBAT

There is so much sweetness in children's voices,
And so much discontent at the end of day,
And so much satisfaction when a train goes by.

I don't know why the rooster keeps on crying,
Nor why the elephant lifts his knobby trunk,
Nor why Hawthorne kept hearing trains at night.

A handsome child is a gift from God,
And a friend is a vein in the back of the hand,
And a wound is an inheritance from the wind.

Some say we are living at the end of time,
But I believe a thousand pagan ministers
Will arrive tomorrow to baptize the wind.

There's nothing we need to do about Saint John.
Whenever he laid his hands on earth
The well water was sweet for a hundred miles.

Everywhere people are longing for a deeper life.
Let's hope some acrobat will come by
And give us a hint how to get into heaven.

NIRMALA'S MUSIC

The music that Nirmala is playing today goes
By two names: The One Who Finds Lost Things,
And The One Through Whom Everything Is Lost.

Tigers go on eating people in the Forest
Of Existence. The Gods agree to this. Saints
Admire whiskers that have been dipped in blood.

Women with their newly washed hair, the souls
Born again and again into sleek, fresh bodies,
Boards leaning against a barn . . . what does it all mean?

Men think ahead, and are mainly providential.
They laid out Egypt. But I like women so much.
They say: "Let the lambs come and be killed."

And women suffer the most. Between every child born,
So many rugs are woven and taken apart. The water
Of a hundred bowls is poured out on the ground.

The hungry tigers follow the disappearing dogs
Into the woods of life. Women understand this,
For this is a world in which everything is lost.

THE FROGS AFTER DARK

I am so much in love with mournful music
That I don't bother to look for violinists.
The aging peepers satisfy me for hours.

The ant moves on his tiny Sephardic feet.
The flute is always glad to repeat the same note.
The ocean rejoices in its dusky mansion.

Bears are often piled up close to each other.
In caves of bears, it's just one hump
After another, and there is no one to sort it out.

You and I have spent so many hours working.
We have paid dearly for the life we have.
It's all right if we do nothing tonight.

We've heard the fiddlers tuning their old fiddles,
And the singer urging the low notes to come.
We've heard her trying to keep the dawn from breaking.

There is some slowness in life that is right for us.
But we love to remember the way the soul leaps
Over and over into the lonely heavens.

THE SYMPATHIES OF THE LONG-MARRIED

Oh well, let's go on eating the grains of eternity.
What do we care about improvements in travel?
Angels sometimes cross the river on old turtles.

Shall we worry about who gets left behind?
That one bird flying through the clouds is enough.
Your sweet face at the door of the house is enough.

The two farm horses stubbornly pull the wagon.
The mad crows carry away the tablecloth.
Most of the time, we live through the night.

Let's not drive the wild angels from our door.
Maybe the mad fields of grain will move.
Maybe the troubled rocks will learn to walk.

It's all right if we're troubled by the night.
It's all right if we can't recall our own name.
It's all right if this rough music keeps on playing.

I've given up worrying about men living alone.
I do worry about the couple who live next door.
Some words heard through the screen door are enough.

THE BLIND OLD MAN

I don't know why so much sweetness hovers around us.
Nor why the wind blows the curtains in the afternoons,
Nor why the earth mutters so much about its children.

We'll never know why the snow falls through the night,
Nor how the heron stretches her long legs,
Nor why we feel so abandoned in the morning.

We have never understood how birds manage to fly,
Nor who the genius is who makes up dreams,
Nor how heaven and earth can appear in a poem.

We don't know why the rain falls so long.
The ditch-digger turns up one shovel after another.
The herons go on stitching the heavens together.

We've never heard about the day we were conceived
Nor the doctor who helped us to be born,
Nor that blind old man who decides when we will die.

It's hard to understand why the sun rises,
And why our children are mostly fond of us,
And why the wind blows the curtains in the afternoon.

FATHER AND SON

There's no end to the going forth on ships,
And the clack of the dog's paws on the floor,
And women who are still lively at eighty.

There's no end to the rumbling of train cars,
And the whine of the twenty-year-old driver turning
The corner, and the dog barking to the end of time.

There's no end to the trampling of horses,
And the way old men throw down their cards,
And the haughty look on the opera singer's face.

There's no end to my ragged stanzas,
And the shirttails blowing in the wind,
And the tree branches broken in the storm.

Have I said there's no end to people dying,
To the drops of sweat on the young girl's shoulder,
And the fatigue of the threshing hands at dusk?

There's a way in which card games finally do end,
And the convict finally turns himself in,
And the father sends his youngest son off on the bus.

II

RAINS

The weather is moody and rainy.
No one knows when Jesus will come.
The long rains have come and gone.
A thousand acres are underwater.

THE ROOF NAIL

A hundred boats are still looking for shore.
There is more in my hopes than I imagined.
The tiny roof nail lies on the ground, aching for the roof.
Some little bone in our foot is longing for heaven.

A DAY IN LATE JUNE

The old man sits in his chair and looks down.
It will come, my dears. The femur leads
To the kneecap, and New Zealand is not
Far behind. They will all catch up.

Schoolchildren are free. Curtains stretch
Out before the window like girls on a picnic.

None of the famous ones have died. The boys
Still hold in them the seeds of Roncevaux.

New people have taken over the motel. It's
All right. What right did we have to throw
Tires into the river? Plotinus nursed
Until he was eleven. He saw the Dear One,

And she is the hardest to see. The hawk's
Wing feathers shine. His eyes are bright.
Some invisible sweetness holds the knee
And the kneecap together. Our tongue

Goes on moving; the fire in the heart
Continues burning. Sparkles of sunshine
Light up the curtains that sway in the wind.
The old man sits in his chair and looks down.

DEALING WITH PARENTS

It's hard to know what to say about parents:
One man said, "I failed my parents." He led his parents
Across a lousy street—two lines of traffic.
Another started a lost colony for his parents.
He rowed across the river, towing his parents.
He bought them boots and pith helmets,
And sent them into battle. One man dressed them
In Austrian uniforms and gave them
Maps of Russia. No one ever saw them again.
Another man who had studied alchemy
Tried to transubstantiate his parents. It used
A lot of heat but there wasn't much change.
Someone else I knew stored his parents

In an empty cistern—the ladder is still sticking out.
Another man tied his parents all one day
And night in a rocking chair. And they
Died all right. . . . But by the end, they
Knew for certain that they'd had children.

THE SENSE OF GETTING OLDER

There's no doubt winter is coming. I see
My London Fog jacket is made in China.
The fall is like a bare writing desk.
The ash tree outside my window
Has no leaves, and Ignatow is gone. . . .
But my pen still moves freely
On this paper. And Vera, where is she?
In a nursing home in Newtonville.
Lamplight shines on the floorboards.
No response. Can I read anything I want
Now, how about *Stalingrad*? Go ahead.
Those I am dear to, those dear to me . . .
I can stand and let my palms sweep
Up over my stomach furnace—
You know, the pot-bellied stove
The Taoists talk about. And maybe
A plume of energy does climb,
As they say, up the spine. The turtles
On the Galápagos don't feel old.
They breathe only once a minute.

THE OLD FISHING LINES

Sometimes I get in my car on a late October day
And drive north. Everything that I haven't done—
Raking, visiting—all those reasons for not living—
Fall away. I pass half-abandoned summer towns,
Admiring the shadows thrown by bare trees
On bare lakes where cold waves lap the sand.

The renegade minister—the one they all gossip
About—would see those waves too, after throwing
His Sunday hat out the window. He'll be
All right. Death hugs the underside of oak leaves.
In each cove you pass you will see
What you had to say no to once.

It's all right if you walk down to the shore.
You'll feel time passing, the way the summer has.
You'll see the little holes that raindrops leave in fine sand
And the old fishing lines driven up on the rocks.

WALKING OUT IN THE MORNING

In the city, whenever you walk out,
The air hits you first . . . abundant,
Nonhuman. Where has it been?
It's like your first college course,

But with better teachers. Farther on,
Your legs begin to feel the cold.
And you learn more. It's like
Graduate school, in which

Your boots keep slipping on
The loose rock as you make
Your way upward through
The shale of the great poems.

If you keep walking anyway,
You'll soon be on top. You'll know
You've read a lot of Germans
When your boots are full of snow.

A POETRY READING IN MARYLAND
For Lucille Clifton

You'd have been surprised at lower Maryland.
This far south we could still sense Washington:
George's powdered hair in the shad blossoms,
So many criminals wanting pardon from Lincoln.
We all admired the great trees, leaning out over
The bay, the English grandeur in the wide lawns.

We came by train to read poems. All of us
Were carrying something—it was hard to say what:
Perhaps luck, or perhaps some recklessness
About truth, or perhaps just a few small stones
We kept in our pockets giving off a fragrance
The students didn't get enough of at home.

We confessed a little—we had to—having brought
So much that was hidden with us, but our intent
Was not to confess. Our intent was to shine a little,
Suggest that we had done well, and drop
A hint about our childhood in the hope that
We too would receive some sort of pardon.

THE LOST TRAPPER

Each time the soprano and the tenor
Kneel and sing to each other,
Somewhere else on stage the baritone
Is about to die.

The Alaskan trapper finds
Blood on his arm, his radio
Dead, and new snow
Falling on the branches.

I don't know why the grasshopper
Doesn't try to wiggle
Out from the bird's claw,
But he doesn't move.

Just forget the idea that
Someone will come and save
You whenever cedars begin
Making that low sound.

STARTING A POEM

You're alone. Then there's a knock
On the door. It's a word. You
Bring it in. Things go
OK for a while. But this word

Has relatives. Soon
They turn up. None of them work.
They sleep on the floor, and they steal
Your tennis shoes.

You started it; you weren't
Content to leave things alone.
Now the den is a mess, and the
Remote is gone.

That's what being married
Is like! You never receive your
Wife only, but the
Madness of her family.

Now see what's happened?
Where is your car? You won't
Be able to find
The keys for a week.

I HAVE DAUGHTERS AND I HAVE SONS

1
Who is out there at six a.m.? The man
Throwing newspapers onto the porch,
And the roaming souls suddenly
Drawn down into their sleeping bodies.

2
Wild words of Jacob Boehme
Go on praising the human body,
But heavy words of the ascetics
Sway in the fall gales.

3
Do I have a right to my poems?
To my jokes? To my loves?

Oh foolish man, knowing nothing—
Less than nothing—about desire.

4

I have daughters and I have sons.
When one of them lays a hand
On my shoulder, shining fish
Turn suddenly in the deep sea.

5

At this age, I especially love dawn
On the sea, stars above the trees,
Pages in *The Threefold Life*,
And the pale faces of baby mice.

6

Perhaps our life is made of struts
And paper, like those early
Wright Brothers planes. Neighbors
Run along holding the wing-tips.

7

I do love Yeats's fierceness
As he jumped into a poem,
And that lovely calm in my father's
Hands, as he buttoned his coat.

THE MOURNING DOVE'S CALL

The mourning dove's call woke me
In the still night, when it was still night
To me. Those sounds were older even
Than the box radio, and they said,

"Your mother is walking along the road.
I saw your dead father last night
Near the cottonwood grove."
I slept all night in a house with dear
Friends asleep in a neighboring room.
The call woke me in the still night.

For Peggy and Frank

TALKING INTO THE EAR OF A DONKEY

I have been talking into the ear of a donkey.
I have so much to say! And the donkey can't wait
To feel my breath stirring the immense oats
Of his ears. "What has happened to the spring,"
I cry, "and our legs that were so joyful
In the bobblings of April?" "Oh, never mind
About all that," the donkey
Says. "Just take hold of my mane, so you
Can lift your lips closer to my hairy ears."

WANTING SUMPTUOUS HEAVENS

No one grumbles among the oyster clans,
And lobsters play their bone guitars all summer.
Only we, with our opposable thumbs, want
Heaven to be, and God to come, again.
There is no end to our grumbling; we want
Comfortable earth and sumptuous heaven.
But the heron standing on one leg in the bog
Drinks his dark rum all day, and is content.

III

A FAMILY THING

I guess it's an old family
Thing. Someone is Napoleon,
Someone is sacrificed. Call in
Jesus, if you don't get it.

Pick up that cookie on the floor.
Let the hired man go on
Wasting his life. He'll find
Someone to waste it with.

It's like a game in which
The game itself loses.
It's like a picnic in which
The basket eats the food.

It's all right if I go to college;
Most people don't. It's all right
To end up bringing your own
Father home. Just be quiet.

Some powers are stronger
Than we are. They never say
When the battle is.
It was last night. You lost.

THE WATER TANK

It's late fall, and the box-elder leaves are gone.
Snow falls on the horses among their hay bales
And on the water tank overturned for winter.
The horses bend their necks toward the white ground to eat.

THE BOX OF CHOCOLATES

He always knew where he had been, and he remembered
The box elder in the fencepost, looked down on men
Who couldn't see the storm coming. He'd learned
To live with the way his bait went deeper.

My mother kept her spirits high with little jobs.
He bought her a heart-shaped box of chocolates
Once a year. One life, one woman,
That was God's rule, and he didn't like it much.

KEEPING QUIET

A friend of mine says that every war
Is some violence in childhood coming closer.
Those whoppings in the shed weren't a joke.
On the whole, it didn't turn out well.

This has been going on for thousands
Of years! It doesn't change. Something
Happened to me, and I can't tell
Anyone, so it will happen to you.

THE DAY THE DOCK COMES IN

So much happens when the dock comes in.
Oak leaves are underfoot. They crackle
As we carry oars to the newly painted shed.
The lake is explaining its early life.

My four hanging apples are gone, I don't
Know where. Little adjustments are every-
Where. We'll have to get ready to read
Seneca—the bookcase will explain.

It's time now to pull up the posts,
Drag the dock in, pile the sections,
Lift the boat on top, and see how
Much subtlety is lost in explaining things.

MORNING PAJAMAS

When you've slept all night in a warm bed, sometimes
You'll find a punky fragrance in your pajamas.
It's a bit low-life, but satisfying.
It's some sort of companionable warmth
That your balls created during the night.
It's a mammal delight, related
To the cow's udder, one
Of the nouns of this earth.
Don't be ashamed, friends;
Don't throw your pajamas in the washer,
Don't open the window;
Forget the pilgrims!
Think how sweet it is
That knowledge should come
From a source so deep.

THAT PROBLEM IN THE FAMILY

I don't know how to say it.
We were bumblers—nothing
Was ever clear. Why the war
Started . . . or why the car didn't . . .

We couldn't do it. Probably
Some people understood, but
We just got on the tractor.
We had no one to call meetings.

"Why do you drink?" No one
Asked that, except my mother. She
Did, and the rest of us said, "I don't
Want to be on her side."

I V

HEARD WHISPERS

The spider sways in October winds; she hears the whisk
Of the bat's foot as it leaves the branch, the groan
The bear makes far out on the Labrador ice,
The cry of the wren as the hurricane takes
The house, the cones falling, the sigh of the nun
As she dies, the whisper Jesus makes to
The woman drawing water, the nearly silent weeping
Of bones eager to be laid away in the grave.

THE SLIM FIR SEEDS

The nimble ovenbird, the dignity of pears,
The simplicity of oars, the imperishable
Engines inside slim fir seeds, all of these
Make clear how much we want the impermanent
To be permanent. We want the hermit wren
To keep her eggs even during the storm.
But that's impossible. We are perishable;
Friends, we are salty, impermanent kingdoms.

For Micah and Chiemi

THE BIG-NOSTRILLED MOOSE

Horses go on eating the Apostle Island ferns,
Also sheep and goats; also the big-nostrilled moose
Who knocks down the common bushes
In his longing for earthly pleasure.
The moose's great cock floats in the lily pads.
That image calms us. His nose calms us.
Slowly, obstinately, we retrieve the pleasures
The Fathers, angry with the Gnostics, threw away.

TURKISH PEARS

Sometimes a poem has her own husband
And children, her nooks and gardens and kitchens,
Her stairs, and those sweet-armed serving boys
Who carry veal in shiny copper pans.
Some poems do give plebeian sweets
Tastier than the chocolates French diners
Eat at evening, and old pleasures abundant
As Turkish pears picked in the garden in August.

THOREAU AS A LOVER

Dear old Thoreau abandoned his scandalous life
To live among the sand cranes and the ants.
He wasn't exactly a crowd-pleaser, but he
Kept company with his handsome language.
Each day he walked alone in the woods,
Bringing along a lover's book which told which flower
Was likely to blossom today. Well, well;
Beyond that, he lived extravagantly alone.

IN A TIME OF LOSSES

We don't want to alarm the heron who's
Guarding the cranberry bog from frost.
But so many hares have been eaten by weasels;
The losses go on night after night.
Foxes slip through the bushes at dusk.
So much we care for has been carried off.
The *air*s and *ar*s we hear in this poem
Belong to the hare who cries out in the night.

SO MUCH TIME

December's foolishness, embers fall, tempters
Fly up into the dreamt palace. Things move so
Slowly in the soul. It must be that we've
Already been grieving for a hundred years.
Old men and women know how much time
Can go by while praying. Let's not try
To cheer each other up. It's all right.
We can stay in grieving another hundred years.

THE GRACKLES

Grackles stroll about on the black floor of sorrow.
Rabbis robed in saffron feed them
Minnow bread. . . . They come to meet you.
Moses and his black wife walk like birds
And dance. Among the stalks of timothy grass
The saddled horses drink from sorrow tanks.
But the grackles' toes are springy—they walk
Over the footprints the dreamer made last night.

FOR THE OLD GNOSTICS

The Fathers put their trust in the end of the world
And they were wrong. The Gnostics were right and not
Right. Dragons copulate with their knobby tails.
Some somnolent wealth rises unconcerned,
Yes, over there! Ponderous stubborn
Sorrow weighs down the flying Gospels.
Scholars cobble together new versions.
The untempered soul grumbles in empty light.

THE PHEASANT CHICKS

"As soon as the master is untied, the bird soars."
That is what Tao Yuan Ming said one day.
"In the sad heat of noon the pheasant chicks
Spread their new wings in the moon dust."
So many body cells recognize their loneliness.
Laughter goes back to the roots of trees.
When I put myself last, an old sorrow comes.
An old sadness returns in the sorrowing dust.

ORION AND THE FARMSTEAD

Orion, that old hunter, floats among the stars
Firmly . . . the farms beneath his feet. How long
It takes for me to agree to walk like him.
Eighty years old, and still placing my feet
So hopefully each night on the ground.
It takes a long time to agree to sorrow.
But that great walker follows his dogs,
Hunting all night among the disappearing stars.

SILENT IN THE MOONLIGHT

Silent in the moonlight, no beginning or end.
Alone, and not alone. A man and a woman lie
On open ground, under an antelope robe.
They sleep under animal skin, looking up
At the old, clear stars. How many years?
The robe thrown over them, rough
Where they sleep. Outside, the moon, the plains
Silent in the moonlight, no beginning or end.

A RAMAGE FOR THE MOUNTAIN

Silent in the moonlight, no beginning or end.
So the binding things are lost, then found again,
The tines dug out of the snow, the singing so low
The other cannot hear it. Some sounds do fit
Thick cords and strong fingers. Slowly the mountain
Enters the man who walks on its slopes alone.
He walks, he sits down, he finds a stone;
No one has seen it, he sits down and is alone.

WHAT IS SORROW FOR?

What is sorrow for? It is a storehouse
Where we store wheat, barley, corn and tears.
We step to the door on a round stone,
And the storehouse feeds all the birds of sorrow.
And I say to myself: Will you have
Sorrow at last? Go on, be cheerful in autumn,
Be stoic, yes, be tranquil, calm;
Or in the valley of sorrows spread your wings.

LOVERS IN THE RIVER

Peony blossoms open in starlight. The lovers
Cross the river carefully, secretly, secretly.
All night horses stamp on the sandy island.
Husbands feel uneasy tonight; their wives,
We know, have gathered with Krishna in the river,
Their bodies sweetened by glad bones.
While David sings, stars fall into the sea; Uriah
Dies . . . It is the madness of the dark-faced God.

THE CAMELS

So many camels kneel to take their burdens on.
What choice do we have but to go down? How
Can I be close to you if I'm not sad? The clam tumbles
In the surf, and amber holds the secret desires
The bee felt before his room grew silent.
The salmon has to weave through so many waters
Before he can return to his old home.
So many stammerers labor to speak one word.

V

SUNDAY AFTERNOON

The snow is falling, and the world is calm.
The flakes are light, but they cool the world
As they fall, and add to the calm of the house.
It's Sunday afternoon. I am reading
Longinus while the Super Bowl is on.
The snow is falling, and the world is calm.

THE TEAPOT

That morning I heard water being poured into a teapot.
The sound was an ordinary, daily, cluffy sound.
But all at once, I knew you loved me.
An unheard-of thing, love audible in water falling.

READY TO SLEEP

Don't be afraid.
The great lettuce of the world
Is all around us.

THE HOUSEFLY

Blessings now on all
Who bend their heads!
Didn't Joseph bend
His head low to kiss
The baker's feet?
The muskrat gives up
His father's house.
The housefly bends his
Head down and gives
Up his elegant
Heaven to live with us.

MY FATHER AT FORTY

I loved him so much. I've said
That before, so don't be surprised.
It was a first love. Go ahead, open
Your hand. Do scissors beat
Paper? Does rock beat scissors?
It's just love and can't be
Explained. Probably it
Happened early. You're looking
At it. The way I found
Of opening a poem I took
From the way he walked into a field.

MY MOTHER

My mother was afraid—oh not
Of the things you imagine—just
Tuberculosis, death,
And my father. She did all right.

There was some sweetness
Bubbling up—a lot of affection
And early happiness. She didn't take
Being a mother too seriously.

Her own mother died of the flu
In the First War. So
Everything was shaky.
People kept leaving.

She had an instinct to
Escape herself. She took a job
In town and bought a piano
With her own money.

She lived a long time
In the old people's home.
The nurses liked her,
But she hardly said a word.

IT'S MORNING AGAIN

It's morning again. Last night I spent hours
In a dream, and I had to keep silent,
As if we were visiting crickets or nuns.

It's a good morning. The cat sleeps all day
Under the lilac bush, and scholars go on
Discovering new maps of Constantinople.

My daughter has found that her girlish things
Were all moonshine. Now she has a baby.
She is the sun and the baby is asleep.

For Bridget

SOMETHING TO DO FOR AUNT CLARA

There's something we hold to in the morning. Maybe
It's just the light, or the way the clock by the bed
Changes slowly, or how wall paintings gradually
Become clear, or the good weight of the eiderdown.
Maybe it's all the books here in this room.
And the sound of dishes rattling, and the teenagers
Waking up, and a child muttering to herself. Now we have time
For the last few sips of coffee before we go to the funeral.

THE MAN AT THE DOOR

Last night in my dream I took some steps
Underground. It seemed to be a holy place—
Perhaps monks a thousand years ago
Thought there. I had almost forgotten them.

How could we forget? Well, it's easy.
A guard at the door—you know the kind,

Those who keep people out—stopped me.
I began singing, "Hum-du-lah,

"Hum-du-lah." I couldn't remember
What those words meant.
But the man at the door grew
Light-headed, and let me slip in.

THE HERMIT

Early in the morning the hermit wakes, hearing
The roots of the fir tree stir beneath his floor.
Someone is there. That strength buried
In earth carries up the summer world. When
A man loves a woman, he nourishes her.
Dancers strew the lawn with the light of their feet.
When a woman loves the earth, she nourishes it.
Earth nourishes what no one can see.

A POETRY READING AT BENEDICTINE COLLEGE IN ATCHISON, KANSAS

TO REMEMBER WILLIAM STAFFORD

We moved the poetry reading to the Exercise Room
For coziness. There we shifted a large bike to the side.
A certain exhilaration entered the room
When the words all agreed to point in one direction.

You said that Lewis and Clark's gang one night
Slept over there by the river, and Amelia Earhart

Lived till she was twelve in that gray house.
Maybe we could all do something brave if we tried.

We, even the heaviest, started to float when we
Remembered the sound of a moth on a screen
Trying to get out. Our lives might change today!
Listening with Sister Faith in the Exercise Room.

VI

UNCERTAINTY

There are so many worlds under the fingernails—
I don't know what to say—probably
We have been keeping slaves alive at night.

I worry about my friends on their lonely road—
They didn't get much good from knowing us—
We kept sending ourselves on the wrong path.

Each day your wife swears she won't leave you,
And each night she is gone; we have to call
Up all our old enemies to find her again.

Most nights the moon returns to its place in the sky.
But there are no messages for twelve hours.
God sends a note saying that he will be late.

Occasionally a victim gets out of prison,
And takes a room across the street. As soon as he waves
To us, policemen appear and take him away.

Each of these stanzas says something, but what?
Each line says something we don't want to hear.
But each is a stone that takes us over the river.

THE THRESHERS

There's no use whining over lost worlds.
The old chicken never picks up the last grains,
And the threshers usually go home when night comes.

Have we thanked the sun for shining so well?
Have we blessed the clouds for their thoughtfulness?
Have we thanked the rain that falls on the fields?

It would be good to go back a hundred years,
And recite some of Wordsworth's sonnets to him.
But it's probably best to let him go on walking.

Let's just agree we're on our own now,
And that we have to wash our own pajamas,
And figure out some way to get home.

We can still tell stories about the Dillinger boys,
And we can still buy balloons for our children,
But it will be hard to make up The Book of Hours.

We know that most lost fathers never return,
And the clocks run only one way,
And the threshers always go home when night comes.

THE LONGING

I don't know why air drops gather on the inside
Of water glasses, and why the shaggy dog
Always seems to be waiting for heaven.

We have had more blessings than our parents had.
Even on Mondays, we can knock on doors
Asking strangers to give us a ticket to heaven.

The porcupine climbs straight up the tree
With his heavy tail hanging down,
But he doesn't give two beans for heaven.

The old man lying in bed writing poems
Feels his brain light up, and he knows
That in some odd way he is approaching heaven.

Men sometimes turn around to see a woman better.
The eyes of beautiful women often glow
When the handsome priest talks of heaven.

I write these poems so happily each day.
I guess it means that I've had a longing
All morning to write the word "heaven."

WHAT DID WE SEE TODAY?

Some days we are passive, listening to the incoming waves.
On other days, we are like a light that sweeps
Out over the husky soybean fields all night.

What did we see today? Horses at the end
Of their tethering ropes, the wing of affection going over,
Flying bulls glimpsed passing the moon disc.

Rather than arguing about whether Giordano Bruno
Was right or not, it might be better to fall silent
And lose ourselves in the curved energy.

We know how many men live alone in their twenties,
And how many women are married to the wrong person,
And how many fathers and sons are strangers to each other.

It's all right if we keep forgetting the way home.
It's all right if we don't remember when we were born.
It's all right if we write the same poem over and over.

Robert, I don't know why you talk so confidently
About yourself in this way. There are a lot of shady
Characters in this town, and you are one of them.

THE LONG-LEGGÉD BIRDS

We know the suffering is about to begin again.
It's in the long-leggéd birds flying over the house,
And in the low strings played by women on Good Friday.

Boys love to play flutes made of grassblades.
And bent trumpets keep on calling to the moon.
But the violin aims for failure and redemption.

The tortoise has a lot of trouble dragging its shell.
You and I have tried in a thousand ingenious ways
To keep up with the suffering expected of us.

There's no use in our trying to be normal.
A dozen times a day we rewrite the details
That would give strangers a glimpse of us.

The musicians were clearly magicians once.
Their sorrow goes on long after the strings are still,
And a hundred sufferings dissolve into a single chord.

None of us old ones are able to find enough suffering.
Each day we remember the long-leggéd birds flying
Over the house and our longing for redemption.

For Noah

HEARING MUSIC AT DAWN

It is sweet to hear music when the night
Is just retreating from the smoky branches
And the sun's enemies are throwing down their gloves.

Music is always reminding us whom we love.
One or two notes dissolve the auditor's mind
So we are swimming once more in the old river.

We are all failed farmers learning to play whist.
We have a lot of hands to play before midnight.
Someone else will have to worry about the time.

I'm always glad when I hear that an old hen
Has been seen crossing the road at dusk.
It means our old teacher is still all right.

We keep remembering Barbarossa's life.
A little whiskey fits in well with our lives.
The time of the Depression is not really over.
Poems like this amount to some form of music.
We dance for two hours. When we look up,
We see that all the musicians have disappeared.

THE HAWK IN HIS NEST

It's all right if this suffering goes on for years.
It's all right if the hawk never finds his own nest.
It's all right if we never receive the love we want.

It's all right if we listen to the sitar for hours.
It doesn't matter how softly the musician plays.
Sooner or later the melody will say it all.

It doesn't matter if we regret our crimes or not.
The mice will carry our defeats into Asia,
And the Tuva throat-singers will tell the whole story.

It's all right if we can't remain cheerful all day.
The task we have accepted is to go down
To renew our friendship with the ruined things.

It's all right if people think we are idiots.
It's all right if we lie face down on the earth.
It's all right if we open the coffin and climb in.

It's not our fault that things have gone wrong.
Let's agree that it was Saturn and the other old men
Who have arranged this series of defeats for us.

MY MOURNFUL ROOM

I don't know why my mournful room is like heaven,
Nor why elephants walk with such a lazy stride,
Nor why the wide-wingéd birds give us so much pleasure.

I don't know why I worry about Hans Brinker,
Nor why I remember so well my old teachers,
Nor why I keep saying blessings on their heads.

It's all right if I forget my own brother,
And pretend I was born before my father,
And erase so many lines I wrote yesterday.

I don't know why I love to sleep under a sheepskin,
Nor why my blanket seems my oldest friend.
And why I am afraid to sleep on the open ground.

Don't ask why the elephants wear such large shoes,
And why the kangaroos are reborn kidnappers,
And why the sailing birds are all Romantics.

We know the salmon follow each other upstream,
And the legislators hire their own nephews,
And the priests pay to get their sons into heaven.

ABOUT MY FATHER

The salty stars experience the ruin of the world.
My father was a nomad on the Mongol plains.
Each day he fed a thousand Astrakhan lambs.

He knew when the dangerous winter would come.
He knew a lot about calving in January,
And how to keep the new lambs from dying.

I couldn't tell you about the calves lost at birth,
Nor the lambs who stood around on wobbly legs,
Nor the ewes who went on eating anyway.

He knew how to put small pins into those farm wagons
In danger of falling apart. He had the gift
Of trying to hold the world together.

I knew how often he had saved other farmers
When times were bad, and kept them from ruin.
He kept a hundred sorrows alive in him.

It's hard to know what to say about Jacob.
I know that he was always fair to Esau.
If you see Jacob, tell him I am his son.

SMOKE-STAINED FINGERS

There is still time for the old days when the musician
Stayed inside his bubble of joy, and the old men
Threw cards down with their smoke-stained fingers.

Let's hope Brooklyn Bridge will remain standing,
That Jacob marries either Rachel or Leah,
And the Appalachians don't wear all the way down.

No one minds if we are scruffy and badly dressed.
The old man who is checking names at the door
Speaks only Hungarian, and is blind as well.

There's no telling how many hours are left to us.
The plateaus in New Mexico lift a little each year.
It's like hearing a dog barking from far away.

Some birdcalls come straight through the walls.
I don't know why we bother to listen to them
When we've never heard our own cries.

Don't give up, friends. Somewhere inside us,
Jacob is tending sheep on our old farm.
The angels are still sending messages to Joseph.

WHAT THE OLD POETS FAILED TO SAY

The sunlight on wheat-heads in August holds me firmly,
For I am in love with the wheat soon to be cut.
Let's thank whoever it was who kept sorrow alive.

Tell me who brought Hafez out of the grave.
Who brings us news of the Thirtieth Kingdom?
I can't stop clapping my hands over this question.

Even though we know God lays our head
On the block, we thank him for it all, and we
Remember the loving we have enjoyed at night.

Tell me why the suffering of the violin string
Goes on for years, why the coyote calls at night,
And why the bird never settles down on one branch.

Tell me why my titles are often so sad,
And why cattle keep on going every day
To the slaughterhouse, and why wars go on so long.

Night after night goes by in the old man's head.
We try to ask new questions. But whatever
The old poets failed to say will never be said.

INDEX OF TITLES
AND FIRST LINES

ABOUT THE AUTHOR

Robert Bly is the author of numerous poetry volumes, as well as books of nonfiction and translation. His honors include the Poetry Society of America's Frost Medal and the National Book Award. He lives in Minneapolis, Minnesota.